Harm Reduction
in Prison

Risikominderung
im Gefängnis

Supported by / Unterstützt durch:

Bundesamt
für Gesundheitswesen

Swiss Federal Office
of Public Health

Harm Reduction in Prison

Joachim Nelles
Andreas Fuhrer
(Eds./Hrsg.)

Risikominderung im Gefängnis

Strategies against Drugs,
AIDS and Risk Behaviour

Strategien gegen Drogen,
AIDS und Risikoverhalten

PETER LANG · BERN

Die Deutsche Bibliothek – CIP-Einheitsaufnahme

Harm reduction in prison : strategies against drugs,
AIDS and risk behaviour = Risikominderung im Gefängnis /
[Bundesamt für Gesundheitswesen ; Universitas Bernensis].
Joachim Nelles ; Andreas Fuhrer (ed.). – Bern : Lang, 1997
NE: Nelles, Joachim [Hrsg.]; Schweiz / Bundesamt für
Gesundheitswesen; Risikominderung im Gefängnis
ISBN 3-906756-97-1

Library of Congress Cataloging-in-Publication Data

Harm reduction in prison = Risikominderung im Gefängnis /
Joachim Nelles & Andreas Fuhrer [editors].
p. cm. English and German. Includes bibliographical references.
ISBN 0-8204-3402-7 (alk. paper)
1. Prisoners–Health and hygiens–Switzerland. 2. Prisoners–
Switzerland–Drug use. 3. Prisoners–Diseases–Switzerland.
4. AIDS (Disease)–Switzerland–Prevention. 5. Drug abuse–
Switzerland–Prevention. I. Nelles, Joachim, 1949-
II. Fuhrer, Andreas, 1965-
HV8844.S9H37 1997   365'.66–dc21

© Peter Lang AG, European Academic Publishers, Berne 1997

Printed in Germany

This book is dedicated to *Sandra Bernasconi* from the Swiss Federal Office of Public Health who was engaged so constantly and expressively in realising the world-wide first project of drug and AIDS-prevention including freely available sterile syringes in prison.

Das vorliegende Buch ist *Sandra Bernasconi* vom Bundesamt für Gesundheitswesen gewidmet, die mit ihrem unermüdlichen und beharrlichen Einsatz die Realisierung des weltweit ersten Projektes zur Drogen- und Aidsprävention mit Abgabe steriler Spritzen im Gefängnis ermöglichte.

Table of contents • Inhaltsverzeichnis

Joachim Nelles   Preface   9
Vorwort   11

Andreas Fuhrer   Harm reduction in prison – Aspects
Joachim Nelles   of a scientific discussion   13
Risikominderung im Gefängnis – Facetten
einer wissenschaftlichen Diskussion   23

Thematische Einführung

Felix Gutzwiller   Schadensreduktion als Teil einer   35
kohärenten Drogenpolitik

Stephan Quensel   Drogen im Gefängnis – muss das sein?   45

Situation und Strategien in der Schweiz

Josef Estermann   Die Verfolgung des Drogenkonsums und
Drogenkonsumierende in Schweizer   61
Gefängnissen

Christophe Koller   La consommation de drogues dans les prisons
suisses. Résultats d'une enquête par interviews
réalisée en 1993   83

8

Andrea Baechtold HIV–Prävention und Spritzenabgabe in der
Frauenvollzugsanstalt Hindelbank –
Paradigma für die Nöte der Vollzugsbehörden? 115

Beat Kaufmann Die kontrollierte Opiatabgabe in der Straf-
Anja Dobler-Mikola anstalt Oberschöngrün – Forschungsplan und
erste Zwischenergebnisse 135

Health Risk and Health Care in Prison

Timothy W. Harding Do prisons need special health policies and
programmes? 161

Monika Frommel Ban on drugs or health care. The dilemma
of a repressive drug policy 181

AIDS and Drug Prevention in Prison

François Wasserfallen AIDS prevention strategies: An overview 189
Dina Zeegers
Pierre G. Bauer

Ambros Uchtenhagen Drug prevention outside and inside 201
of prison walls

Kate Dolan AIDS, drugs and risk behaviour in prison:
State of the art 213

Joachim Nelles Provision of syringes and prescription of
Anja Dobler-Mikola heroin in prison: The swiss experience in the
Beat Kaufmann prisons of Hindelbank and Oberschöngrün 239

List of authors · Autorenverzeichnis 263

Preface

When Sandra Bernasconi from the Federal Office of Public Health asked me in early 1992 if I would be prepared to design a pilot project for drug and HIV prevention at Hindelbank Prison for women, which would include providing inmates with sterile syringes, I did not hesitate. In many prisons, covert drug use and the exchange of used syringes were a part of everyday life. Those familiar with the problem were clear in their conviction that only harm reducing measures – which had already proved their value outside prisons – were capable of improving the unsatisfactory state of affairs within prison walls. However, the political unfashion-ability of such measures meant that the discussion was usually restricted to a small group. Indeed, prison services themselves had most often total-ly neglected the drug problem and its consequences. The planned project provided an opportunity to subject the various arguments to scientific investigation.

Even though the management of Hindelbank Prison itself and the cantonal prisons authority gave the «green light» for the project, it was to take more than two years before it could get underway when, on 13.6. 1994, syringe dispensers were set up in the six sections of the prison. This delay was primarily due to the fact that the project was given a rough ride by the various political authorities.

The results of this 12-month project are now available. The outcomes, entirely positive, allay all the fears described before the project start. Most importantly, the exchange of used syringes between drug dependents all but disappeared.

A basic aim of the Hindelbank pilot project was to identify general recommendations for the introduction of preventive measures in other prisons. In view of the considerable international interest, we decided to place the results obtained in Hindelbank within a wider context. Financial assistance from the Federal Office of Public Health allowed us to conduct a symposium on this subject between 28.2 and 1.3.1996 at the University Psychiatric Clinic of Bern. Here, specialists from a range of disciplines gathered to exchange their knowledge.

This volume includes all the lectures presented during the symposium. They are, according to the organisation of the symposium, printed in either English, German or French. An article summarising the discussions has been added to cater for readers who are keen to acquire a rapid overview of the question. Eight short paragraphs present the various facets of this scientific discussion and serve as the basis for an attempt to come to an initial conclusion, in so far as this is possible at all given our current state of knowledge.

The main purpose of the symposium was to prepare a scientific basis for subsequent political decisions. The purpose of this book is to make the results available for a wider discussion. If the results presented here are taken into account in political decisions, or in the planning and implementation of further projects, then both aims will have been achieved. In order to ensure the continuing improvement of preventive and harm reducing measures in other prisons, I hope that our book will meet with the adequate reception.

Last but not least, I should like to give my personal thanks for the exceptional commitment of everyone involved in the realisation of the present book.

Bern, November 1996
Joachim Nelles, MD

Vorwort

Als mich Sandra Bernasconi vom Bundesamt für Gesundheitswesen im Frühjahr 1992 anfragte, ob ich bereit wäre, für die Frauenstrafanstalt in Hindelbank ein «Pilotprojekt Drogen- und HIV-Prävention» auszuarbeiten, welches die Abgabe von sterilen Spritzen vorsah, zögerte ich nicht lange. Versteckter Drogenkonsum und der Tausch gebrauchter Spritzen gehörten zum Alltag vieler Gefängnisse. Unter den mit der Problematik Vertrauten wurde zwar rege darüber diskutiert, dass nur schadensbegrenzende Massnahmen, wie sie sich bereits ausserhalb von Gefängnismauern bewährt hatten, geeignet seien, diese unbefriedigenden Verhältnisse innerhalb der Gefängnisse zu verbessern. Doch infolge fehlender Politikfähigkeit solcher Massnahmen blieb die Diskussion zumeist auf einen engen Kreis begrenzt. Von offizieller Vollzugsseite wurden das Drogenproblem im Gefängnis und dessen Folgen über lange Zeit sogar gänzlich negiert. Das vorgesehene Projekt bot die Chance, die vorgebrachten Argumente einer sachlichen Überprüfung zu unterziehen.

Obschon die Verantwortlichen der Strafanstalt Hindelbank wie auch die kantonale Vollzugsbehörde «grünes Licht» für das Projekt signalisierten, sollte es mehr als zwei Jahre dauern, bis es am 13.6.1994 mit dem Aufstellen von Spritzenautomaten in den sechs Abteilungen des Gefängnisses seinen Anfang nehmen konnte. Das lag im wesentlichen daran, dass das Projekt einen dornigen Weg durch verschiedene politische Instanzen zu überstehen hatte. Die nun vorliegenden Resultate aus dem zwölfmonatigen Pilotprojekt sind ermutigend. Sie widerlegen die im Vorfeld geäusserten Befürchtungen. Das wichtigste Resultat besteht darin, dass der Tausch gebrauchter Spritzen in Hindelbank praktisch verschwunden ist.

Ziel des Pilotprojektes war es auch, generelle Empfehlungen für die Einführung präventiver und schadensbegrenzender Massnahmen in anderen Vollzugseinrichtungen zu erarbeiten. Angesichts des grossen internationalen Interesses entschlossen wir uns deshalb, die Resultate von Hindelbank in einen grösseren Kontext zu stellen. Mit finanzieller Hilfe durch das Bundesamt für Gesundheitswesen wurde es möglich, vom 28.2.-1.3.1996 in der Psychiatrischen Universitätsklinik Bern eine Fachtagung zu dieser Thematik durchzuführen. Fachleute aus verschiedenen Disziplinen tauschten dabei ihr Wissen untereinander aus.

Alle Vorträge dieser Tagung sind im vorliegenden Buch aufgenommen und, analog der Aufgliederung der Tagung, entweder in deutscher, französischer oder englischer Sprache verfasst. Ein zusammenfassender Beitrag soll es dem eiligen Leser erlauben, sich einen raschen Überblick über die Thematik zu verschaffen. In acht knappen Abschnitten wurden die Facetten der wissenschaftlichen Diskussion abgehandelt; sie münden in dem Versuch, ein erstes übergreifendes Fazit zu ziehen, sofern dies beim heutigen Stand des Wissens überhaupt schon möglich ist.

Ziel der Tagung war es, wissenschaftliche Grundlagen für spätere politische Entscheidungsprozesse zu erarbeiten. Ziel des vorliegenden Buches ist es, die Ergebnisse einer breiten öffentlichen Diskussion zugänglich zu machen. Fliessen die vorliegenden Resultate in spätere politische Prozesse oder in die Planung und Realisierung anderer Projekte ein, sind beide Ziele erreicht. Im Interesse einer nachhaltigen Verbesserung präventiver und schadensbegrenzender Massnahmen auch in anderen Vollzugsinstitutionen wünsche ich mir eine entsprechende Rezeption dieses Bandes.

An dieser Stelle richte ich zum Schluss meinen Dank an alle, die am Entstehen dieses Buches mitgewirkt haben.

Bern, November 1996
Dr. med. Joachim Nelles

Harm Reduction in Prison
Aspects of a scientific discussion

Andreas Fuhrer
Joachim Nelles

The need for preventive health care in prison

The usual punishment for serious infringements of the law in enlightened countries is the withdrawal of personal freedom. For organisational, economic and, not least, historical reasons, individuals who have been taken into custody are locally concentrated in prisons. Because criminal activity is frequently associated with personal deficiencies in the delinquent, prisons also concentrate a range of problems associated with the inmates: a tendency towards violence, drug use, risk of suicide and poor physical and mental state of the inmates are everyday realities for many prisons. However, because of their very purpose, places of detention are not equipped to deal with this type of problem. As a result, the prison service faces the task of at least preventing the term of imprisonment from having a directly harmful effect on the health of inmates, quite apart from the need to offer appropriate individual care. Harm reduction – the attempt to minimise the avoidable consequences of potentially deleterious conditions and modes of behaviour – is becoming a precondition for one of the most important objectives of the penal system, the resocialisation of imprisoned individuals.

Illegal drug use provides a potent illustration of the importance of harm reduction in prisons. It is not only the scale of drug use in prisons that arouses anxiety (there are prisons in which well over half of the inmates use illegal drugs), but also the disastrous link between covert drug use and the transmission of infectious diseases. HIV and viral hepatitis, both life–threatening infections, propagate with relative ease within the restrictive confines of prison life as a result of unprotected sexual contacts and the sharing of used syringes. Furthermore, when infected prisoners are released, the danger spreads beyond the narrow group of prison inmates. For example, in the longer term, unprotected sexual contacts (casual relationships, contact with prostitutes) may directly or indirectly expose wider sectors of the population to risk.

Despite the significance of these problems, prisons have in the past been largely ignored in the formulation of healthcare and prevention policies. The first pilot projects in Switzerland aimed at enhancing drug and HIV prevention in prisons through pragmatic assistance (needle exchange and controlled heroin prescription programs) gave rise to the exchange of scientific knowledge which is documented in this volume. The discussion focused primarily on the problems of drug use and infection. In this field of preventive health care it would appear to be especially important to raise awareness of the harm reduction approach.

The prison world – a distorting mirror of life?

In many ways, prison walls create an isolated, self–enclosed world. Just as outside, prison life is an alternation of work and free time; prisons have their own economiy, where privileges are the negotiating chips and cigarettes are not the sole means of payment. Prisons have their own culture of hierarchies, routines, stabilised coalitions, written and unwritten laws (Quensel)[1]. Thus, at first glance, prisons appear as a mirror of society.

However, it only takes a glance at the demography of prison populations to show how distorted the analogy between the 'prison microcosm' and the outside world actually is: 95 percent of inmates are male, most of

---

[1] References in this article refer to the respective papers in the present volume.

them are young (source for Switzerland: Koller, Estermann) and, in particular, there are significant differences in terms of general health. Physical and medical disorders are frequent and the consumption of medicaments by prison inmates runs at a significantly higher level than in the normal population (Koller for Switzerland). The occurrence of infectious diseases – hepatitis, tuberculosis, sexually transmitted diseases – is disproportionally high among prisoners and the occurrence of HIV is up to 60 times higher than in the general public (Dolan, Harding, Nelles). Many inmates suffer from psychiatric disorders – an estimated 170,000 prisoners in the USA fall into this category – frequently without receiving appropriate treatment (Harding).

This accumulation of acknowledged social problems in prisons is all the more significant in view of the fact that prisons play a pivotal role in the random mixing of society (Dolan). More than four million people are detained in the world's prisons – this figure does not include the Far East, Asia, South America and Africa. In industrialised countries, the constant prison population typically amounts to 100 prisoners per 100,000 inhabitants. In the USA this number reaches 529/100,000. The total number of individuals who have suffered penal sanctions at any time is, of course, significantly higher. Contrary to what is generally assumed, inmates rarely remain separated from society for long periods: home visits, transfers, parole and the increasing frequency of short terms of imprisonment result in the high levels of fluctuation which are typical of prison populations. As a result, over a period of years large sections of the population may come into contact with the prison world and its problems.

The fateful principle «drug equals crime»

In recent decades, an increasing number of people world–wide have been imprisoned for drug–related offences and drug procurement. On the one hand, the increase in the number of drug–related sentences is connected with the increase in the availability and use of illegal drugs since the 1960s. However, it is equally the consequence of the policy of criminalising drug use and drug possession. Since infringements of the laws on narcotics, for example drug use, usually don't produce victims who wish to file a report with the police, the number of drug–related sentences is primarily a function of the level of police repression. In Switzerland, for example, increased repression has resulted in above–average growth in the number of sentences of this type from just a few cases in the mid 1960s to over 9000 in 1994 (Estermann). A quarter of the inmates currently held in German prisons are there because of infringements of the drugs laws (Quensel).

A large–percentage of inmates who are serving drug–related sentences are themselves drug dependent and it is precisely because of their dependence that they were arrested, whether simply for drug use or for crimes committed in order to finance the purchase of drugs. Most of them find ways and means to continue their drug use in prison (Nelles) and this can only be prevented, if at all, by maintaining total supervision and sacrificing basic human rights. As expected, studies of drug use in prisons reveal some worrying statistics. A survey conducted by the Swiss Federal Office for Statistics reveals that at present 25–50 percent of the prison population is dependent on drugs (Koller). This figure is representative of many industrialised countries and it appears that the proportion of drug dependent women prisoners is considerably higher (Nelles et al 1995). The problems are aggravated by the fact that drug dependent prisoners are frequently ineligible for release on parole due to their drug–related behaviour during imprisonment (Quensel).

Covert drug use has become the major problem confronting many prisons, sometimes obviously, when inmates die from overdoses, but mostly by indirect consequences such as exceptionally high rates of viral hepatitis and HIV infection or relapses following release. There is now scientific evidence that HIV is transmitted in prison (Dolan). Given this situation, it has to be asked whether prison is really the right institution in which to detain drug dependents or whether the penal system needs to come up with new methods for handling such people (Baechtold). For example, alternative models propose suspended sentences for the duration of external therapy or creation of drug therapy wards inside the prison. Quensel, in contrast, asserts that the separate treatment of drug users will constantly create new dependencies and privileges and argues that the cause underlying the association of drug problems and penal sanction, that is to say the politically constructed equivalence of drugs and criminality, has to be reconsidered.

Drug prevention and the principle of equivalence

Drug prevention in the population at large and in special target groups is an established element in the health policies of many countries. Information campaigns, health education and personal counselling, improvements in the quality of life and drug control are the key strategies which are pursued as a function of the objective in question, for example preventing people from starting to use drugs or reducing the number of drug dependents (Uchtenhagen).

An evaluation of prevention programmes in Europe and the USA has shown that the most effective strategies are those that concentrate on the ability of potential drug users to cope with life, their social skills and their self–esteem. Although prevention can modify people's knowledge of and attitude towards drugs, this has only an indirect influence on drug use. If preventive measures are to succeed then it is necessary to continue or repeat them over an extended period (Uchtenhagen). Alongside information and education (primary or secondary prevention), the «acceptance approach», for example provision of sterile syringes or controlled prescription of drugs, has proved to be a successful strategy for reducing the health risks associated with drug use (Dobler–Mikola and Nelles).

One of the problems in drug prevention lies in the fact that it is precisely the individuals at the greatest risk whom it is most difficult to reach (Uchtenhagen). This is particularly true of prisoners, both users and non–users alike. The principle of equivalence – the ethical principle, embodied in health policy, that prevention should be equally available both within and without the prison walls – has long been largely neglected, especially in so far as the politically divisive question of harm reduction measures is concerned (Nelles). To date, preventive health measures in prisons have rarely been systematically documented and even more rarely assessed. Nevertheless, carefully introduced pilot projects seem likely to make it possible to provide drug dependent prisoners with pragmatic assistance (Uchtenhagen).

Harm reduction: an established component of drug prevention

Drug prevention policy uses the term «harm reduction» to refer to measures which do not primarily aim to treat dependence but instead attempt to combat the risks associated with an existing dependence. These measures include the provision of sterile syringes, disinfectants and condoms, education in safer drug use, injecting rooms and the controlled prescription of methadone and heroin (Gutzwiller, Quensel).

On the one hand, such initiatives for harm reduction are justified by the fact that it is less the drugs themselves than the circumstances in which they are used (because of their illegality) that constitute the health risk; for example, abscesses caused by injections and the transmission of HIV and hepatitis result from the re–use of old syringes. Overdoses and poisoning often result from ignorance of the composition and purity of illegally obtained substances. Controlled drug prescription means that drug dependents do not have to find the money for drug purchase and consequently acts as a brake on criminality and prostitution. At the same time, such measures create the preconditions for a life outside the confines of poverty and criminality and thus increase the probability that recipients will successfully overcome their dependence.

Harm reduction demands that drug dependence is, at least for the moment, accepted as a fact. Dependence itself is generally disapproved of. Survival aid by means of harm reduction is continuously criticised for this apparent duality of standards, for example when the provision of syringes and toleration of dependence is construed as a trivialisation of drug use. However, the acceptance of our ethical obligation to help, together with the positive, and now scientifically documented results lead to increased promotion of low risk modes of behaviour for drug dependents and a high level of acceptance of these measures in the general population (Gutzwiller).

Politics and pragmatism

The drug problem is to a large extent a political problem. The drug debate is an arena of ideologies, myths and fears (Quensel). Thus the mass criminalisation of drug users, which confronts the penal system with all but insoluble problems, is primarily driven by the ideologically motivated emphasis on abstinence despite the fact that, in a liberal society, criminal theory does not demand any such criminalisation (Frommel). The politicisation of the drug problem can be seen in the different phases of its development in Switzerland, starting from the social construction of the drug problem around 1968, through the extension of repressive drug policies, superseded by the primacy of health policy between 1987 and 1990 and the return to intensified repression as of 1991 (Estermann). It can also be seen in the attempt to press the drug problem into the service of other political aims, for example when the fight against drugs was misused to justify the introduction of more severe immigration laws (Quensel).

As a result of this ideologically–influenced approach to the real question, drug policy has often helped to fuel the problem it sets itself to address (Quensel). In contrast to this, we have witnessed and are continuing to witness, often under aggravated conditions, a more pragmatic approach to drug dependence in places where the real problem is to be found. As the drugs scene continues to deteriorate and AIDS becomes more widespread, survival support has become a standard healthcare component outside prisons.

Harm reduction in prison: a dilemma?

Harm reduction measures have long ceased to be implemented within the walls of our prisons. Measures which have proved their worth in the population at large are subject to renewed doubt, since it is in prison that the discrepancy between the demand for abstinence and the primacy of health is at its most pronounced. The sceptical interpretation is that certain survival support measures (provision of disinfectants and syringes and the controlled prescription of drugs in prisons) confirm inmates in the very behaviour which brought them to prison or, indeed, might be an incentive for drug use.

However, discrepancies between rhetorically proclaimed objectives and everyday reality are an *inherent* part of the penal system. Prisons form such a deterministic world that contradictions cannot fail to become glaringly obvious. The drug problem and in particular the provision of syringes in prison has, as it were, torn down the veil which normally covers such dilemmas (Baechtold). Yes or no decisions are clearly incapable of fulfilling the disparate tasks facing the penal system, such as the obligation to ensure prisoners' welfare and the need to prepare them for a law–abiding life. The task of the penal system thus becomes one of optimisation which demands that services are graded in order of priority (Baechtold). It is, furthermore, a great advantage if personnel can clearly separate the two areas of responsibility «enforcement» and «welfare». However, the fundamental dilemma will remain as long as the dogma of abstinence persists (Frommel).

Courage and caution

In Switzerland, the harm reduction measures introduced in Hindelbank Prison for women next to Berne (pilot project involving the installation of freely accessible syringe exchange machines) and in Oberschöngrün Prison in Solothurn (syringe provision followed by a pilot project for heroin prescription) represent a new direction in drug and HIV prevention in prisons. These projects met with considerable interest among international experts and in the international press. Within the framework of Swiss drug policy which is explicitly based on the four pillars of prevention, repression, therapy and survival support (Gutzwiller), the measures tested in Hindelbank and Oberschöngrün represent, admittedly, small, but logically consistent steps. The time taken to introduce survival support measures in prisons makes it clear that such a step is by no means self–evident. How, then, did it become possible?

In *Hindelbank Prison*, it was the institution's own health service that initially demanded the introduction of harm reduction measures after a survey which they conducted revealed worrying statistics on the prevalence of HIV and the level of risk–related behaviour in the prison. Following a long period of political deliberation at the level of the cantonal prison authority the introduction of a scientifically supervised drug and HIV prevention programme became possible (Nelles). The Federal Office of Public Health gave the project considerable support during the development stage and financed its implementation. In *Oberschöngrün Prison*, the prison doctor decided, at his own responsibility, to distribute sterile syringes to dependent inmates as a measure to prevent HIV. His actions were subsequently legitimated by the relevant political authority. The positive results of syringe provision is reflected by a high level of acceptance among the prison's management and staff. Using this experience as a springboard, it then became possible to test the results of controlled heroin prescription in Oberschöngrün, a project which was also supported and largely financed by the Federal Office of Public Health (Kaufmann).

What characterises these two projects is the fact that they were both initiated by concerned prison personnel and subsequently won the commitment of an active public health authority which guaranteed systematic project design, scientific supervision, and funding of the project implementation. In the final analysis, it is this combination of *courageous action, circumspect support and scientific appraisal* that has made the projects politically acceptable and practicable.

Conclusions

People in prisons are exposed to exceptionally high health risks. This is the result of the local concentration of unfavourable factors such as drug dependence, mental and social deficiencies, overcrowding, stress, inadequate hygiene practices and restricted access to medical care. Prisons today play a decisive role in the spread of AIDS through the re–use of used syringes and unprotected sexual contact. Since prisons act as hubs of social interaction, the health risks may, in the long term, affect broad sectors of the population – the conception of a prison as an isolated system is far removed from reality.

After many decades when prisons were excluded from both health policy and research, we are now becoming increasingly aware of the disastrous health situation in prisons. Growing numbers of scientific studies of the prevalence of infections and risk–related behaviour in prisons confirm this bleak picture. At the same time, the view that the State is responsible for the health of prisoners is gaining ground: It has withdrawn their liberty. If it also refuses them the necessary medical care then it also places their health at risk.

In contrast to the consensus on the need to integrate prisoner care within health policy, the question of *which* strategies for the improvement of the prison health situation are acceptable and relevant continues to be hotly debated. Prevention through information, counselling and education is widely welcomed. However, most prisons lack the resources for systematic training. Equally, the elimination of unhealthy environmental conditions (prison overcrowding, inadequate hygiene provision etc.) is also limited by the lack of resources. Measures which imply acceptance of the situation, such as the distribution of condoms, disinfectants, syringes and controlled drug prescription, remain contentious. In prisons, where the twin obligations of enforcement and welfare – punishment and help – are juxtaposed, the door still appears to be locked to the widespread introduction of harm reduction measures; health care equivalent to the measures implemented outside the prison walls remain unavailable to most inmates. But Switzerland's initial experience shows that harm reducing drug and HIV prevention measures can also be successful in prison. An examination of this positive approach under different conditions (e.g. in larger institutions, in remand detention centres) might prove to be the starting point for a comprehensive improvement in prison health.

Risikominderung im Gefängnis

Facetten einer wissenschaftlichen Diskussion

Andreas Fuhrer
Joachim Nelles

Die Notwendigkeit der Gesundheitsvorsorge im Gefängnis

Die übliche Strafe, mit welcher schwere Gesetzesverstösse in aufgeklärten Staaten geahndet werden, ist der Entzug der persönlichen Freiheit. Aus organisatorischen, ökonomischen und nicht zuletzt historischen Gründen werden die Freiheitsstrafen in Gefängnissen, d.h. örtlich konzentriert vollzogen. Weil Straffälligkeit oft im Zusammenhang mit persönlichen Defiziten steht, konzentrieren sich im Gefängnis mit den Inhaftierten auch eine Reihe von Problemen: Gewaltbereitschaft, Drogenkonsum, Suizidgefahr und schlechte körperliche und psychische Verfassung der Insassen gehören zum Alltag vieler Gefängnisse. Doch Strafanstalten sind ihrer Bestimmung nach nicht für den Umgang mit derartigen Problemen eingerichtet. In der Folge sehen sich Gefängnisverantwortliche vor die Aufgabe gestellt, wenigstens einen unmittelbar schadenden Einfluss eines Gefängnisaufenthalts auf die Gesundheit der Inhaftierten zu vermeiden, weit entfernt davon, die notwendige individuelle Betreuung anbieten zu können. *Risikominderung* («Harm Reduction») – *der Versuch, vermeidbare Folgen gesundheitsgefährdender Umstände und Verhaltensweisen zu minimieren* – wird zur Voraussetzung für eines der

wichtigsten Ziele des Vollzugs, der Resozialisierung straffällig gewordener Menschen.

Wie notwendig Risikominderung im Gefängnis ist, zeigt sich ein-
drücklich am Beispiel des illegalen Drogenkonsums. Nicht nur das Ausmass des Drogenkonsums im Gefängnis ist besorgniserregend (es gibt
Anstalten, in denen weit mehr als die Hälfte der Insassen illegale Drogen
konsumieren), sondern vor allem die unheilvolle Verknüpfung des ver-
steckten Drogenkonsums mit der Übertragung von Infektionskrankheiten.
HIV und Virale Hepatitis, beides lebensbedrohliche Infektionen, können
sich im geschlossenen Rahmen des Gefängnisses über mehrfach benutzte
Injektionsspritzen oder ungeschützte Sexualkontakte vergleichsweise
leicht ausbreiten. Spätestens mit der Entlassung infizierter Häftlinge beschränkt sich die Gefährdung aber nicht mehr auf den engen Kreis der
Gefängnisinsassen. Über den Weg ungeschützter sexueller Kontakte (Ge-
legenheitsbeziehungen, Beschaffungsprostitution) beispielsweise sind
längerfristig auch weite Bevölkerungskreise direkt oder indirekt von den
Infektionsrisiken betroffen.

Ungeachtet der Tragweite dieser Probleme fanden die Gefängnisse in
der Gesundheitspolitik und –prävention bisher kaum Beachtung. Erste
Pilotversuche in der Schweiz mit dem Ziel, die Drogen– und HIV–Prävention im Gefängnis um pragmatische Hilfsangebote (Spritzen– und
Heroinabgabe) zu erweitern, waren Anlass zu dem im vorliegenden Band
dokumentierten wissenschaftlichen Austausch. Die Diskussion befasste
sich schwergewichtig mit der Drogen– und Infektionsproblematik. In
diesem Bereich der Gesundheitsprophylaxe scheint die Aufwertung
risikomindernder Ansätze besonders notwendig und dringlich.

Gefängniswelt – ein Zerrspiegel des Lebens?

Gefängnismauern schaffen in mancher Hinsicht eine eigene, abgeson-
derte Welt. Im Gefängnis spielt sich wie ausserhalb der Alltag zwischen
Arbeit und Freizeit ab; es existiert ein eigenes Wirtschaftssystem, wo mit
Privilegien gehandelt und nicht nur mit Zigaretten bezahlt wird; es

herrscht eine eigene Kultur der Hierarchien, Routinen, stabilisierten Koalitionen, geschriebenen und ungeschriebenen Gesetze (Quensel)[1]. Oberflächlich betrachtet erscheinen Gefängnisse so als Spiegelbild der Gesellschaft.

Doch schon ein Blick auf die Demographie der Gefängnisbevölkerung zeigt, wie verzerrt die Verhältnisse im «Mikrokosmos Gefängnis» im Vergleich zur übrigen Welt tatsächlich sind: 95 Prozent aller Inhaftierten sind Männer, die meisten von ihnen im jugendlichen Alter (für die Schweiz: Koller, Estermann). Markante Unterschiede zeigen sich insbesondere bezüglich der Gesundheitssituation. Körperliche und psychische Leiden sind häufig, der Medikamentenkonsum bei Inhaftierten ist, verglichen mit der Normalbevölkerung, deutlich erhöht (Koller für die Schweiz). Infektionskrankheiten – Hepatitis, Tuberkulose, Geschlechtskrankheiten – sind unter Gefangenen überproportional häufig; die HIV–Prävalenz ist in Gefängnissen bis zu 60 mal höher als in der Allgemeinbevölkerung (Dolan, Harding, Nelles). Viele Gefangene leiden, oft unbehandelt, an psychiatrischen Erkrankungen – in US–Amerikanischen Gefängnissen schätzungsweise fast 170'000 Menschen (Harding).

Diese Kumulierung an sich bekannter gesellschaftlicher Probleme im Gefängnis ist um so bedeutender, als die Gefängnisse in der ansonsten zufällig durchmischten Gesellschaft eine eigentliche Angelpunktfunktion einnehmen (Dolan). Weltweit leben mehr als vier Millionen Menschen in Gefangenschaft (Asien, der Ferne Osten, Afrika und Südamerika nicht miteingeschlossen), in den Industrieländern beträgt die *ständige* Gefangenenzahl typischerweise 100 Gefangene pro 100'000 Einwohner, in den USA gar 529/100'000. Die Gesamtzahl jemals straffällig Gewordener ist natürlich noch wesentlich höher. Anders als gemeinhin angenommen, bleiben die Häftlinge selten über lange Zeit von der Gesellschaft isoliert: Urlaube, Verlegungen, vorzeitige Entlassungen und eine zunehmende Zahl an Kurzstrafen führen zu der für Gefängnisse typischen hohen Fluk-

---

[1] Referenzen in diesem Artikel beziehen sich auf die Beiträge des vorliegenden Bandes.

tuation. Über die Jahre hinweg kommen auf diese Weise beachtliche Be-
völkerungsteile mit der Gefängniswelt in Berührung.

Die verhängnisvolle Gleichsetzung von Drogen und Kriminalität

In den vergangenen Jahrzehnten wurden weltweit mehr und mehr Personen wegen Drogendelikten oder Beschaffungskriminalität inhaftiert. Der
Anstieg der Zahl drogenbedingter Gefängnisstrafen steht einerseits im
Zusammenhang mit der zunehmenden Verbreitung illegaler Drogen seit
den 60er Jahren, ist andererseits aber auch als Folge der Politik der Kriminalisierung des Drogenkonsums und -besitzes zu werten. Weil bei
Verstössen gegen Betäubungsmittelgesetze, etwa beim Konsum, kaum je
anzeigeerstattende Geschädigte zu finden sind, wird die Anzahl drogenbedingter Verurteilungen wesentlich durch die Intensität der polizeilichen
Repression beeinflusst. In der Schweiz beispielsweise stieg die Zahl
solcher Verurteilungen im Zuge zunehmender Repressionstätigkeit überproportional von wenigen Fällen Mitte der 60er Jahre bis über 9000 im
Jahr 1994 (Estermann). In deutschen Gefängnissen sitzt gegenwärtig ein
Viertel der Gefangenen wegen Verstössen gegen das Betäubungsmittelgesetz ein (Quensel).

Ein Grossteil der drogenbedingt Inhaftierten ist selbst drogenabhängig
und gerade aufgrund der Sucht, sei es wegen blossen Konsums oder
durch Delikte, die der Finanzierung des Konsums dienten, überhaupt erst
straffällig geworden. Die meisten von ihnen finden Mittel und Wege, den
Drogenkonsum im Gefängnis fortzusetzen (Nelles), und nur um den Preis
totaler Kontrolle und unter Opferung elementarer Menschenrechte wäre
dies, wenn überhaupt, zu verhindern. Untersuchungen über den Drogenkonsum in Gefängnissen liefern entsprechend besorgniserregende Zahlen.
So sind gemäss einer Erhebung des Bundesamtes für Statistik der
Schweiz gegenwärtig 25–50 Prozent der Gefängnispopulation drogenabhängig (Koller). Dieser Anteil ist repräsentativ für viele Industrieländer,
wobei unter straffälligen Frauen die Proportion der Drogenabhängigen
noch einmal deutlich höher ist (Nelles et al 1995). Die Problematik wird

akzentuiert durch den Umstand, dass Abhängige oft aufgrund ihres sucht-spezifischen Verhaltens nicht in den Genuss einer vorzeitigen Entlassung kommen (Quensel).

Versteckter Drogenkonsum ist zum Hauptproblem vieler Gefängnisse geworden, mitunter offenkundig, etwa wenn es zu überdosisbedingten Todesfällen kommt, meist aber durch indirekte Auswirkungen, wie aus-sergewöhnlich hohe Infektionsraten mit Viraler Hepatitis und HIV oder drogenbedingte Rückfälle nach der Entlassung. Für HIV–Übertragungen im Gefängnis gibt es mittlerweile wissenschaftliche Evidenz (Dolan). Angesichts dieser Situation stellt sich die Frage, ob das Gefängnis über-haupt die geeignete Institution zur Verwahrung Drogenabhängiger sei, oder ob für sie zumindest neue Formen des Strafvollzugs entwickelt wer-den müssten (Baechtold). Alternative Modelle sehen etwa die Strafaus-setzung für die Dauer einer externen Therapie oder gefängniseigene The-rapieabteilungen vor. Quensel gibt demgegenüber zu bedenken, dass die gesonderte Behandlung der Drogenkonsumierenden stets neue Abhän-gigkeiten und Privilegien schaffe und spricht sich dafür aus, die *Ursache* für die zwangsweise Verknüpfung von Drogenproblem und Strafvollzug, d.h. die politisch konstruierte Identität von Drogen und Kriminalität, neu zu überdenken.

Drogenprävention und das Äquivalenzprinzip

Drogenprävention in der Allgemeinbevölkerung und in speziellen Ziel-gruppen ist fester Bestandteil der Gesundheitspolitik vieler Länder. Infor-mationskampagnen, Gesundheitserziehung und persönliche Beratung, die Verbesserung der Lebensqualität sowie die Kontrolle der Suchtmittel sind Hauptstrategien, welche entsprechend der jeweiligen Ziele, bei-spielsweise der Verhinderung des Einstiegs oder der Reduktion der An-zahl Abhängiger, eingesetzt werden (Uchtenhagen).

Die Evaluation von Präventionsprogrammen in Europa und den USA hat gezeigt, dass vor allem jene Strategien wirksam sind, welche auf die Lebenstüchtigkeit, soziale Kompetenz und Selbstachtung der potentiellen

Drogenkonsumenten abzielen. Das Wissen und die Einstellung bezüglich Drogen kann zwar durch Prävention verändert werden, allerdings mit nur mittelbarem Einfluss auf den Drogenkonsum. Notwendig für den Präventionserfolg ist die Fortsetzung bzw. Wiederholung der Massnahmen über längere Zeit (Uchtenhagen). Neben der informierenden/erziehenden Prophylaxe (primäre bzw. sekundäre Prävention) hat sich der «akzeptierende Ansatz», etwa die Abgabe steriler Spritzen oder die Verschreibung von Betäubungsmitteln, als taugliche Strategie zur Verringerung der mit dem Drogenkonsum verbundenen Gesundheitsrisiken erwiesen (Dobler–Mikola und Nelles).

Eine Schwierigkeit der Drogenprävention besteht darin, dass gerade jene Personen nur ungenügend erreicht werden, die besonderen Risiken ausgesetzt sind (Uchtenhagen). Für Häftlinge, konsumierende wie nicht–konsumierende, gilt das in besonderem Masse. Das *Äquivalenzprinzip* – die aus gesundheitspolitischer und ethischer Sicht erforderliche Gleichstellung der Präventionsangebote innerhalb und ausserhalb der Gefängnismauern – ist, insbesondere was die politisch umstrittenen risikomindernden Massnahmen betrifft, bislang kaum realisiert (Nelles). Gesundheitspräventive Massnahmen in Gefängnissen wurden bisher kaum systematisch dokumentiert und noch seltener evaluiert. Sorgsam eingeführte Pilotprojekte scheinen jedoch geeignet, pragmatische Drogenhilfe auch Gefangenen zugänglich zu machen (Uchtenhagen).

Risikominderung: ein etabliertes Element der Drogenprävention

Die Drogenprävention fasst unter dem Begriff der *Risikominderung* Massnahmen zusammen, welche nicht primär auf eine Therapie der Sucht abzielen, sondern Folgerisiken einer bestehenden Abhängigkeit bekämpfen. Zu diesen Massnahmen zählen die Abgabe von sterilem Spritzenbesteck, von Desinfektionsmitteln und Kondomen, die Anleitung zum sicheren Drogengebrauch, Spritzenräume sowie die Verschreibung von Methadon und Heroin (Gutzwiller, Quensel).

Hilfsangebote zur Risikominderung werden zum einen durch die Tatsache legitimiert, dass es weniger die Drogen selbst als die illegalitäts-bedingten Konsum*umstände* sind, welche gesundheitsgefährdend sind; so sind z.B. Spritzenabszesse, HIV– und Hepatitis–Übertragungen eine Folge der mehrfachen Verwendung gebrauchter Spritzen. Überdosierungen und Vergiftungen resultieren oft aus der Unkenntnis der Zusammensetzung und Reinheit des illegal erworbenen Stoffs. Die Verschreibung von Betäubungsmitteln entlastet die Abhängigen von der Notwendigkeit, Geld für die Droge aufzutreiben und beugt damit der Kriminalität und Prostitution vor. Zum anderen schaffen solche Massnahmen die Voraussetzungen für ein Leben abseits von Verelendung und Kriminalität und erhöhen damit die Chance für einen erfolgreichen Ausstieg aus der Abhängigkeit.

Risikominderung bedingt, dass die Drogenabhängigkeit zumindest vorübergehend als Faktum hingenommen wird. Die Sucht selbst bleibt in der Regel missbilligt. Diese scheinbare Doppelbödigkeit wird der Überlebenshilfe immer wieder zum Vorwurf gemacht, etwa wenn die Spritzenabgabe und –tolerierung als Bagatellisierung des Konsums gewertet werden. Die Einsicht in die ethische Verpflichtung zur Hilfe ebenso wie positive, mittlerweile auch wissenschaftlich dokumentierte Erfahrungen haben dazu geführt, dass sich die Förderung risikoärmerer Verhaltensweisen im Umgang mit Drogenabhängigen dennoch durchsetzen konnte und in der Bevölkerung akzeptiert wird (Gutzwiller).

Politik und Pragmatismus

Das Drogenproblem ist zu einem guten Teil ein politisches Problem. Die Drogendebatte ist geprägt von Ideologien, Mythen und Ängsten (Quensel). So ist die breite Kriminalisierung der Drogenkonsumenten, welche den Strafvollzug vor kaum lösbare Probleme stellt, vornehmlich durch das ideologisch gefärbte Abstinenzaxiom motiviert, während strafrechtstheoretisch dafür in einem liberalen System die Notwendigkeit fehlt (Frommel). Die politische Prägung der Drogenproblematik zeigt sich

beispielhaft in ihrer phasenweisen Entwicklung in der Schweiz, ausgehend von der sozialen Konstruktion des Drogenproblems um 1968,
über den Aufbau drogenpolitischer Repression, deren Ablösung durch
das Primat der Gesundheitspolitik zwischen 1987 und 1990, zurück zu
einer ab 1991 belegten Intensivierung der Repression (Estermann); oder
aber im Versuch, die Drogenproblematik für andere politische Zwecke zu
instrumentalisieren, etwa wenn die Rauschgiftbekämpfung als Begründung für die Verschärfung des Ausländerrechts missbraucht wird (Quensel).

Als Folge dieses ideologisierten Umgangs mit dem eigentlichen Problem agiert die Drogen*politik* oft geradezu als problemtreibende Kraft
(Quensel). Gleichsam im Gegenzug fand und findet, vielfach unter er-
schwerten Bedingungen, eine Pragmatisierung des Umgangs mit Drogensüchtigen dort statt, wo sich das Drogenproblem wirklich abspielt. Im
Zuge zunehmender Verelendung der Drogenszene und der Ausbreitung
von AIDS wurde Überlebenshilfe zu einem Standardangebot des Gesundheitswesens ausserhalb der Gefängnisse.

Risikominderung im Gefängnis: ein Dilemma?

Vor Gefängnismauern haben Massnahmen der Risikominderung bislang
weitgehend Halt gemacht. In Freiheit längst Erprobtes wird neu hinter-
fragt, denn deutlicher als ausserhalb tritt im Gefängnis die Diskrepanz
zwischen Abstinenzanspruch und Gesundheitsprimat zu Tage. Verurteilte
würden, so die skeptische Interpretation, durch gewisse Überlebenshilfe–
Angebote (Abgabe von Desinfektionsmitteln, Spritzen und Betäubungsmitteln im Gefängnis) mitunter gerade in jenem Tun unterstützt, das sie
ins Gefängnis gebracht hat, oder gar zum Drogenkonsum verleitet.

Doch Diskrepanzen zwischen rhetorischen Zielen und Alltagsrealität
gehören *inhärent* zum Strafvollzug. Gefängnisse bilden eine so sehr
determinierte Welt, dass Widersprüche nur allzu deutlich werden müssen.
Das Drogenproblem und insbesondere die Spritzenabgabe im Gefängnis
hat nur gleichsam den Vorhang geöffnet, welcher solche Dilemmata nor-

malerweise verdeckt (Baechtold). Mit binären Entscheidungen sind Vollzugsaufgaben wie Fürsorgepflicht und Vorbereitung auf ein straffreies Leben offensichtlich nicht zur gleichen Zeit adäquat erfüllbar. Der Strafvollzug mündet damit in eine Optimierungsaufgabe, welche die Abstufung der Leistungen nach ihrer Priorität verlangt (Baechtold). Dazu ist es von Vorteil, wenn die konkurrenzierenden Aufgabenbereiche «Vollzug» und «Betreuung» personell klar getrennt werden. Das Grunddilemma bleibt allerdings bestehen, solange das Abstinenzdogma aufrechterhalten bleibt (Frommel).

Mut und Umsicht

In der Schweiz wurden mit den Massnahmen zur Risikominderung in der Frauenstrafanstalt Hindelbank/Bern (Pilotprojekt mit Aufstellung frei zugänglicher Spritzentausch–Automaten) und in der Vollzugsanstalt Oberschöngrün/Solothurn (Spritzenabgabe, später zusätzlich Pilotprojekt zur Heroinverschreibung) neue Wege der Drogen– und HIV–Prävention im Gefängnis eingeschlagen. Die Versuche stiessen international in Fachkreisen und in den Medien auf grosses Interesse. Im Rahmen der schweizerischen Drogenpolitik, die sich explizit auf die vier Säulen Prävention, Repression, Therapie und Überlebenshilfe stützt (Gutzwiller), stellen die in Hindelbank und Oberschöngrün getroffenen Massnahmen zwar nicht mehr als kleine, aber immerhin folgerichtige Schritte dar. Die zeitliche Verzögerung, mit der die Überlebenshilfe im Gefängnis installiert wird, zeigt auf, dass diese Entwicklung keineswegs selbstverständlich ist. Wie wurde sie dennoch möglich?

In der Strafanstalt *Hindelbank* war es der anstaltsinterne Gesundheitsdienst, der ultimativ Massnahmen zur Risikominderung forderte, nachdem eine in eigener Regie durchgeführte Erhebung besorgniserregende Zahlen über die HIV-Prävalenz und das Risikoverhalten in der Anstalt ergeben hatte. Nach einem längeren politischen Entscheidungsprozess auf der Ebene der kantonalen Gefängnisbehörden entstand ein wissenschaftlich begleitetes Drogen– und HIV–Präventionsprojekt (Nelles). Das

Bundesamt für Gesundheitswesen unterstützte das Projekt während seiner Entwicklung massgeblich und finanzierte dessen Durchführung.

In der Strafanstalt *Oberschöngrün* gab der Gefängnisarzt als Massnahme zur HIV–Prävention in eigener Verantwortung sterile Spritzen an drogenabhängige Insassinnen ab. Sein Vorgehen wurde nachträglich durch die politisch verantwortliche Behörde legitimiert. Die positiven Erfahrungen mit der Spritzenabgabe führten zu einer hohen Akzeptanz dieser Massnahme in der Leitung und beim Personal der Anstalt. Aufgrund dieser Ausgangslage konnte in Oberschöngrün die versuchsweise Heroinabgabe, ebenfalls in Zusammenarbeit mit und weitgehend finanziert durch das Bundesamt für Gesundheitswesen, eingeführt werden (Kaufmann).

Kennzeichnend für die beiden Projekte ist, dass sie durch die Initiative besorgter AnstaltsmitarbeiterInnen ausgelöst wurden, gefolgt vom Engagement einer aktiven Gesundheitsbehörde, welche die systematische Konzeption und wissenschaftliche Begleitung gewährleistete und für die finanzielle Starthilfe aufkam. Erst dieses *Zusammenspiel couragierten Vorangehens, umsichtiger Begleitung* und wissenschaftlicher Auswertung hat die Projekte letztlich politikfähig und realisierbar gemacht.

Fazit

Menschen in Gefängnissen sind ausserordentlichen Gesundheitsrisiken ausgesetzt. Dies als Resultat der örtlichen Konzentration ungünstiger Faktoren wie Drogensucht, psychischer und sozialer Defizite, Enge, Stress, ungenügender hygienischer Verhältnisse und beschränkter Möglichkeiten der medizinischen Betreuung. Gefängnisse spielen heute für die Ausbreitung von HIV über gebrauchte Spritzen oder ungeschützte Sexualkontakte eine entscheidende Rolle. Weil Gefängnisse als eigentliche Angelpunkte in der gesellschaftlichen Durchmischung wirken, betreffen die Gesundheitsgefahren langfristig weite Bevölkerungskreise – die Vorstellung vom Gefängnis als isoliertem System ist fern aller Realität.

Nachdem Gefängnisse jahrzehntelang von der Gesundheitspolitik wie von der Forschung weitgehend ausgeklammert blieben, ist man sich heute der mitunter katastrophalen Gesundheitssituation in Gefängnissen zunehmend bewusst. Mehr und mehr wissenschaftliche Studien über Infektionsprävalenzen und das Risikoverhalten in Gefängnissen bestätigen das düstere Bild. Gleichzeitig wächst die Einsicht, dass der Staat für die Gesundheit der Gefangenen Verantwortung trägt: zum Freiheitsentzug hat er sie verurteilt; verwehrt er ihnen die nötige Gesundheitsvorsorge, setzt er ausserdem ihre Gesundheit aufs Spiel.

Im Konstrast zum Konsens über den gesundheitspolitischen Handlungsbedarf wird die Frage, *welche* Strategien zur Verbesserung der Gesundheitssituation im Gefängnis vertretbar und sinnvoll seien, nach wie vor kontrovers diskutiert. Allgemein begrüsst wird Prophylaxe durch Information, Beratung und Ausbildung. Meistens fehlen den Gefängnissen allerdings die Ressourcen für systematisches Training. Ebenso werden der Sanierung gesundheitsfeindlicher Umgebungsbedingungen (Überfüllung der Anstalten, mangelnde hygienische Verhältnisse u.a.) durch Beschränkung der Mittel Grenzen gesetzt. Umstritten bleiben akzeptierende Ansätze, wie die Abgabe von Kondomen, Desinfektionsmitteln, Spritzen und die kontrollierte Drogenabgabe. Im Gefängnis, wo sich Vollzugs- und Betreuungsverantwortung – Strafe und Hilfe – gegenüberstehen, scheint die breite Einführung risikomindernder Massnahmen nach wie vor blockiert; eine zu den Massnahmen ausserhalb der Gefängnisse äquivalente Gesundheitsvorsorge bleibt den meisten Häftlingen vorenthalten. Erste Erfahrungen in der Schweiz haben gezeigt, dass risikomindernde Drogen- und HIV-Präventionsangebote auch im Gefängnis erfolgreich sein können. Eine Überprüfung dieser positiven Ansätze unter veränderten Bedingungen (z.B. in grossen Anstalten, in Untersuchungsgefängnissen) könnte der Ausgangspunkt einer umfassenden Verbesserung der Gesundheitssituation im Gefängnis sein.

Schadensreduktion als Teil einer kohärenten Drogenbekämpfungsstrategie

Felix Gutzwiller

1 Die Schweiz: hohe Suchtbereitschaft

Seit Ende der 60er Jahre werden in der Schweiz illegale Drogen im Sinne des Betäubungsmittelgesetzes in nennenswertem Ausmass gebraucht (1). Stand vorerst der Konsum vor allem von Cannabis im Vordergrund, folgte Mitte der 70er Jahre der Konsum von Heroin und in den 80er Jahren derjenige von Kokain. In den 80er und 90er Jahren hat sich der Konsum in der Schweiz auf einem hohen Niveau weitgehend stabilisiert. Rund ein Viertel der Bevölkerung gab in verschiedenen Untersuchungen an, Erfahrung mit Cannabis-Produkten zu haben. Die Lebenszeitprävalenzen für Opiate liegen je nach Befragung bei 2–4%. Beunruhigend sind zur Zeit insbesondere die individuellen (körperlichen, sozialen) und kollektiven (z.B. Kriminalität) Auswirkungen des Heroinkonsums, aber auch neue Formen des Konsums, wie etwa das sogenannte Folienrauchen (Heroin). Wenig ist bekannt über neue Entwicklungen z.B. in der sogenannten Techno-Szene (Ecstasy).

Werden schliesslich die Konsumziffern bzw. die Gesundheitsschäden hinzugezogen, welche durch den legalen Konsum von Suchtmitteln in der Schweiz zustande kommen, so zeigt sich insgesamt eine hohe Suchtbereitschaft.

2 Ein kohärentes Konzept zur Drogenbekämpfung ist nötig

Aufgrund der hohen Suchtbereitschaft sowie der individuellen und gesellschaftlichen Folgeschäden von Abhängigkeiten ist es heute ein breit
abgestütztes Ziel einer kohärenten Drogenpolitik, das Ausmass an Sucht
und Abhängigkeit möglichst klein zu halten. Zudem muss ein kohärentes
Drogenbekämpfungskonzept die individuellen (z.B. gesundheitlichen
oder sozialen) bzw. gesellschaftlichen Auswirkungen (Beschaffungskriminalität, organisierter Drogenhandel) eindämmen können (2, 3).

Dabei geht es um zwei grundsätzliche Strategien zur Erreichung die-
ser Ziele: einerseits darum, die *Drogennachfrage* zu senken bzw. die
Konsumschäden möglichst gering zu halten, andererseits darum, das
Drogenangebot zu kontrollieren und dadurch möglichst zu reduzieren
(*Abbildung 1*).

Zur Umsetzung dieser Strategien ist einmal von allgemeinen gesellschaftlichen Voraussetzungen auszugehen, welche für die Gesundheit der
Bevölkerung, insbesondere der Heranwachsenden, von Bedeutung sind
(Familienstrukturen, Erziehungswesen, Zukunftsperspektiven, Arbeits-
markt etc.). Zum anderen gelten generelle rechtsstaatliche Grundsätze.

Auf der Nachfrageseite geht es einmal um eine umfassende, moderne
Gesundheitsförderung im Sinne der eigentlichen Verhütung (*primäre
Prävention*).

Das moderne Konzept der Gesundheitsförderung und Prävention beruht auf der sogenannten Ottawa-Charta der Weltgesundheitsorganisation
(1986). Danach zielt «Gesundheitsförderung auf einen Prozess, allen
Menschen ein höheres Mass an Selbstbestimmung über ihre Lebensum-
stände und Umwelt zu ermöglichen und sie damit zur Stärkung ihrer
Gesundheit zu befähigen. Gesundheit steht für ein positives Konzept, das
in gleicher Weise die Bedeutung sozialer und individueller Ressourcen
für die Gesundheit ebenso betont wie die körperlichen Fähigkeiten».

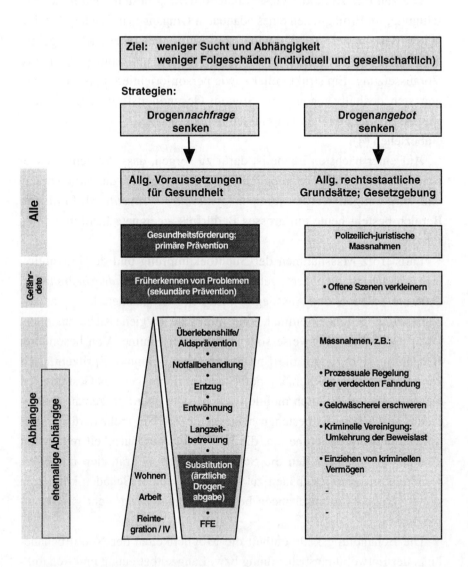

Abbildung 1: Kohärente Drogenbekämpfung

Die zentrale Rolle der Gesundheitsförderung besteht also in der Befähigung, im Ermöglichen eines adäquaten Umganges mit sich selbst. Ein hohes Mass an Selbstbestimmung bzw. Autonomie, aber auch an gesellschaftlichen Massnahmen, welche diesen Prozess unterstützen, sind dazu Voraussetzung. Ein struktureller sowie person-orientierter Ansatz bedingen sich deshalb gegenseitig. Sowohl Gesundheitsförderung als auch spezifische Suchtprävention müssen beide Ansätze in ihre Massnahmen einbeziehen (4).

Auf einer nächsten Ebene ist dafür zu sorgen, dass Probleme, insbesondere bei Jugendlichen, möglichst früh und möglichst dezentral erkannt und aufgefangen werden können *(sekundäre Prävention)*. In diesem Bereich besteht heute ein grosses Bedürfnis, geeignete Institutionen zu schaffen.

Falls trotz Massnahmen der Suchtbekämpfung und der Prävention eine Abhängigkeit entsteht, geht es vorerst um die *Schadensbegrenzung*, dann um Therapie und Ausstieg (5). Zu den Massnahmen der Schadensbegrenzung gehört es einmal, eine minimale Hygiene sicherzustellen. Dazu dienen beispielsweise sogenannte Fixer-Räume. Von besonderer Bedeutung sind zudem die Spritzentauschprogramme. Spritzentausch kann vor Ort (Fixer-Räume, Apotheken, Einrichtungen des Gesundheitswesens), aber auch durch mobile Equipen oder aber Spritzentauschautomaten geschehen. Es bestehen heute keine Zweifel mehr darüber, dass Spritzentauschprogramme u.a. die HIV-Infektionshäufigkeit reduzieren können. Insgesamt sollen die Schadensreduktionsstrategien mithelfen, weitere Konsumfolgeschäden zu vermeiden. Solche Schäden können ja spätere Rehabilitationschancen beeinträchtigen, wenn nicht gar verunmöglichen.

Die Behandlungskette enthält die Möglichkeiten der Notfallbehandlung, der Entwöhnungsbehandlung bzw. Langzeitbetreuung und Rehabilitation sowie des Entzugs. Zudem werden in der Schweiz zur Zeit Versuche zur diversifizierten ärztlichen Drogenabgabe (inklusive Heroin) durchgeführt. Ziel der Heroinabgabe ist es also, eingebettet in ein therapie-orientiertes Umfeld Abhängigen einen Ausstieg aus der Kriminalität bzw. der Szene, eine physische und psychische Stabilisierung sowie die längerfristige Rehabilitation zu gestatten (6).

Mit der Behandlungskette werden nur Fortschritte erzielt, wenn gleichzeitig Massnahmen zur Deckung der existentiellen Grundbedürfnisse ergriffen werden (d.h. Reintegrationsangebote sowie begleitetes Wohnen, Arbeiten etc.).

Schliesslich dürfen Massnahmen zur Senkung der Drogennachfrage und solche, welche das illegale Drogenangebot eindämmen, möglichst wenig Widersprüche beinhalten. Einige der polizeilich-juristischen Massnahmen sind in *Abbildung 1* beispielhaft angegeben, auch wenn sie hier nicht weiter diskutiert werden sollen.

3 Die aktuellen drogenpolitischen Positionsbezüge: Ein «dritter Weg»?

Nach jahrelangen drogenpolitischen Diskussionen, die weitgehend durch eine extreme Polarisierung und ein Verharren an Ort gekennzeichnet waren, ist nun deutlich Bewegung in die Drogenpolitik gekommen.

Drei Richtungen markieren die Pole dieser drogenpolitischen Diskussion, die auch über die Zukunft von Massnahmen der Schadensbegrenzung mitentscheiden wird.

Als erste von zwei *Volksinitiativen* wird wohl 1997 die Initiative «Jugend ohne Drogen» zur Abstimmung kommen. Diese Initiative sieht vor, über die Verfassung den Bund zu einer restriktiven und ausschliesslich auf Abstinenz ausgerichteten Drogenpolitik zu verpflichten. Bundesrat und Parlament stellen sich gegen diese Initiative, da sie essentielle Elemente einer breitgefächerten drogenpolitischen Strategie verunmöglichen würde. Zu diesen Elementen gehört auch die Schadensreduktion. So sind nach Ansicht der bundesrätlichen Botschaft etwa Spritzentauschprogramme, aber auch die Methadonsubstitution nach einer eventuellen Annahme dieser Initiative kaum mehr durchführbar (7).

Auf der anderen Seite des drogenpolitischen Spektrums steht die ebenfalls eingereichte Volksinitiative der DROLEG. Hier geht es im

Prinzip um eine Legalisierung der entsprechenden Betäubungsmittel ohne ärztliche Kontrolle. Auch diese Initiative wird von Bundesrat und Parlament abgelehnt. Hauptgrund dabei ist wohl der mit Annahme dieser Initiative verbundene drogenpolitische Alleingang der Schweiz, die schon heute mit den Heroinabgabeversuchen international nicht nur auf Beifall stösst. Zudem wird geltend gemacht, dass die Vorteile einer Zerschlagung des Schwarzmarktes bzw. der organisierten Kriminalität durch die Legalisierung der entsprechenden Substanzen auf der Hand liege, umgekehrt aber nicht sicher sei, welches Ausmass an zusätzlichen Abhängigen zu verzeichnen wäre.

Nicht einfach als Kompromiss, sondern als echter «dritter Weg» sieht dagegen die bundesrätliche Drogenpolitik eine 4-Säulen-Strategie vor, die nun seit einigen Jahren in der Schweiz umgesetzt wird (Prävention, Schadensreduktion, Therapie, Repression). In dieser Beziehung ergibt sich auch Übereinstimmung mit dem schon früher zitierten Konzept von drei Bundesratsparteien (3). Um die notwendigen gesetzlichen Veränderungen vorzubereiten (insbesondere diejenigen des Betäubungsmittelgesetzes BtmG) hat der Bundesrat eine Expertenkommission eingesetzt. Der entsprechende Bericht liegt seit Februar 1996 vor (8). Unter den vorgeschlagenen Gesetzesänderungen befinden sich auch Aussagen zur Entkriminalisierung des Konsums bzw. zur Medikalisierung der Heroinabgabe. Mit der Revision des Betäubungsmittelgesetzes wird das Eidgenössische Departement des Innern (EDI) wohl bis nach der Abstimmung über die Initiative «Jugend ohne Drogen» zuwarten wollen. Dannzumal könnte eine baldige Revision – aufgrund der Vorbereitungen der erwähnten Expertengruppe – in einem konkreten indirekten Gegenvorschlag auf Gesetzesstufe resultieren.

Es spricht heute einiges dafür, dass dieser «dritter Weg» in der Schweiz mehrheitsfähig werden wird und dass damit auch Massnahmen der Schadensreduktion für die Zukunft gesichert sein werden.

4   Eine kohärente Drogenbekämpfungsstrategie: mehrheitsfähig?

In der vom Institut für Sozial- und Präventivmedizin der Universität Lausanne sowie von IPSO Sozialforschung durchgeführten Repräsentativbefragung (1994, n=1'202) wurde auch der Akzeptanz von verschiedenen Massnahmen zur Drogenbekämpfung nachgegangen (9). Zudem konnten die Antworten mit einer gleichartigen, ebenfalls repräsentativen Befragung von 1991 verglichen werden. Aus *Abbildung 2* geht folgendes hervor: Massnahmen, welche einer aktiven Prävention oder Frühbehandlung zugeordnet werden können, weisen heute eine hohe Akzeptanz auf. Das gleiche gilt für die Bestrafung des Drogenhandels bzw. der Geldwäscherei.

Ebenfalls klar mehrheitsfähig scheinen Massnahmen der Schadensreduktion zu sein. So weisen sogenannte Fixer-Räume heute eine Akzeptanz von rund 70% auf. Die ärztlich kontrollierte Drogenabgabe schliesslich wird heute ebenfalls von rund 70% der Befragten befürwortet – ein klarer Anstieg seit 1991 (63,8%). Umstritten bzw. nicht akzeptabel sind für eine Mehrheit weitere Postulate wie der öffentliche Konsum, oder aber der freie Verkauf von Cannabis-Produkten. Insgesamt scheinen diese Daten darauf hinzuweisen, dass sich nach jahrelangen, teilweise äusserst kontrovers geführten Diskussionen nun die Erkenntnis durchsetzt, dass es zur Lösung der Drogenproblematik keine einfachen Rezepte gibt.

Nur eine kohärente Strategie, welche unterschiedlichste Massnahmen zu einem möglichst kohärenten Ganzen verbindet, wird Fortschritte bringen können. Eine vorurteilslose Beurteilung verschiedener Massnahmen ist also nötig.

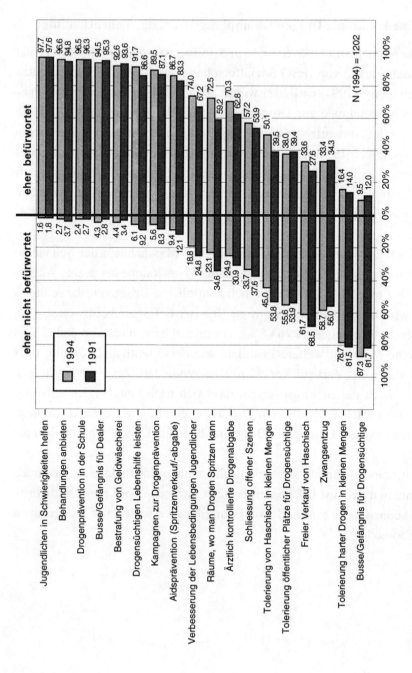

Abbildung 2: Zustimmung der Bevölkerung zu verschiedenen Lösungen für das Drogensuchtproblem

Literatur

1   Uchtenhagen A. Suchtrisiko und Suchtbehandlung in der Schweiz. Aus: *Drogenpolitik wohin?* Sachverhalte, Entwicklungen, Handlungsvorschläge. Wolfgang Böker; Joachim Nelles (Hrsg.), S. 201-219, Verlag Paul Haupt Bern und Stuttgart (Publikation der Akademischen Kommission der Universität Bern).

2   Lagebericht und Gesamtkonzept für Massnahmen im Bereich des Suchtmittelkonsums; Kantonale Kommission für Drogenfragen, Zürich, 1992.

3   «Für eine kohärente Drogenpolitik» (Konzept und Massnahmen). FDP, SP und CVP Schweiz, 24.6.1994.

4   Suchtpräventionskonzept. Bericht der Arbeitsgruppe «Suchtprävention/ Gesundheitsförderung. Gesundheitsdirektion des Kantons Zürich und Institut für Sozial- und Präventivmedizin der Universität Zürich (Hrsg.), Zürich, Oktober 1991.

5   Uchtenhagen A. Erkenntnisse aus einigen Behandlungsansätzen und Behandlungserfahrungen. Aus: *Drogenpolitik wohin?* Sachverhalte, Entwicklungen, Handlungsvorschläge. Wolfgang Böker; Joachim Nelles (Hrsg.), S. 201-219, Verlag Paul Haupt Bern und Stuttgart (Publikation der Akademischen Kommission der Universität Bern).

6   Uchtenhagen A, Dobler-Mikola A, Gutzwiller F. Ärztlich kontrollierte Verschreibung von Betäubungsmitteln: Grundlagen, Forschungsplan, erste Erfahrungen. In: Bundesamt für Gesundheitswesen. Hrsg. von M. Rihs-Middel... Ärztliche Verschreibung von Betäubungsmitteln: wissenschaftliche Grundlagen und praktische Erfahrungen. Bern. Huber, 1996; 26-49.

7   Botschaft des Bundesrates zu den Volksinitiativen «Jugend ohne Drogen» und «Für eine vernünftige Drogenpolitik» vom 19. Juni 1995. Bundesblatt 1995 III, S. 1250.

8   Bericht der Expertenkommission für die *Revision des Betäubungsmittelgesetzes vom 3. Oktober 1951* an die Vorsteherin des Eidgenössischen Departementes des Innern, Bundesamt für Gesundheitswesen, Bern, Februar 1996.

9   Evaluation der Massnahmen des Bundes zur Verminderung der Drogenprobleme: Phase II, 1992–1994. Dubois-Arber F. et al. Einstellungen der Schweizer Bevölkerung zum illegalen Drogenkonsum. Institut für Sozial- und Präventivmedizin der Universität Lausanne, Lausanne, 1994.

Drogen im Strafvollzug – muß das sein?

Stephan Quensel

Die hier anstehende Diskussion gleicht der in den USA heftig diskutierten Frage, welches die beste Hinrichtungsart sei: Gas, Erschießen, Gift oder Hängen – eine Entscheidung, die man im Einzelfall sogar dem Verurteilten überläßt – anstatt die Todesstrafe abzuschaffen.

Dies war mein Eindruck, als wir vor 12 Jahren im Gottlieb Duttweiler Institut über «Sondereinrichtungen für Drogenabhängige im Strafvollzug» diskutierten (Bachmann 1985).

Ich meine, daß auch unsere Diskussion hier diesem Dilemma nicht entgehen kann – auch wenn wir mit viel gutem Willen gleichsam an der vordersten Front der Drogenpolitik agieren. Da ich von den praktischen Details nicht allzuviel verstehe, möchte ich deshalb versuchen, aus soziologischer Sicht etwas zum Hintergrund unserer Diskussion zu sagen, wobei ich zunächst kurz allgemein auf die drogenpolitische Entwicklung der letzten Jahre eingehen möchte, um sodann drei konkretere Problembereiche anzusprechen, die bei der Einführung von Harm Reduction im Strafvollzug zu beachten sind – auch wenn ich damit in diesen informierten Kreisen eher offene Türen einrennen werde. Zum Abschluß versuche ich, das Ergebnis in zehn Thesen zusammenzufassen.

1. Beobachtet man die *Entwicklung der Drogenpolitik* in diesen letzten 12 Jahren, lassen sich – zumindest aus deutscher Sicht – je zwei gegenläufige Trends festhalten:

1.1 Wir können zunächst eine sehr deutliche Tendenz feststellen, den *Soft–Drogen–Bereich* faktisch zu entkriminalisieren und den Gebrauch von Cannabis und Ecstasy weitgehend zu normalisieren (vgl. BISDRO 1995). Eine Tendenz, die freilich regional sehr unterschiedlich ausfällt, und die noch immer mit erheblichen Widerständen zu rechnen hat. Während wir bei uns – insbesondere nach der recht verklausulierten Entscheidung des Bundesverfassungsgerichts von 1994 – in den norddeutschen Ländern fast niederländische Verhältnisse haben, und in den Niederlanden zunehmend der Eigenanbau des Nederweeds auch für die Koffieshop–Belieferung geduldet wird, schickt man in Bayern und Frankreich noch immer Cannabis–Konsumenten in den Strafvollzug oder in die «Zwangs–Therapie» (wobei die Franzosen den «Konsum» direkt, wir dagegen den Konsumenten über den «Besitz» bestrafen; vgl. Siebel 1996). Diese Entwicklung entspricht etwa den Vorschlägen der Schweizer Expertenkommission, den Konsum zu entkriminalisieren.

1.2 Im Bereich der *harten Drogen* erleben wir in der Drogen–Praxis im Gefolge von Aids wie aber auch aus zunehmender Einsicht in das faktische Ausmaß der Verelendung eine fast explosionsartige Entfaltung eines akzeptierenden Ansatzes nach niederländisch–schweizerischem Vorbild. Dies reicht von der ständig zunehmenden Methadon–Vergabe – auch vereinzelt in Strafanstalten, über die akzeptierende Betreuung, den Nadeltausch und Druckräume (etwa in Frankfurt) bis hin zu den z.Z. umkämpften Versuchen, Heroin–Programme einzuführen.

Ein akzeptierender Ansatz, der auf der einen Seite der Drogen–Sozialarbeit den abgerissenen Kontakt zum Abhängigen wieder eröffnet hat, ohne doch die klassische Therapie zu beeinträchtigen, die ihrerseits ebenfalls neue, realitätsnähere Therapieformen entwickelt hat: Kurzzeit–Therapie, Paartherapie, ambulanttherapeutische Begleitung (vgl. zu deren Vielfalt und zu den damit verbundenen Risiken: Neue Zürcher Zeitung vom 26.2.96, S.13f: «Sinkende Nachfrage nach Drogentherapien»). Ein Ansatz freilich, der auf der anderen Seite sowohl von der Bevölkerung wie auch von Seiten der Polizei stets in seinen Grenzen gehalten wird:

vom Platzspitz–Syndrom bis hin zum Rotterdamer Bürger–Aufstand, den wir in ähnlicher Weise auch bei uns beobachten können, wenn es etwa darum geht, einen Nadel–Automaten aufzuhängen oder eine Wohnung für Drogenabhängige anzumieten.

1.3 In der vom Tagesgeschehen abgehobenen *Politik* verschärft sich dagegen die repressive Komponente, und zwar um so deutlicher, je «höher» die Politik–Ebene liegt.

Auf den «unteren» Ebenen sind die *Kommunen* in ihrer Sozial–Politik mit den direkten Folgen konfrontiert, die bei uns in den sozialdemokratisch regierten Bundesländern bis hin zu entsprechenden Bundesrats–Initiativen auch ernst genommen werden: so etwa die Schleswig–Holsteinische Initiative, Koffieshops zu erproben, die von den Gesundheitsministern der Bundesländer weitgehend unterstützt wird, oder der Hamburger und Frankfurter Antrag für ein Heroinprogramm, die bisher beide abgelehnt wurden, die Methadonvergabe in den Strafanstalten in Bremen und Hamburg sowie die niedersächsischen Experimente zur Nadelvergabe in je einer Männer– und einer Frauen–Strafanstalt.

Im länderübergreifenden Bereich der *großen Verbände* wie der *Polizei* dagegen dominieren nach wie vor die alten Interessen, mit Hilfe des «Drogen–Problems» Ressourcen materiell–finanzieller Art einzuwerben bzw. mit dem Druckmittel der organisierten Drogen–Mafia rechtsstaatsfremde Befugnisse – Lauschangriff, V–Männer etc. – zu erhalten.

Auf der *Bundesebene* herrscht nach wie vor ungebrochen der repressive Ansatz, mit der Angst vor den Drogen «Politik» zu betreiben. Ein Ansatz, der schließlich zusammen mit den USA, Frankreich und in Zukunft verstärkt auch mit den neu in die EU eingetretenen skandinavischen Ländern die *internationale Ebene* entscheidend beeinflußt: im Wirken der Pompidou–Gruppe, im Schengener Abkommen, im anstehenden Disziplinierungs–Besuch von Chirac und Kohl in den Niederlanden und – last but not least – in der von Deutschland mit vorangetriebenen und inzwischen bei uns auch ratifizierten Wiener Konvention von 1988.

1.4 Diese noch immer «moderne» repressive Basis schlägt sich ganz unmittelbar im *Strafvollzugs–Bereich* nieder. Hier zeigt sich viel deutlicher noch als bei den fast beliebig manipulierbaren Zahlen der Drogentoten oder bei den polizeilich gelieferten Daten die katastrophale problemtreibende Kraft unserer offiziellen Drogenpolitik. Ein Sachverhalt, der vielleicht auch erklären kann, warum der Strafvollzug bei den sonst so vernünftig vermittelnden Vorschlägen der Schweizer Experten–Kommission (zumindest in den Zeitungsberichten) nicht vorkommt.

Wir rechnen heute bei uns damit, daß einem guten Viertel aller strafrechtlichen *Verurteilungen* zu einer Freiheitsstrafe von mehr als zwei Jahren (die nicht mehr zur Bewährung ausgesetzt werden kann) als Hauptdelikt ein Verstoß gegen das Betäubungsmittel–Gesetz (BtMG) zugrundeliegt, daß diese Täter also die größte Gruppe unserer «Schwerstverbrecher» stellen. Dementsprechend finden wir in unseren *Strafanstalten* etwa ein Viertel reine BtMG–Täter und ein weiteres Viertel «Beschaffungs–Kriminelle» (BISDRO 1995), denen überdies wegen ihrer Drogenabhängigkeit (und der damit zusammenhängenden Mißerfolge bei den Probeurlauben etc.) sehr häufig die vorzeitige Entlassung verwehrt und damit die ohnehin überlange Strafzeit gegenüber ihren Mitgefangenen sogar faktisch noch verlängert wird; Zahlen, die in den Frauenanstalten und in den Untersuchungshaft–Anstalten noch höher ausfallen sollen.

Wir stoßen hier auf eine Entwicklung, die bei uns in den letzten Jahren den guten Trend zur Liberalisierung und Einschränkung der Freiheitsstrafe gestoppt hat, die in Frankreich und insbesondere in den Niederlanden die Zahl der Gefangenen enorm ansteigen ließ, und die in den USA letztlich dafür verantwortlich ist, daß sie mit 530 Gefangenen auf 100'000 Einwohner etwa 6mal mehr Haftplätze benötigen als ihre genötigten europäischen Partner (Harrison 1995).

1.5 Sehen wir einmal von den *Kosten* ab, die bei uns allein für diese ca. 20'000 inhaftierten modernen «Ketzer und Hexen» ca. eine Milliarde DM ausmachen (ein Betrag, der in der kleineren Schweiz für die gesamte «teure Repression» aufzuwenden ist: s. Der Bund vom 23.2.1996, S.18), dann läßt sich diese Entwicklung aus der lokalen Bremer Sicht auch *praktisch* recht eindrucksvoll belegen:

(1) In unserem Straffälligen–Hilfe–Verein, der in Bremen fünf Häuser betreibt, hatten wir vor Jahren beschlossen, drogenabhängige Strafgefangene nicht in das Haupthaus aufzunehmen und die anderen Häuser nur im Verhältnis von einem Abhängigen zu drei «normalen» Strafentlassenen zu belegen. Heute, wenige Jahre später, wird auch das Haupthaus zu 80% von Drogentätern bewohnt. Man mag dies als Indiz dafür nehmen, wie sehr diese Art repressiver Drogenpolitik gleichsam von hinten in die klassische *Sozialarbeit* hineinwirkt.

(2) Noch deutlicher wird dies, wenn wir feststellen, daß in den letzten Jahren unsere drogenabhängigen Knast–Klienten immer jünger und schwieriger werden mit einer wachsenden Belastung durch Haftzeiten und Hafterfahrungen: *Karrieren*, die schon äußerlich sichtbar werden, die aber in ihrer prisonisierten Lebensuntauglichkeit immer mehr dem Junkie–Bild entsprechen, nach dem diese Art der Drogenpolitik entworfen wurde. Ein Foucault'scher Traum – der Strafvollzug produziert sein Problem – der selbst in der niederländischen Regierungserklärung wie auch im Schweizer Gesprächskreis der Wirtschaftsführer oder jetzt jüngst bei der Schweizer Expertenkommission den Ruf nach kasernierter Zwangstherapie bzw. nach dem Ausbau fürsorgerischer Freiheitsentziehung laut werden läßt, obwohl wir doch in unserem insofern sicher vorbildlichen Drogen–Maßregel–Vollzug inzwischen fast 100 Prozent Mißerfolg konstatieren müssen (Schulzke 1993), und in der Schweiz die geschlossene Drogenstation Oberhalden in Egg mangels Nachfrage schließen muß (Neue Zürcher Zeitung vom 27.2.96, S.53: «Betriebseinstellung der Drogenstation in Egg»).

(3) Vollzugserfahrungen, die schließlich auch dazu führen, daß die *Szene* selber rauher und roher wird, weil man auf der einen Seite gar nichts mehr zu verlieren hat, und auf der anderen Seite eben nur noch dies im

Gefängnis gelernt hat: sich gewaltsam das Notwendige zu nehmen und alles einmal durchzuprobieren. Gewalt, Raub und kaum vertuschter Diebstahl paart sich hier mit breitem Drogenmißbrauch, in dem Methadon allenfalls die Basisversorgung garantiert, Alkohol, Tabletten und zunehmend Kokain dagegen den Lebensstandard bilden (Kemmesies 1996).

2. Der Versuch, Harm Reduction in das Gefängnis einzuführen, muß drei Problemfelder berücksichtigen: das Gefängnis–System, die Funktion der Droge und die noch immer dominierende Drogen–Ideologie.

2.1 *Gefängnisse* sind – im Regelfall und sicher ungewollt – perfekte *Asozialisierungs–Apparate*, die selektiv diejenigen Störungen verstärken, mit denen ihre Insassen eingeliefert wurden, und zwar um so perfekter, je länger die Insassen prisonisiert werden, je größer die Anstalt ist und je mehr sie auf Sicherheit und Ordnung zu achten hat.

Dies galt schon immer ganz allgemein für den Ausschluß vom üblichen Normalleben wie umgekehrt für die Notwendigkeit, sich an den anderen Gefangenen zu orientieren. Eine Wirkung, die aber auch spezifisch den Gewalttäter für sein gewaltsames Handeln belohnt, dem Betrüger die wenigen Vorzugs–Inseln reserviert (Bibliothek oder Behandlungsplätze) und die «grauen Mäuse» als problemlos auch «drinnen» übersieht.

Dieser selektive Verstärkungsmechanismus funktioniert in eben dieser Weise auch heute für die neuartige *Drogen–Klientel*: der Abhängige wird im Zweifel noch abhängiger, da ihm die Alternativen fehlen, und der Dealer erwirbt in dieser «Hochschule des Verbrechens» – wie man diesen Mechanismus früher benannte – sein Dealer–Diplom.

Die bekannten Rückfallzahlen belegen diesen Sachverhalt ebenso wie die zunehmende Verelendung vielfach bestrafter Drogentäter.

2.2 Gefängnisse sind als solche weithin *reformresistent*, so sehr man auch seit Beginn ihrer vierhundertjährigen Geschichte an solchen Reformen arbeitete – wobei wiederum zumeist personengebundene Ausnahmen die Regel bestätigen.

Diese Resistenz ergibt sich u.a. daraus, daß Gefängnisse nur dann funktionieren können, wenn die beiden Subsysteme der Insassen– und der Personal–Kultur einen modus vivendi gefunden haben, die das jeweils andere Subsystem möglichst ungestört läßt.

(1) Im Rahmen der *Insassen–Kultur* bilden sich dabei informelle Macht– und Interaktions–Strukturen, die jedem Insassen eine jeweils bestimmte Position zuordnen – als Leader, Händler, Schläger, Sexualobjekt oder Sündenbock – um auf diese Weise einerseits Ruhe und Ordnung zu bewahren, andererseits die knappen Ressourcen interessengelenkt zu verteilen.

Der «Einbruch» der neuen Drogen–Klientel hat diese Ordnung anfangs erheblich gestört, bis sie heute in einer – bisher wenig untersuchten – neuartigen Mischkultur aus «Droge und Kriminalität» ein neues Gleich-gewicht gefunden hat. Ein Anpassungs–Prozess, den Mathiesen (1969) als «defences of the weak» schon früh für therapeutische Institutionen beobachtet hat, und für den das Scheitern spezifischer «Drogen–Abtei-lungen» beredtes Zeugnis ablegt.

Die Einführung von Harm–Reduction–Techniken – Nadeltausch, Methadon, Safer–use–training, Heroin–Vergabe, drogenfreie Abteilungen und bedingt vorzeitige Entlassung – schafft neue Privilegien und zerstört alte Abhängigkeiten. Sie führt zu neuen «Koalitionen» mit der anderen Seite und gefährdet insgesamt das eingefrorene Gleichgewicht der Kräfte.

(2) Aber auch die *Personal–Kultur* hat sich in ihrer Anstalt ebenso eingerichtet wie die «Lebenslangen» auf der anderen Seite. Auch hier gibt es die formellen wie informellen Machtzentren – in der Dienstauf-sichtsleitung oder dem Personalrat – die eingeschliffenen Routinen und kleinen Privilegien, die stabilisierten «Koalitionen» zur anderen Seite hin. Eingebunden in ein ebenso abstraktes wie detailliertes Regelwerk, dessen Funktionieren nur bei ständigem Regelverstoß garantiert ist und dessen Funktion in der Verlagerung der Verantwortung für den Krisenfall besteht, wird jeder Reform–Versuch über kurz oder lang absorbiert – die

Anweisung «von oben» ebenso wie die Angliederung des «Behandlungs–Personals», das alsbald außerhalb seiner therapeutischen Inseln der Grundmatrix der Personal–Kultur zu folgen hat, will es nicht ins Leere laufen.

Die Einführung neuartiger Harm–Reduction–Techniken kann dieses Hierarchie–Gebäude stören, eingeschliffene Wechselbeziehungen zur Insassen–Kultur beeinträchtigen und neue Sozialaufgaben mit sich bringen bzw. zusätzlichen Aufwand zur Aufrechterhaltung von Ordnung und Sicherheit erforderlich machen.

(3) Eine fast einverständliche Reform–Resistenz also, die ebenso auf Widerständen wie auf erfolgversprechenden Absorptionsprozessen beruht, und die eine Veränderung um so mehr erschweren wird, je länger diese Kulturen erfolgreich existieren, je größer die Anstalt ist, und je gewichtiger «Sicherheit und Ordnung» die Anstalt regieren.

3. Diese Reform–Resistenz begleitet das Gefängniswesen von seinen Ursprüngen an; sie hat uns diese weithin untaugliche, mittelalterliche Apparatur zur Verwahrung von Problemfällen bis heute erhalten. Die *Drogen* erfüllen sie heute mit neuem Leben.

3.1 Gleichwohl hat es immer schon Drogen im Gefängnis gegeben, den Tabak, den selbstgebrauten Schnaps, die Kaffee–Bombe oder die geröstete Bananenschale.

Sie erfüllen dort eine *dreifache Funktion*: Sie *kompensieren* zunächst – weitaus stärker noch als «draußen» – die ungeheure Freizeit–Öde, die Isolation, das Bewußtsein des Versagens. Sie schaffen kleine Inseln des Wohlbehagens, des Abschaltens und Vergessens. Das galt für die Zigarette und den eingeschmuggelten oder selbstgebrauten Alkohol ebenso wie heute für Cannabis und Heroin oder Kokain.

Drogen gerieten damit zum anstaltsinternen *Zahlungsmittel*, zur Tabakwährung wie bei uns nach dem zweiten Weltkrieg, zum Alkohol-Deal und heute zum doppelt verbotenen Drogenhandel; zum Zahlungsmittel für Händler, Bänker, Schuldner und Gläubiger, zum Schmiermittel der Insassen–Kultur.

Und Drogen können auf dieser Basis zum *Status–Kriterium* werden, wiederum ähnlich wie «draußen», wenn auch vergröbert und verzerrt. Da gibt es die Haves und Have–not, diejenigen, die großzügig einen spendieren, und die Unterwürfigen mit dem «Haste nicht mal 'ne Zigarette für mich». Mit Drogen demonstriert man Zugehörigkeit zur «in–group», festigen sich Knast–Freundschaften und lassen sich interne Hierarchien absichern. Drogen regulieren auch die Beziehung zur anderen Subkultur; weniger wegen manifester Korruption, sondern weitaus häufiger im Rahmen eines je spezifisch eingependelten Drogen–Kontroll–Verhaltens. Ein Verhaltensspielraum, der von permanenter Zellen–Revision über Urin–Kontrollen bis hin zum laissez faire, zum offensichtlichen Übersehen der Schnapsfahne oder Haschisch–Seligkeit reichen kann. Eine allgemeine Anstalts–Strategie, deren wahrer Kontroll–Charakter dann jeweils im abweichenden Einzelfall zu Tage tritt: vom «das übersehe ich heute noch mal» bis hin zur Anzeige Renitenz–verdächtiger Haschisch–Krümel.

3.2 Das wachsende Gewicht zunehmend *verelendeter Drogentäter* in unseren Strafanstalten dürfte die Bedeutung der Drogen für das innere Anstalts–System entscheidend verstärkt haben, da nun erstmals eine zumeist für längere Zeit einsitzende Tätergruppe das Anstaltsgeschehen mitbestimmt, die ausdrücklich als «Drogen»–Täter definiert ist. Und zwar in doppelter Weise definiert: von außen mit einem rechtlich abgesicherten Sonderstatus (die Paragraphen 35ff BtMG bei uns bzw. die besondere Drogenabteilung). Und von innen her mit einem inneren Selbstverständnis, das sich weithin um die Droge dreht, die schon draußen zum zentralen Lebensmittelpunkt wurde, weil andere Lebensweisen nie erlernt oder zunehmend verlernt wurden, und weil sie nur dadurch – mit wachsender «Politoxikomanie» – noch einen Lebensinhalt finden können.

Diese ihre spezifischen Erfahrungen, Haltungen, Techniken, die ihrerseits noch in vorangegangenen Therapien psychologisch geschult und in früheren Hafterfahrungen mit Praxis aufgeladen wurden, bestimmen heute in einer sicher noch weiter vorantreibbaren Weise das Gesicht der inneren Anstalts–Struktur zumindest in unseren größeren Sicherheits–Anstalten.

3.3 Die Einführung von Harm-Reduction–Angeboten wird sicherlich im Einzelfall Entlastung bringen, gesundheitlich wie aber auch als Chance, die Verstrickungen in die Insassen–Kultur zu lockern – sofern solche Chancen etwa im Freizeitangebot, bei der Ausbildung und insbesondere im Rahmen von Lockerungsmaßnahmen auch tatsächlich angeboten werden können.

Anderenfalls werden sie – wie alle anderen «Behandlungs–Angebote» auch – den Sonderstatus der Drogentäter untermauern und nach anfänglicher Irritation rasch in das innere System integriert – als Chance an Heroin heranzukommen, als Methadon–Coming–Out, als Kontroll–Instrument im Nadel–Bereich.

4. Die wohl entscheidende Problem–Dimension, die heute die Realisierung von Harm Reduction im Strafvollzug behindert, liegt im *mentalen Bereich*, also in unserer Drogen–Ideologie, unseren Drogen–Vorstellungen und unseren Gedanken–Gefängnissen – weshalb manche annehmen, man könne sie relativ einfach durch «rationale» Aufklärung beseitigen.

Tatsächlich jedoch sind solche Gedankengefängnisse stets dreifach *fest verankert*: in einem allgemein übergreifenden Konsens – etwa dem Drogenfreiheits–Axiom, sodann emotional fundiert in unseren Ängsten, Sorgen und Hoffnungen, und schließlich interessegebunden insbesondere bei denjenigen, deren professionell–berufliches Schicksal von der Fortexistenz dieser Gedankengefängnisse abhängt. Die vom VPM (Verein für psychologische Menschenkenntnis) mitgetragene Schweizer Initiative «Jugend ohne Drogen» demonstriert diese Verstrickung beispielhaft

(s. Neue Zürcher Zeitung vom 19.2.1996, S.13 «Giftpfeile gegen die Heroinversuche»).

Für unsere Fragestellung sehe ich drei *Mentalitäts–Barrieren*, die in wachsender Reihenfolge Hindernisse aufwerfen:

4.1 Vordergründig geht es zunächst darum, mit den üblichen *Drogen–Mythen* aufzuräumen – eine klassische Aufgabe der Aufklärung. Dies betrifft weniger die Insassen oder das Anstaltspersonal, da die einen aus eigener Erfahrung, die anderen im direkten «Front–Kontakt» relativ realitätsnahe denken. So sehr auch hier auf der einen Seite konkret-praktische Hinweise – etwa bei der Aids–Prophylaxe – notwendig sind, und auf der anderen Seite in der jeweiligen Subkultur deren spezifische Ängste, Vorurteile, Stereotype und Abwehr–Mechanismen abzubauen wären; Sichtweisen, die jedoch eher allgemeiner denn drogenspezifischer Art sind.

Viel gewichtiger ist wohl die Aufklärung der sogenannten Entscheidungs–Träger von der Politik über die Bürokratie, aber auch die Medien, bis hinein in die höhere Anstalts–Hierarchie.

Drei miteinander verbundene Mythen unterstützen hier die allgemeine Sorge, neuartige Entscheidungen zu treffen: *die Fixierung auf die Gefährlichkeit der Drogen, die Idee der Sucht–Persönlichkeit und das Abstinenz–Denken*. Drei Grundlagen unserer gegenwärtigen Drogen–Politik, die wir zur Genüge aus der allgemeinen Methadon– und Akzeptanz–Diskussion kennen. Drogen–Axiome, die jedoch bei unserer Fragestellung dann an Gewicht gewinnen, wenn der «Staat» selber sein rhetorisches Ziel der Fürsorge und Resozialisierung dadurch in Frage gestellt sieht, daß er durch das Bereitstellen von akzeptierenden Angeboten «die ihm anvertrauten Süchtigen immer weiter in die Sucht hineintreiben soll».

4.2 Eine zweite, tiefergreifende Barriere ergibt sich aus dem uralten *«less eligibility»*–Prinzip, nach dem es den Gefangen nicht besser gehen darf als dem gesetzestreuen Mitbürger. Hinter diesem ursprünglich aus dem

Abschreckungs–Gedanken heraus entwickelten Prinzip steht heute die
Sorge, auf diese Weise Böses mit Gutem, Straftaten mit Heroin–Vergabe
zu belohnen – eine Sorge, die etwa vor dem «Hotel–Vollzug» warnt und
die nicht verstehen kann, daß verwahrloste Jugendliche auf eine Segel–
Tour gehen dürfen. Ein durch rationale Argumente nur schwer fassbarer
emotionaler Hintergrund, der – gleichviel ob real oder nicht – vor allem
in parteipolitischen Überlegungen und den daraus folgenden vollzugspraktischen Entscheidungen eine nicht geringe Rolle spielen dürfte.

4.3 Die entscheidende Barriere aber dürfte darin liegen, daß solche
Harm–Reduction–Maßnahmen die *Doppelbödigkeit der eigenen Drogenpolitik* evident machen werden: Spritzentausch als Beihilfe zu strafbarem
Tun? Safer–use–Training als Anleitung zum Drogen–Mißbrauch? Oder
gar Heroin–Vergabe an diejenigen, die eben deswegen zur Freiheitsstrafe
verurteilt wurden? Oder umgekehrt, bei Verweigerung dieser Maßnahmen, obwohl die tatsächliche Situation ja bekannt ist: Beihilfe zur dro-
henden Ansteckung der dem Staat anvertrauten Gefangenen? Oder gar
Förderung der Ausbreitung von HIV und Hepatitis auf die künftigen
Sexualpartner dieser Gefangenen? Eine Doppelbödigkeit, die schon früher damit beginnt, Personen mit der rechten Hand zu strafen, die man mit
der linken zu Süchtigen erklärt; eine Doppelbödigkeit, die letztlich jedoch
darin gründet, mit repressiven Mitteln Erwachsenen vorschreiben zu
wollen, welche Drogen sie genießen und welche sie meiden sollen.

Fasst man das bisher Gesagte zusammen, ergeben sich die folgenden
zehn Thesen zur Frage der Harm–Reduction in Strafanstalten:

1. Die gegenwärtige *Drogen–Politik* schafft sich ihr Drogen–Problem;
der *Strafvollzug* produziert – ungewollt – den typischen Drogen–Täter.
Man opfert so vergeblich Drogen–Tote, HIV–Erkrankte und Langzeit–
Gefangene auf dem Altar der Abstinenz–Ideologie und korrumpiert damit
Rechtsstaat und Strafjustiz–System.

2. Während die «Drogen»–Politik auf der unteren Ebene der Kommunen und kleineren Länder realitätsnah zu arbeiten beginnt, verharrt die Drogen–«Politik» auf der übergeordneten Ebene der großen Staaten – Deutschland, Frankreich und USA – wie auf der von ihnen beeinflußten internationalen Ebene im überkommenen Repressions–Schema.

3. Die wachsende Einsicht in das Scheitern der Drogen–Repression sowie die zunehmenden menschlichen und finanziellen Kosten werden – wie bei allen anderen im historischen Prozess eingebürgerten Drogen – à la longue dazu führen, Repression durch Enkulturation auch der derzeit illegalisierten Drogen zu ersetzen.

4. Das Ziel einer rationalen Drogen–Politik ist – wie bei allen «legalen» Drogen – die Akzeptanz eines kulturell gebändigten Drogen–Konsums; der Weg führt über seine Normalisierung; die Strategie ist die schrittweise Entkriminalisierung.

5. Drogen–Konsumenten, Drogen–Besitzer, Klein–Dealer, abhängige Dealer und leichtere Beschaffungs–«Kriminalität» gehören – auch im Wiederholungsfall – schon heute nicht in das Gefängnis. Auf dem Wege der Entkriminalisierung werden auch Dealer und Beschaffungs–Täter die Gefängnisse verlassen. Dies dient den Betroffenen, erhöht die Sicherheit der Bürger und öffnet dem Strafvollzug die Chance zur notwendigen Reform.

6. Solange Drogen–Täter noch im Strafvollzug sind, gilt es,

a) möglichst jeden Sonderstatus zu vermeiden (wie z.B. «drogenfreie» Sonderabteilungen u.ä.), und

b) sie – entgegen der heutigen Praxis – so früh wie möglich zu entlassen (probeweise Beurlaubung, Zwei–Drittel–Entlassung).

7. Solange Drogen–Abhängige noch im Strafvollzug sind, sollten sie – wie draußen – die Möglichkeit zu einer möglichst unauffälligen «Substitution» erhalten; hierbei verdient die Heroin/Kokain–Abgabe den

Vorzug vor der Substitution, da in der Anstalt die täglich mehrmalige Abgabe keine Probleme bereitet. Bei der (vorzeitigen) Entlassung ist eine bruchlose Fortsetzung der «Substitution» vorzusehen.

8. Bei der Einführung von Harm–Reduction–Maßnahmen sind rechtzeitig drei spezifische Widerstandsbereiche zu berücksichtigen:

(1) Die aufeinander bezogenen kulturellen Subsysteme der Insassen und des Personals;
(2) die Funktion der Droge zur Kompensation, als Währung und zum Status–Gewinn;
(3) die aufklärungsbedürftigen Mentalitäts–Barrieren insbesondere bei den Entscheidungs–Trägern. Diese Widerstandsbereiche korrelieren – auch auf der internationalen Ebene – mit der Größe der Anstalt und dem Ausmaß von Sicherheits– und Ordnungs–Denken.

9. Die Forschung sollte nicht nur die direkten Auswirkungen solcher Harm–Reduction–Maßnahmen evaluieren, sondern zugleich die Art der Implementation und deren Wechselwirkungen mit den drei in These 8 erwähnten Widerstands–Bereichen untersuchen.

10. Da die Drogen–Problematik im Strafvollzug – zumindest im westeuropäischen Bereich – weithin ähnlich ausfällt, sind die Schweizer Pionier–Erfahrungen (ähnlich wie bei der Methadon–Vergabe) gut auf andere Länder übertragbar, sofern auf nationaler Ebene der recht unterschiedliche Einfluß der in These 8 benannten Widerstände beachtet wird.

Literatur

Bachmann, Urs u.a.: Drogenabhängige im Strafvollzug. Sondereinrichtungen? Verlag Schweizerische Fachstelle für Alkoholprobleme 1985

BISDRO (Bremer Institut für Drogenforschung): Gutachten zur Cannabis–Situation in der Bundesrepublik. Bremen 1995

Bundesverfassungsgericht: Beschluß vom 9.3.94. NJW 1994:1577–90

Foucault, Michel: Überwachen und Strafen. Frankfurt 1974

Gesprächskreis Wirtschaftsführer und Drogenpolitik: Für eine kohärente und nachhaltige Drogenpolitik. Manuskript. 6.11.1995

Harrison, Lana u.a.: Cannabis Use in the United States: Implications for Policy. Final Report. Newark 1995

Kemmesies, Uwe: Kompulsive Drogengebraucher in den Niederlanden und Deutschland. Dissertation Bremen 1996

Mathiesen, Thomas: Defences of the Weak. Oslo 1969

Niederländisches Ministerium für Auswärtige Angelegenheiten u.a.: Die niederländische Drogenpolitik, Kontinuität und Wandel. Rijswijk 1995

Rechtspflegestatistik für 1992. Statistisches Bundesamt, Wiesbaden 1995

Schulzke, M. u.a.: Wissenschaftliche Begleitung der Fachklinik Brauel. Endbericht. Hannover 1993

Siebel, Andreas: Vergleich des deutschen und französischen Drogenstrafrechts. Dissertation Bremen 1996

Die Verfolgung des Drogenkonsums und Drogenkonsumierende in Schweizer Gefängnissen

Josef Estermann

Ohne Zweifel ist die Bedeutung des Drogenproblems in Schweizer Gefängnissen seit den frühen achtziger Jahren gestiegen. Der Ursprung seiner aktuellen Form, nämlich der breiten Kriminalisierung des Konsums und der Darstellung des Drogenhandels als beinahe schlimmstes Verbrechen überhaupt, ist in den späten sechziger Jahren zu suchen. Vorher gab es mit Sicherheit keine Überrepräsentation von Heroin– und Kokainkonsumierenden in Schweizer Gefängnissen. Was heute in der schweizerischen Öffentlichkeit als Drogenproblem wahrgenommen wird, ist wesentlich bestimmt durch die Repression (vgl. Boller, 1995). In der öffentlichen Diskussion steht in erster Linie Heroin, weniger Kokain und Cannabis und selten Alkohol oder Nikotin. Dies obwohl der Markt für die legal handelbaren Substanzen Nikotin und Alkohol, ausgedrückt in Endverbraucherpreisen, etwa viermal grösser ist als derjenige für illegale Drogen.

Die für die Repression eingesetzten Mittel und die Anzahl der von der Repression betroffenen Personen sind bedeutend und haben in den vergangenen Jahren zugenommen. Masszahlen für diese Effekte liefern die polizeiliche Kriminalstatistik, die Statistik der in das Strafregister eingetragenen Urteile und die Statistik der Gefängniseinweisungen (vgl. Estermann/ Rônez, 1995).

Die von den Instanzen sozialer Kontrolle in den Repressionsbereich investierten Ressourcen haben den massiven Anstieg der Verzeigungen und Verurteilungen erst ermöglicht. Da bei den Verstössen gegen das Betäubungsmittelgesetz, insbesondere beim Konsum, keine beteiligten Geschädigten, also kaum je Anzeigeerstattende zu finden sind, muss die Polizeitätigkeit proaktiv sein. Aus diesem Grunde ist die Anzahl der Verfahren von den durch die Polizei eingesetzten Ressourcen bestimmt. Die Repression hat sich als kriminalpolitische Möglichkeit durchgesetzt und etabliert.

Daten der polizeilichen Verfolgung des Drogenkonsums und Drogenhandels sind seit 1974 verfügbar (*Tabelle 1*). Bis 1990 ist ein annähernd linearer Anstieg zu sehen, mit einem leicht verstärkten Anstieg in den Jahren 1981 und 1982. Zwischen 1988 und 1990 stagniert die Zahl der Verzeigungen. Die Jahre 1991 bis 1993 hingegen sind durch einen rasanten Anstieg gekennzeichnet, der 1994 abflacht und 1995 zum Stehen kommt. Insbesondere die Verdoppelung der Verfahrenszahlen zwischen 1990 und 1993 weist auf die Rolle und die Arbeit der Polizei als zentrale Grösse für die gesellschaftlich wahrgenommene Bedeutung des Drogenkonsums und die stark expandierende Drogenrepression hin. Die Anzahl der durch die Polizei erfassten Personen stieg nicht so stark wie die Zahl der Verfahren, aber doch immerhin um 74%. Im Jahre 1994 waren es etwa 40'000 von der Polizei initiierte Verfahren, die 27'000 erfasste Personen betreffen. Im Jahre 1995 stieg die Anzahl der Verfahren nochmals leicht auf 42'000 ohne wesentliche Änderung der Zahl der erfassten Personen. Im Vergleich dazu nimmt sich der Justizbereich geradezu bescheiden aus.

Die Gerichte entdeckten das Drogenproblem für die Schweiz erst im Jahre 1968. Abgesehen von zwei Konsolidierungsphasen Mitte der siebziger und Ende der achtziger Jahre zeigt sich ein bedeutender Zuwachs der im Strafregister eingetragenen Verurteilungen. Der Rückgang der eingetragenen Verurteilungen im Jahre 1992 ist als Artefakt der Änderung der Strafregisterverordnung geschuldet: Seither sind sogenannte blosse

Tabelle 1: Polizeiliche Verzeigungen, angezeigte Personen, Verurteilungen und Einweisungen in den Strafvollzug auf Grundlage des Betäubungsmittelgesetzes im Zeitverlauf

Jahr	polizeiliche Verzeigungen	angezeigte Personen	Verurteilungen	unbedingte Freiheitsstrafen	Einweisungen Straf- und Massnahmenvollzug	BetmG-Strafgefangene am Stichtag 1. Mai
1965			9			
1966			16			
1967			51			
1968			80			
1969			332			
1970			1 158			
1971			1 791			
1972			2 373			
1973			2 448			
1974	4 704		2 367			
1975	5 725		2 587			
1976	5 546		2 328	762		
1977	5 820		2 658	853		
1978	6 299		2 707	802		
1979	7 045		3 239	973		
1980	8 224		3 387	1 010		
1981	9 699		3 839	1 216		
1982	11 951		4 090	1 314		
1983	13 168		4 533	1 612		
1984	13 689		5 383	1 678	1 416	1 067
1985	15 361		5 681	1 822	1 493	1 190
1986	15 815		6 043	2 073	1 709	1 301
1987	17 179		6 297	1 994	1 612	1 360
1988	18 739		6 751	2 141	1 647	1 306
1989	18 780		6 658	2 162	1 741	1 175
1990	18 880	14 768	6 711	2 237	1 721	1 272
1991	23 470	17 575	7 941	2 578	1 805	1 276
1992	30 860	21 252	7 653	2 530	1 846	1 462
1993	38 206	25 364	8 943	2 929	1 951	1 582
1994	40 378	26 321	9 055	2 999		1 661
1995	42 001					

Quellen: Bundesamt für Statistik (BFS), Bundesamt für Polizeiwesen (BAP)

Übertretungsbussen, sofern sie nicht zusammen mit anderen Strafnorm-verletzungen abgeurteilt werden, nicht mehr eingetragen. Dies betrifft vor allem Verurteilungen wegen blossen Konsums.

Unbedingte Freiheitsstrafen und Gefängniseinweisungen nehmen seit Mitte der siebziger Jahre stetig zu. Der Bestand an Insassen, die aufgrund des Betäubungsmittelgesetzes verurteilt wurden, stagnierte hingegen zwischen 1986 und 1991 und legte erst im Jahre 1992 deutlich zu. In der zweiten Hälfte des vergangenen Jahrzehnts haben anscheinend die Vollzugsbehörden, zumindest was den Aufenthalt von Drogenkonsumierenden in den Gefängnissen betrifft, eine eher restriktive Politik betrieben.

Bei Betrachtung der einzelnen indizierten Variablen der Drogenrepression wird deutlich, dass die Bereiche Polizei, Justiz und Gefängnis bis 1990 parallel verlaufen (*Abbildung 1*). Erst 1991 bricht diese parallele Entwicklung ab und zeigt die Vorreiterrolle der polizeilichen Ermittlungen. Ohne Zweifel steht dies in Zusammenhang mit der Änderung der Drogenpolitik in der Schweiz im Jahre 1991. In der Öffentlichkeit ist seit der Verabschiedung des Massnahmenpaketes gegen den Drogenmissbrauch durch den Bundesrat der Eindruck entstanden, dass sich die Drogenpolitik in der Schweiz unter der Flagge der Forschungsprogramme zur diversifizierten Verschreibung von Betäubungsmitteln stark liberalisiert hätte. Die Daten zur Strafverfolgung zeigen jedoch das pure Gegenteil. Die Repression hat seit 1990 massiv zugenommen, allerdings auch die Anzahl der Methadonverschreibungen (Bundesamt für Gesundheitswesen, Methadonbericht, 1995).

Die soziodemografischen Merkmale der auf Grundlage des Betäubungsmittelgesetzes verurteilten Insassen unterscheiden sich wesentlich von der erwachsenen ständigen Wohnbevölkerung der Schweiz. Diese Gruppe der Insassen besteht zu 93% aus Männern und zu 80% aus zwischen 20 und 35 Jahre alten Personen. Die Altersverteilung steigt steil an und erreicht mit 25 bis 26 Jahren ihr Maximum. Der Median beträgt 29 Jahre und der Durchschnittswert 31 Jahre. Insgesamt sind die 21– bis 40jährigen überrepräsentiert. In bezug auf die übrige Gefängnispopulation ergeben sich kleinere Unterschiede. Das Durchschnittsalter sämtli-

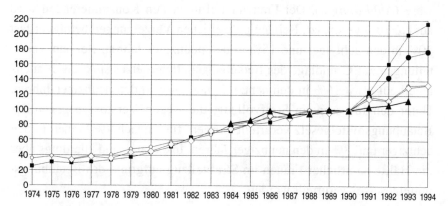

— Polizeiliche Verzeigungen

— Verzeigte Personen

— Verurteilungen

— Unbedingte Freiheitsstrafen

— Einweisungen in den Straf- und Massnahmenvollzug

Abbildung 1: Indizes zur Betäubungsmittelrepression, 1974–1994 (Index 1990=100)

cher Insassen liegt bei 33 Jahren und der Frauenanteil bei knapp 6%. Vom Freiheitsentzug in Gefängnissen sind meistens nur Personen betroffen, die ihr zwanzigstes Lebensjahr hinter sich haben. In einigen Fällen finden sich auch Achtzehn– und Neunzehnjährige im Gefängnis, für die in der Regel Jugendvollzug oder Arbeitserziehung, Massnahmen und so weiter vorgesehen sind. Jugendstrafen werden im Strafregister in der Regel nicht erfasst. Unter anderem wegen Drogenkonsums in Heime eingewiesen werden allerdings schon Personen im Alter von unter fünfzehn oder sechzehn Jahren, die häufig später ihre sogenannten kriminellen Karrieren fortsetzen und im Gefängnis landen (vgl. Estermann, 1986). Die Zahl dieser Kinder und Jugendlichen geht in die Tausende.

Unter verhafteten, verurteilten und strafgefangenen Drogenkonsumierenden, auch unter den Drogentodesfällen, finden sich sehr viel weniger

Frauen als es nach ihrem Anteil unter den Konsumierenden zu erwarten wäre (*Abbildung 2*). Der Frauenanteil unter den Konsumierenden wird auf ca. 30% geschätzt. Bei den polizeilichen Verzeigungen beträgt er fast 20% in den achtziger und 15% in den neunziger Jahren. Bei den Verurteilungen auf Grundlage des Betäubungsmittelgesetzes sinkt der Frauenanteil auf etwa 16% in den achtziger und 14% in den neunziger Jahren. Unter den Insassen im Strafvollzug, die wegen Verstössen gegen das Betäubungsmittelgesetz verurteilt wurden, finden sich 7% Frauen in den achtziger und 8% in den neunziger Jahren. Insgesamt sind allerdings über die Hälfte sämtlicher Frauen im Strafvollzug aufgrund des Betäubungsmittelgesetzes verurteilt worden.

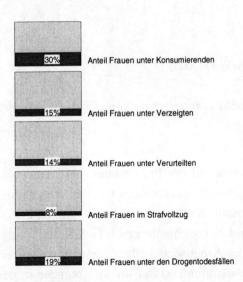

Abbildung 2: Frauen
und die Verfolgung
des Drogenkonsums

Frauen verfügen über eine grössere Verfolgungsimmunität und allgemein über eine geringere Sterblichkeit, vor allem in den hier interessierenden Altersklassen. Unter den polizeilich gemeldeten Drogentodesfällen der Jahre 1988 bis 1994 waren 19% Frauen. Diese Zahl liegt etwas höher als der Anteil der Frauen unter den polizeilich verzeigten Personen in den neunziger Jahren. Ein grosser Teil der Personen, die im Zusammenhang mit dem Gebrauch illegaler Drogen starben, in der Regel wegen Opiaten, waren schon wegen Verstössen gegen das Betäubungsmittelgesetz in das Strafregister eingetragen (*Abbildung 3*): 50% der Männer waren einschlägig vorbestraft, weitere 20% wegen anderer Delikte eingetragen. Es verbleiben immerhin 30%, die bis zu ihrem Tode ohne Kontakt zum Strafjustizsystem blieben. Bei den Frauen sind dies 50%; der Anteil der einschlägig Vorbestraften liegt bei 40%, plus 10% wegen anderer Delikte eingetragene Frauen.

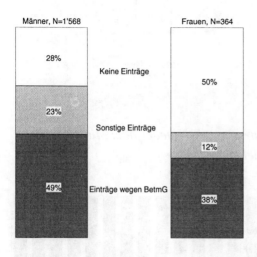

Abbildung 3: Gemeldete identifizierbare Drogentodesfälle nach Geschlecht und Strafregistereintrag

Epidemiologische Ergebnisse weisen darauf hin, dass sich die Inzidenz in den vergangenen Jahren kaum wesentlich verändert hat, dass jedoch der Anteil älterer Konsumierender immer grösser wird. Die Inzidenz konzentriert sich bei einem Alter von etwa zwanzig Jahren. Bei einigen Konsumierenden beträgt die Dauer des mehr oder weniger intensiven Konsums 15, 20, 25 Jahre oder mehr. Vor 1980 gab es bedeutend weniger vierzigjährige Konsumierende als heute, da in der Schweiz der Gebrauch von Heroin und Kokain in den fünfziger und frühen sechziger Jahren sehr wenig verbreitet war. Dieser Alterungseffekt ist bei den Drogentodesfällen deutlich zu sehen (*Abbildung 4*). Die Tendenz in der Repressionsstatistik weist in die gleiche Richtung (*Abbildung 5*).

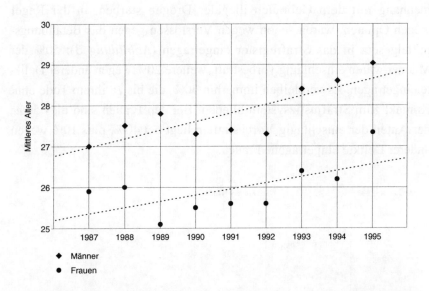

Abbildung 4: Polizeilich registrierte Drogentodesfälle: Mittleres Alter der verstorbenen Personen nach Geschlecht

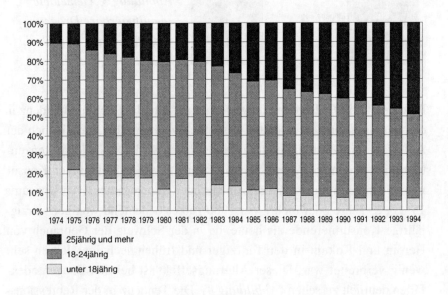

Abbildung 5: Verzeigte Personen nach Altersgruppen, 1974-1994

Die aktuelle Diskussion um Drogenkonsum und Drogenhandel steht in sehr engem Zusammenhang mit der Diskussion des Ausländer– und Asylrechts, der organisierten Kriminalität und dem Ausbau der Ermittlungskompetenzen und –instrumente der verschiedenen Polizeistellen. Offiziell war in der Schweiz 1994 das Jahr der Inneren Sicherheit. Insbesondere die Verschärfung des Ausländerrechts wurde mit der Bekämpfung ausländischer Rauschgifthändler legitimiert.

Verurteilungen wegen Verletzungen des Bundesgesetzes über Aufenthalt und Niederlassung der Ausländer (ANAG) übertrafen die Fallzahlen im Betäubungsmittelbereich seit 1990 bei weitem (*Abbildung 6*). Verurteilungen auf Grundlage des Betäubungsmittelgesetzes wuchsen in den letzten fünf Jahren um etwa 30%, ANAG–Verurteilungen hingegen um 100%. Polizei und Strafjustiz fokussieren im Bereich der Überschneidung von ANAG und Betäubungsmittelgesetz vor allem dunkelhäutigere Menschen afrikanischer oder mediterraner Herkunft. Die äussere Erscheinung, insbesondere die Hautfarbe, macht diesen Personenkreis leicht identifizierbar und häufiger Routineüberprüfung durch die Polizei zugänglich.

Der Ausländeranteil in den Schweizer Gefängnissen ist tatsächlich ausserordentlich hoch. Gemessen am mittleren Insassenbestand betrug der Ausländeranteil im Jahre 1993 etwa 45%, gemessen an den eingewiesenen Personen jedoch bloss ein Drittel. Dies liegt daran, dass Ausländer im Durchschnitt längere Freiheitsstrafen verbüssen als Schweizer. Seit 1991 überschreitet der Ausländeranteil unter denjenigen Strafgefangenen, die aufgrund des Betäubungsmittelgesetzes verurteilt wurden, die 50%–Marke. Wiederum ungefähr die Hälfte davon hat keinen regulären Wohnsitz in der Schweiz. Der Anteil dieser Personen nimmt allerdings zur Zeit im Zuge der verschärften Ausschaffungspolitik ab. Der hohe Ausländeranteil in den Gefängnissen führt zu Kommunikationsschwierigkeiten mit dem in der Regel einheimischen Personal, das eher selten über die entsprechenden Sprachkenntnisse verfügt. So entstehen Subkulturen, die den Betrieb der Gefängnisse nicht gerade erleichtern. Entsprechend verschlechtert sich auch die medizinische Versorgung. Ein Teil der

Ausländer sitzt wegen Handels und nicht wegen gleichzeitigen Konsums, was allerdings nicht ausschliesst, dass auch diese Personen im Gefängnis illegale Drogen konsumieren. Mehr als die Hälfte der ca. 1300 Verurteilungen von Ausländern ohne Wohnsitz in der Schweiz wegen Verstosses gegen das Betäubungsmittelgesetz im Jahre 1993 betrifft Handel ohne Konsum. Bei den Ausländern mit Wohnsitz in der Schweiz (2200 Verurteilungen) beträgt dieser Anteil ein Viertel, bei den Schweizerinnen und Schweizern (5400 Verurteilungen) nur ein Zehntel.

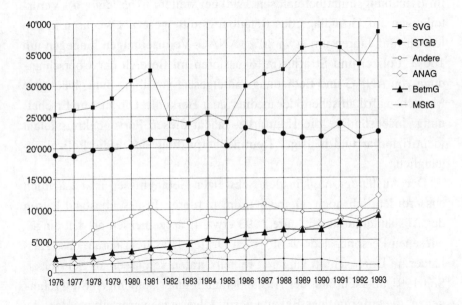

Abbildung 6: Verurteilungen nach verschiedenen Gesetzen

Die rechtlichen Grundlagen im Betäubungsmittelstrafrecht der Schweiz sind verglichen mit denen anderer Länder eher neueren Datums. Wegen eines liberalen Staatsverständnisses und wegen konkreter Interessen der pharmazeutischen Industrie beugte sich die Schweiz nur widerwillig und spät dem internationalen Druck zur Kriminalisierung von Herstellung, Handel und Konsum der noch anfangs dieses Jahrhunderts hochgelobten und stark beworbenen Medikamente Kokain, Opiumtinktur, Morphium und Heroin sowie der alten Kulturpflanze Hanf. So war beispielsweise Opium im vergangenen Jahrhundert nicht nur als Analgetikum geschätzt, sondern auch als das effizienteste und erfolgreichste Medikament zur Bekämpfung der Cholera und anderer Durchfallerkrankungen, insbesondere bevor Infusionen zur Rehydrierung breit angewendet werden konnten und diese Behandlungsweise allgemein anerkannt war. Laudanum, ein alkoholischer Opiumauszug, fand sich in jeder besseren Hausapotheke. Vor allem zu Kriegszeiten war der Nachschub an Opium ein wichtiges Anliegen der Militärbürokratie. Die Geschichte geht natürlich auch weiter zurück: Nicht nur THC–haltige Hanfpflanzen lassen sich aus vorrömischen Zeiten in der Schweiz archäologisch nachweisen, sondern auch geritzte Schlafmohnkapseln.

In der Schweiz beschäftigte sich die Gesetzgebung erst nach dem ersten Weltkrieg mit den sogenannten Betäubungsmitteln. Das erste Schweizer Betäubungsmittelgesetz vom 2. Oktober 1924 bezieht sich zwar auf Opium und Kokain, stellt aber Produktion und Vertrieb an sich nicht unter Strafe, schon gar nicht den Konsum oder den Besitz, schränkt aber den freien Verkehr ein. Am 1. Juni 1952 trat das Betäubungsmittelgesetz vom 3. Oktober 1951 nach längeren Auseinandersetzungen in Kraft. Auch in diesem Gesetz ist von der Strafbarkeit des Konsums keine Rede. In den Jahren 1968 und 1969 hingegen, zur Zeit des Höhepunkts der Studentenrevolten, beschäftigte sich das Bundesgericht mit der Frage, ob der Besitz von Betäubungsmitteln, der ursprünglich als Auffangtatbestand für den illegalen Handel gedacht war, auch im Zusammenhang mit blossem Konsum strafbar sei. Die Frage wurde in der Folge bejaht. Dieser wohl auch politisch bestimmte Entscheid führte dazu, dass anschliessend vielerorts blosse Konsumentinnen und Konsumenten wegen Besitzes von Betäubungsmitteln verurteilt wurden. Die Revision des Jahres 1970 brachte allerdings vorläufig nur Anpassungen an internationale Abkommen ohne Verschärfung des strafrechtlichen Teils des Betäubungsmittelgesetzes.

Erst eine neuerliche Revision im Jahre 1975 führte zur expliziten Strafbarkeit des Konsums im Sinne der bundesgerichtlichen Interpretation der Strafbarkeit des Besitzes. Konsumierende konnten in extremis nun selbst dann bestraft werden, wenn sie gar nicht wussten, welche Substanzen sie zu sich nahmen. Die Jahre zwischen 1985 und 1992 sahen etliche Revisionen der Betäubungsmittelverordnung, in der immer neue Stoffe Aufnahme fanden, so dass zur Zeit etwa 160 Substanzen und eine unbestimmte Zahl von Derivaten strafrechtlich relevant werden können.

Das Engagement der Repression im Bereich des sogenannten Drogenproblems lässt sich in Phasen aufgliedern, Phasen, die allerdings durch eine Zeitreihenanalyse der Repressionsdaten alleine nicht abzuleiten sind, sondern sich nur unter Bezugnahme auf das soziale und politische Umfeld im jeweiligen Zeitabschnitt definieren lassen. Bis 1968 gab es kein sogenanntes Drogenproblem, der Konsum war nicht strafbar. In der Schweiz wurde erst im Zeitraum zwischen 1968 und 1975, abgesehen von der Drogendiskussion der zwanziger und dreissiger Jahre dieses Jahrhunderts, das Drogenproblem sozial konstruiert und empirisch gemessen. Dies geschah im Umfeld der Jugend– und Studentenunruhen und des Vietnamkriegs, durch den auch viele junge amerikanische Soldaten erstmals mit Opiaten in Kontakt kamen. Die Hippie–Kultur prägte das Lebensgefühl eines grossen Teils der Jugend. Viele Leitfiguren, insbesondere Musiker, waren bekennende Konsumentinnen und Konsumenten von illegalen Drogen. Die Lebenswelt dieser Jugend implizierte den Gebrauch weiterer psychotroper Genussmittel neben den von ihren Eltern bevorzugten Substanzen Alkohol und Tabak.

Mit der endgültigen gesetzlichen Kriminalisierung eines Aspekts dieser Lebensform in der Schweiz setzte 1975 bis 1979 eine Konsolidierung ein. Die Prohibitionisten und Moralunternehmer siegten über die den Drogenkonsum befürwortende Jugendkultur, die diese Niederlage allerdings nicht unbedingt als solche begriff, sondern quasi autonom neben der Norm lebte. Die Phase 1980 bis 1982 sah eine Respezifizierung der

Jugendkultur im Rahmen der Jugendunruhen, der sogenannten Hausbesetzerbewegung und der harten, militärisch geprägten Auseinandersetzung in den grösseren Städten. In dieser Zeit wurde von repressiver Seite eine Diversionspolitik betrieben, die den Drogen– und Waffenhandel im «unkontrollierten Ghetto» geradezu förderte. Es gab sogar Stimmen, die bestimmten Institutionen sozialer Kontrolle vorhielten, Heroin gezielt in politisch aktive Gruppen zu schleusen, um diese zu kompromittieren und handlungsunfähig zu machen.

In den Jahren 1982 bis 1986 folgte dann die Konsolidierung einer sich stetig verstärkenden Repression auch im medizinischen Bereich, die im Verbot des Verkaufs von Injektionsbesteck durch den damaligen Zürcher Kantonsarzt gipfelte. Tiefere Einsichten in den Prozess der Verbreitung von Infektionskrankheiten und die Diskussion um AIDS als eine auch durch heterosexuellen Geschlechtsverkehr verbreitete Krankheit leiteten dann die nächste Phase ein, die kurze Phase des gesundheitspolitischen Primats in der Drogenpolitik. Sie dauerte von 1987 bis 1990. Was die öffentliche Diskussion anging, war sie flankiert von Überlegungen zu sich prostituierenden Fixerinnen. Sie galten als grosse Gefahr für die Gesundheit ihrer Freier und in der Folge deren Frauen und ihrer Kinder. Viele betrachteten Fixerinnen als die eigentliche Keimzelle der heterosexuellen Epidemie. Zu Beginn war die infektionsepidemiologische Situation tatsächlich durch eine sehr hohe Prävalenz von HIV unter injizierenden Drogenkonsumierenden gekennzeichnet (*Abbildung 7*).

Das AIDS verursachende Virus drang in den Jahren 1983 bis 1987 massiv in die Gruppe der injizierenden Drogenbenutzer ein. Durch ein verändertes Bewusstsein der Konsumierenden und durch eine Verbesserung der hygienischen Infrastruktur konnte die HIV–Inzidenz stark zurückgedrängt werden. In diesem Zusammenhang spielten Spritzentauschprogramme und das Projekt ZIPP–AIDS, das Prävention und medizinische Betreuung in der offenen Zürcher Szene am Platzspitz sicherstellte, eine wichtige Rolle. Dieses Projekt wurde zum Jahreswechsel 1991/92 liquidiert, kurz vor der Schliessung des Platzspitzes für die offene Drogenszene. In der Folge bekam die Einrichtung von Injektionsräumen zur

Überlebenshilfe eine wesentliche Bedeutung. Die HIV–Prävalenz unter den injizierenden Drogenkonsumierenden sank zum Ende der Periode des gesundheitspolitischen Primats auf ca. 10%. Hepatitis–Infektionsraten, also HAV, HBV und vor allem HCV–Prävalenzen blieben hingegen fast unverändert hoch. Das Hepatitis–B–Virus kennt dieselben Infektionswege wie HIV, ist jedoch bedeutend infektiöser. Bei HBV wurden auch Infektionen ohne Geschlechtsverkehr oder Spritzentausch beschrieben. Das Hepatitis–C–Virus kann sogar über verschmutztes, umgebungskontaminiertes Spritzbesteck und Löffel oder Kontamination von Hautverletzungen übertragen werden. Unterdessen sind HCV–Infektionen nach längerem Aufenthalt in der offenen Szene schon beinahe die Regel. Mangelnde Hygiene führt auch immer noch zu einer hohen Ansteckungsrate mit dem fäkal–oral übertragenen Hepatitis–A–Virus. Alle diese Infektionen spielen natürlich auch in den Gefängnissen eine Rolle. Immer-

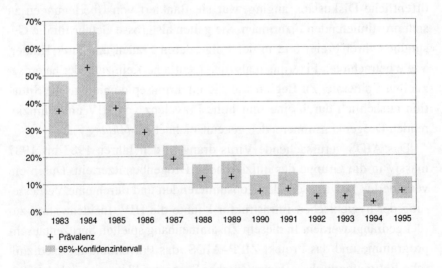

Abbildung 7: HIV–Prävalenz: Ergebnisse von Testreihen (seit 1985 anonyme Tests) bei injizierenden Drogenkonsumierenden in der Schweiz, 1983–1995

hin konnte die Ideologie des gesundheitspolitischen Primats bis heute soweit aufrechterhalten werden, als dass die Notwendigkeit der Verfügbarkeit von sauberen Spritzen auch in den Gefängnissen kaum mehr bestritten wird.

Das Repressionsprimat kehrte im Jahre 1991 unter dem Banner der Aufrechterhaltung der öffentlichen Ordnung wieder an seinen angestammten Platz zurück. Die Gesundheitspolitik schien selbst die kümmerlichsten Ansätze einer eigenständigen ordnungspolitischen Kompetenz zu verlieren. Der Prozess der Verdrängung des gesundheitspolitischen Primats war 1994 abgeschlossen und die Gesundheitspolitik im Wesentlichen auf die erweiterten niederschwelligen Methadonprogramme mit zur Zeit ca. 14'000 Klienten sowie auf die wissenschaftlichen Versuche zur Heroinabgabe beschränkt. Ein Schauplatz der politischen Auseinandersetzungen blieben die kommunalen Injektionsräume für Fixer: In Luzern beispielsweise wurde deren Einrichtung durch Volksabstimmung unter massiver Intervention von Mitgliedern des sektenähnlichen Vereins zur Förderung der psychologischen Menschenkenntnis (VPM) und von der Initiative «Jugend ohne Drogen» nahestehenden Kreisen sowie von innerstädtischen Gewerblern abgelehnt, in Basel hingegen angenommen. Die Bekämpfung der «Unordnung» und der «Schande für die Städte», welche die offenen Szenen im Bewusstsein weiter Teile der Bevölkerung und der Institutionen sozialer Kontrolle darstellen, schien nun wieder wichtiger als die gesundheitliche Versorgung der Betroffenen. Präventionsbemühungen und die dazu vorgesehenen Etats richteten sich wieder zunehmend an die nicht drogenbenutzende Bevölkerung, um für Verständnis für die armen Drogensüchtigen zu werben und durch Darstellung des Drogengrauens weitere Personen abzuschrecken. Im Jahre 1995 zeichnet sich eine Konsolidierung der grossen Repressionsbemühungen ab.

Die Bekämpfung des Drogenkonsums und Drogenhandels mit repressiven Mitteln gestaltet sich ausserordentlich aufwendig. Der Umfang der Repressionskosten ist aufgrund der Analyse von Aggregatdaten durch das Bundesamt für Statistik für das Jahr 1991 mit 500 Millionen Franken zu beziffern (Estermann, 1995). Dieser Betrag entspricht immerhin einem

Sechstel der Gesamtausgaben für die Hochschulen, 50% der Kosten der Universitätskliniken eingeschlossen. Die Tendenz ist steigend, so dass beinahe von einer Kostenexplosion der Drogenrepression gesprochen werden kann. Diese halbe Milliarde Franken stellen die Regulierungskosten des schweizerischen Drogenschwarzmarktes dar. Der Markt besitzt ein Volumen von ca. 2,5 Mia. Franken jährlich. Die Konfiszierungen reduzieren das Volumen um etwa 2%. Der Aufwand, umgerechnet auf ein konfisziertes Gramm Heroin, beläuft sich auf mehrere Tausend Franken. Der Herstellungspreis von Diacetylmorphin–HCl beträgt hingegen weniger als zehn Franken pro Gramm.

Kosten sind jedoch durchaus auch mit umgekehrtem Vorzeichen zu versehen: Sie schlagen sich als Einkommen von Polizisten und Gefängniswärtern, als Investitionen im Baubereich oder im Bereich der Informatik nieder. Weitere positive ökonomische Effekte zeigen sich in der Filmindustrie, in der Presse, der Forschung und der Reisetätigkeit. Die Kosten sind ein Ausdruck der Bedeutung des mit kostspieligen Mitteln bekämpften Problems selbst.

Sicherlich wäre es falsch, den Drogenkonsum oder auch nur die häufig damit einhergehenden gesundheitlichen Probleme alleine als Artefakt repressiver Tätigkeit aufzufassen. Aber die mangelnde Hygiene als Ursache schwerer gesundheitlicher Schäden und als Grund für den grössten Teil der Übermortalität unter Drogenkonsumierenden, in erster Linie Opiatkonsumierenden und Politoxikomanen, hängt eng mit dem repressiv bestimmten Umfeld dieser Population zusammen.

Für Drogentodesfälle existieren verschiedene Erfassungssysteme. Bei deren Ergebnissen fällt auf, dass der Anstieg sowohl der polizeilich registrierten als auch der in der Mortalitätsstatistik des BFS verzeichneten Drogentodesfälle in den Jahren 1986 bis 1990 stattfand, also bevor eine massiv verstärkte polizeiliche Repression im Jahre 1991 einsetzte (*Abbildung 8*). Die Erfassung der Drogentodesfälle beruht auf zwei vollständig unabhängigen Systemen. Die Mortalitätsstatistik beruht auf den durch den Arzt ausgestellten Todesscheinen, die Polizeistatistik hingegen auf

Polizeiberichten an das Bundesamt für Polizeiwesen. Trotzdem sind die Abweichungen zwischen den beiden Messsystemen nicht sehr gross.

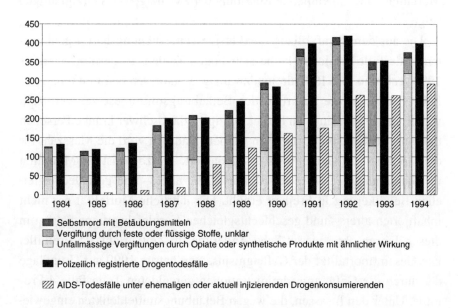

Selbstmord mit Betäubungsmitteln

Vergiftung durch feste oder flüssige Stoffe, unklar

Unfallmässige Vergiftungen durch Opiate oder synthetische Produkte mit ähnlicher Wirkung

Polizeilich registrierte Drogentodesfälle

AIDS-Todesfälle unter ehemaligen oder aktuell injizierenden Drogenkonsumierenden

Abbildung 8: Verschiedene Erfassungssysteme für Drogentodesfälle, 1984–1994

Der Anstieg der Drogentodesfälle läuft parallel zu dem Anstieg der AIDS–Todesfälle unter injizierenden Drogenkonsumierenden und hat eher etwas mit dem sich verschlechternden Gesundheitszustand unter den Konsumierenden zu tun. Zwischen 1992 und 1994 stagniert die Zahl der AIDS–Todesfälle auf einem Niveau von 250 bis 300, jene der Drogentodesfälle auf einem Niveau von 350 bis 400. Nicht inbegriffen sind Todesfälle unter Konsumierenden, die auf anderen Todesursachen beruhen, etwa als Folge von Hepatitisinfektionen, Herzversagen, Verkehrsunfällen und so weiter.

In den vergangenen zehn Jahren hat sich die gesamte Belastung mit unnatürlichen Todesfällen in der Schweiz nicht erhöht, sondern vermindert. Die Zunahme der Drogentodesfälle brachte keine Veränderung der Gesamtmortalität, während sich, im Zusammenwirken mit der AIDS–Mortalität, eine zunehmende Belastung der Zwanzig– bis Vierzigjährigen zeigt.

Die aus dem Strafvollzug – exklusive Untersuchungshaft – gemeldeten Todesfälle erreichen keine sehr hohen Zahlen. Insgesamt waren es 1990 sechzehn und 1991 dreiundzwanzig. Von diesen betrafen 6 bzw. 12 Fälle Personen, die aufgrund des Betäubungsmittelgesetzes verurteilt waren. Es ist allerdings zu berücksichtigen, dass schwer kranke Personen meistens in Kliniken überwiesen werden. Dadurch wird die Masszahl für die Mortalität im Gefängnis selbst reduziert. Trotzdem ist die Mortalität im Gefängnis gegenüber der Mortalität der alters– und geschlechtsgleichen Bevölkerung in Freiheit erhöht. Die jährliche Mortalität der nicht inhaftierten alters– und geschlechtsgleichen Vergleichsgruppe beträgt in diesen Jahren ohne wesentliche Änderung im Zeitverlauf 1,5 Promille. Die Gesamtmortalität der Gefängnisinsassen betrug 1990 auf Grundlage der durch die Gefängnisadministrationen gemeldeten Todesfälle 4 Promille. Unter den Insassen, die wegen Betäubungsmitteldelikten eingewiesen wurden, betrug sie 5 Promille. Im Jahre 1991 verschärfte sich die Situation dramatisch: Die Gesamtmortalität im Gefängnis betrug 6 Promille, unter den Insassen mit Verurteilungen nach dem Betäubungsmittelgesetz sogar ein Prozent. Aufgrund neuerer Schätzungen entspricht dies auch der aktuellen Situation. Demzufolge liegt die Übersterblichkeit im Gefängnis insgesamt beim Faktor vier, für Insassen mit Verurteilungen nach dem Betäubungsmittelgesetz beim Faktor sechs. Die Sterblichkeit der zur Zeit auf ca. 30'000 schwer abhängige Personen geschätzte Kerngruppe der Drogenkonsumierenden in der Schweiz liegt jedoch bei über zwei Prozent. Für diese Gruppe scheint prima vista der Gefängnisaufenthalt selbst keine erhöhte Sterblichkeit zu bedeuten. In Anbetracht dessen, dass Schwerkranke in der Regel in Kliniken verbracht und von der Administration als Überweisungen beziehungsweise Entlassungen registriert werden, und in Anbetracht dessen, dass viele Todesfälle durch Überdosierung mehr oder weniger unmittelbar nach Gefängnis–

und Haftaufenthalten vorkommen, kann jedoch keinesfalls von einem günstigen Einfluss des Gefängnisaufenthaltes auf die Mortalität ausgegangen werden.

Der Themenkomplex Drogen ist für den heutigen Strafvollzug in der Schweiz zentral. Ein Blick auf die Gesundheit und Mortalität zeigt auch ein strafrechtsdogmatisches und ethisches Problem: NIL NOCERE ist ein Grundsatz des Strafvollzugs. Der Staat hat sicherzustellen, dass die Gesundheitsversorgung der Gefängnisinsassen mindestens dem Minimalangebot für Menschen in Freiheit entspricht. Nicht schaden, sondern fördern und erziehen ist das im Strafgesetzbuch festgelegte Ziel des Strafvollzugs. Der blosse Sicherungsaspekt betrifft alleine die Gemeingefährlichkeit bestimmter Insassen, den Schutz der Gesellschaft. Hier geht es um schwere Verbrechen, Raubmord, Vergewaltigung, absichtliche schwere Körperverletzung und ähnliches. Nach Thomas von Aquin sind durch menschliches Gesetz zu strafen «VITIA GRAVIORA … ET PRAECIPUE QUAE SUNT AD NOCENDUM ALIORUM, SINE QUORUM PROHIBITIONE SOCIETAS HUMANA CONSERVARI NON POTEST, SICUT PROHIBENTUR LEGE HUMANA HOMICIDIA, FURTA ET HUIUS MODI». Gemäss der Regel von Aquinus sind Drogenkonsumierende mit Sicherheit nicht zu bestrafen (vgl. Schultz, 1991 und 1995).

Neben der Verdeckung der offenen Drogenszene könnte als Erfolg der verstärkten Repression der letzten Jahre die sich erhöhende Erfassungsdichte und der polizeiliche Bekanntheitsgrad der Konsumierenden gewertet werden. Nur: Ein Einfluss auf Inzidenz und Prävalenz ist auch damit nicht verbunden. Einflüsse der Konjunktur der Drogenrepression sind zwar in den Repressionszahlen selber zu sehen, nicht jedoch in der epidemiologischen Entwicklung. Die Zahl der Konsumierenden bewegt sich weitgehend unabhängig von den verschiedenen staatlichen Massnahmen, hingegen ist der allgemeine Gesundheitszustand der Konsumierenden, der sich in den letzten zehn Jahren verschlechtert hat, für deren Sterblichkeit von wesentlicher Bedeutung.

Jedenfalls ist es der Drogenrepression in über 25 Jahren nicht gelungen, das Angebot auf dem Drogenmarkt nachhaltig zu reduzieren, nicht einmal im Strafvollzug selbst und insbesondere nicht in den vergangenen fünf Jahren verstärkter Repressionsbemühungen. Der Anteil der konfiszierten illegalen Substanzen in der Schweiz ist mit 2 bis 3 Prozent zu gering, um irgendwie marktrelevant sein zu können. Daran ändern auch spektakuläre Fänge von 20 oder 100 Kilogramm nichts. Die Situation in anderen Ländern unterscheidet sich nicht wesentlich von der Situation in der Schweiz. Bestimmte amerikanische Quellen sprechen zwar von einem kontrollierten Anteil von bis zu 30%, aber wahrscheinlich ist auf dem Wege der Übermittlung eine Null vor das Komma gerutscht oder der genannte Anteil betrifft das Volumen, über dessen Marktpräsenz die Behörden oder die verdeckten Fahnder oder die Informanten der Polizei zu irgend einem Zeitpunkt Kenntnis hatten. Bei den Versuchen, Produktion, Verkäufer und Käufer ermittlungstechnisch zu durchdringen, besteht immer die Gefahr, aus Sicht der Polizei sicher auch die Notwendigkeit, dass Organe der Strafverfolgung selber in unterschiedlichen Funktionen auf dem Markt auftreten. Solche Verhaltensweisen stellt das Betäubungsmittelgesetz bei gesetzeskonformem Vorgehen straffrei.

Das Repressionsprimat und die Prohibition bewiesen und beweisen immer noch grosses Beharrungsvermögen. Vor Ende der sechziger Jahre – immer unter Ausklammerung der Zwischenkriegszeit – waren Drogen noch nicht als soziales Problem entdeckt. Das Jahr 1968 mag hier zu Recht Assoziationen wecken. Nach diesem Zeitpunkt waren die Rahmenbedingungen für die im Schwarzmarkt zu erzielenden Profite ohne Unterbruch gewährleistet (zur Schwarzmarktproblematik siehe Pommerehne/Hartmann, 1980 und Pommerehne/Hart, 1991). Nur in der kurzen Zeit des infektionsepidemiologisch bestimmten gesundheitspolitischen Primats der zweiten Hälfte der achtziger Jahre schien sich das Repressionsprimat aufzuweichen. Als Exponenten und Garanten dieser Rahmenbedingungen sind neben der medial vermittelten Öffentlichkeit die Instanzen sozialer Kontrolle, Polizei, Justiz und Gesundheitsverwaltung zu nennen. Ausserdem wird eine generelle Überwachungssituation legitimiert. Der Komplex «illegale Drogen» kann neben dem Drogenhandel auch die Bereiche Waffenhandel, organisierte Kriminalität und politische Kriminalität umfassen.

Für die Beurteilung der Drogenpolitik spielen in erster Linie Kosten– und Effizienzüberlegungen eine Rolle, aber auch Überlegungen zum Grenznutzen bei immer mehr zusätzlich erkannten Konsumierenden, Überlegungen zu Marktvolumen, Marktkosten und Steuern im Vergleich zu den Märkten von legalen Drogen und die Rechtssicherheit für alle Beteiligten. Eine isolierte Betrachtung des sogenannten Drogenproblems als Problem der Konsumierenden führt in die Irre. Die aktuelle, auch rechtsdogmatisch beeinflusste Diskussion um die Strafbarkeit von Besitz und Konsum bestimmter Substanzen bietet Gelegenheit für eine umfassendere Betrachtungsweise (Schultz, 1991 und 1995). Wie die rechtliche Situation zur Zeit gegeben ist, erscheint es allerdings notwendig, im Sinne von «HARM REDUCTION» die gesundheitliche Situation der Insassen zu verbessern, insbesondere spezifische Verschreibungs– und Substitutionsprogramme auch in den Gefängnissen in ausreichendem Masse anzubieten. Mittel– und längerfristig wären ein Rückzug des Strafrechts aus dem Betäubungsmittelbereich zu Gunsten verwaltungsrechtlicher Regelungen und die Verdrängung des Schwarzmarktes durch einen ordentlich besteuerten Medikamentenmarkt anzustreben. Als erster Schritt ist die Straffreiheit des Konsums und seiner Vorbereitungshandlungen wie des Besitzes zum Eigengebrauch zu gewähren. Die entsprechenden Vorschläge der Expertenkommission zur Revision des Betäubungsmittelgesetzes sind ein Schritt in die richtige Richtung. Jedenfalls würde ihre Durchführung den Strafvollzug entlasten.

Besonderer Dank für die Unterstützung bei der Aufarbeitung der Daten, Herstellung der Grafiken und Diskussion der Ergebnisse gebührt Simone Rônez und George Muriset, BFS.

Literatur

Boller, Boris: Drogen – Medienthema und Medien–Selbstdarstellung. Drogenbe-
richterstattung in der Schweizer Presse in den Jahren 1993 und 1994. Bull.
BAG, Nr. 33/95, Bern 1995.

Bundesamt für Gesundheitswesen: Methadonbericht. Suchtmittelersatz in der
Behandlung Heroinabhängiger in der Schweiz. 3. Aufl., Bern 1995.

Estermann, Josef: Die Bedeutung von Erziehungsheim– und Erziehungsan-
staltsaufenthalten für kriminelle Karrieren. In: Kriminologisches Bulletin,
1984; 10:27–40.

Estermann, Josef: Kriminelle Karrieren von Gefängnisinsassen. Eine empirische
Untersuchung. Lang, Frankfurt/M, Bern, New York 1986.

Estermann, Josef; Hermann, Ute; Hügi, Daniela; Nydegger, Bruno: Sozial-
epidemiologie des Drogenkonsums. Zu Prävalenz und Inzidenz des Heroin-
und Kokaingebrauchs und dessen polizeiliche Verfolgung. Berlin, 1996.

Estermann, Josef und Rônez, Simone: Drogen und Strafrecht in der Schweiz.
Zeitreihen zu Verzeigungen, Strafurteilen und Strafvollzug, 1974–1994,
*Drogues et droit pénal en Suisse. Séries chronologiques des dénonciations,
jugements pénaux et exécutions de peines, 1974–1994.* Bundesamt für Statistik (Hg.), Reihe Statistik der Schweiz, Bern 1995.

Estermann, Josef: Die Kosten der Drogenrepression. Schätzungen für die
Schweiz 1991. *Consommation et trafic de drogues: les coûts de la repression
1991.* Bundesamt für Statistik (Hg.), Reihe Statistik der Schweiz, Bern 1995.

Fahrenkrug, Hermann et al.: Illegale Drogen in der Schweiz, 1990–1993. Zürich
1995.

Pommerehne, Werner W. und Hartmann, Hans C.: Ein ökonomischer Ansatz zur
Rauschgiftkontrolle. Jahrbuch für Sozialwissenschaft, 31/1980, 102–143.

Pommerehne, Werner W. und Hart, Albert: Man muss den Teufel nicht mit dem
Beelzebub austreiben wollen: Drogenpolitik aus ökonomischer Sicht. In: W.
Böker, J. Nelles (Hrsg.): Drogenpolitik wohin? Haupt, Bern 1991, 241–270.

Schultz, Hans: Zur strafrechtlichen Behandlung der Betäubungsmittel. Eine kriminalpolitische Skizze. In: Studi in memoria di Pietro Nuvolone, Volume
Secondo, giuffrè editore, 1991, 233–252.

Schultz, Hans: Die Revision des Betäubungsmittelgesetzes 1975: Gründe, Ergebnisse, Auswirkungen, in: Schweizerische Zeitschrift für Strafrecht
113/1995, 273–278.

Spuhler, Thomas: Todesursachenstatistik. Tabellen 1994, Bundesamt für Statistik (Hg.), Bern 1995.

La consommation de drogues dans les prisons suisses

Résultats d'une enquête par interviews réalisée en 1993

Christophe Koller

1 Introduction

Avec l'augmentation des problèmes liés à la drogue ainsi que la forte présence de l'épidémie de sida en milieu carcéral, le thème de la santé dans les prisons ainsi que le rôle de la prison dans la société est devenu l'un des thèmes importants de la politique médico–légale en Suisse. Même si, à l'heure actuelle, la consommation de drogues dans les prisons reste souvent mal connue, ou minimisée, force est de constater que la consommation de tabacs, de médicaments ou de drogues illicites est proportionellement bien plus élevée en milieu carcéral que pour la population hors institution. De plus, la prise de drogues illicites par voie intraveineuse (en particulier l'héroïne) constitue un comportement à haut risque pour la transmission du VIH.

Nous partirons de l'idée qu'un mauvais état de santé, même s'il est d'abord lié à l'isolement, à la surpopulation ainsi qu'aux pressions psychologiques dans les prisons, est aussi à mettre en relation avec la consommation de drogues et la manière de consommer celle–ci. En effet, plus cette consommation sera marquée et plus l'état de santé sera pressentit comme mauvais, ce qui se traduira par des possibilités de réinsertion sociale amoindries ainsi qu'une augmentation des risques de récidives et de contamination de la population générale (hépatite, tuberculose, sida).

Le but de cet article est de présenter, sur la base de notre échantillon, la problématique de la consommation de drogue en milieu carcéral, les liens existant entre les différentes drogues (douces et dures), la fréquence de leur absorption et les relations entre ces comportements et l'état de santé. Nous nous placerons principalement dans le cadre d'une approche comparative (prisons et population hors institution) en tenant compte du caractère très hétérogène du système carcéral suisse.

Les limites de l'enquête
- Echantillon de petite dimension: impossibilité de dégager des résultats représentatifs pour de petites unités géographiques (commune ou canton) ainsi que pour des institutions particulières ou des mois précis.
- Ne permet pas de déterminer les causes des maladies.
- Ne permet pas d'observer ou d'interroger des individus sur une longue durée (par exemple dans le sens d'une étude longitudinale).
- L'enquête ne prévoit aucun examen médical.
- La cause de l'entrée, le type de condamnation ainsi que la durée de la peine sont inconnus.
- L'évolution de la consommation en milieu carcéral ne peut pas être estimé,
- Il n'est pas possible de distinguer la consommation «in muros» et «extra muros».
- Pour la consommation de drogues dures «in muros» et «extra muros», il n'est pas possible de faire la distinction entre consommation illégale et prescription médicale.

---

2 Méthodes

2.1 L'enquête auprès des prisons dans le contexte de l'Enquête suisse sur la santé

L'enquête menée dans le milieu carcéral suisse poursuit les mêmes objectifs que l'enquête menée auprès des ménages, à savoir: l'étude de l'état de santé et de ses facteurs déterminants, l'observation chronologique de l'évolution de l'état de santé de la population ainsi que les effets engendrés par les mesures de politique de la santé.

Cette enquête a été effectuée en deux temps: tout d'abord une enquête par interviews réalisées auprès des ménages en 1992 et, l'année suivante, une enquête face à face menée auprès des personnes résidant en institution.

Réalisée au niveau suisse sur la base du même questionnaire, cette enquête fournit pour la première fois des statistiques portant sur l'état de santé et les conditions de vie de la population carcérale, l'utilisation des services de santé, les symptômes de maladies ainsi que les comportements ayant une influence sur la santé pour les personnes vivant en institution. Elle permet d'établir des comparaisons avec la population générale résidant en Suisse et âgée de 15 ans et plus (seuls les étrangers avec permis B (annuel) ou C (établissement) sont inclus).

Contenu de l'Enquête suisse sur la santé:
- caractères sociodémographiques
- état de santé physique et psychique
- comportements ayant une influence sur la santé
- symptômes de maladies et problèmes de santé
- aspects de la promotion de la santé
- handicaps et conséquences sociales associées
- utilisation des services de santé
- problèmes de santé des retraités

La méthode de sélection des personnes interrogées diffère sur deux points:

- Tout d'abord, l'enquête auprès de la population générale a été réalisée à partir d'un échantillon de 23'000 ménages de toute la Suisse disposant d'un raccordement téléphonique, une personne par ménage ayant été tirée au hasard. Pour l'enquête auprès des institutions, le tirage s'est opéré à partir d'une pré–enquête, réalisée sur la base du registre des entreprises. Cette pré–enquête a couvert 2088 institutions, comptant

97'000 pensionnaires résident dans un établissement depuis une durée égale ou supérieure à trois mois. Plusieurs personnes ont été tirées au hasard dans chacune des institutions. Sur cette base, un échantillon de 134 établissements (dont 24 institutions carcérales) représentatif du type et de la taille des établissements a été retenu.

- Deuxièmement, la méthode diffère quant à la forme des interviews. En effet, si les interviews ont été réalisées par téléphone auprès des ménages, les entretiens avec les personnes vivant en institution ont été effectuées au niveau personnel (face à face).

Finalement, 15'300 interviews ont été réalisées auprès de la population générale (de mai 1992 à avril 1993) et 1303 entretiens ont pû être menés à bien auprès des personnes séjournant en institution (de juillet à novembre 1993). Parmi ces derniers, 201 l'ont été auprès des détenus qui représentaient une population carcérale de 2804 personnes âgées de 18 ans et plus et répondant aux critères de l'enquête.

Les entretiens auprès des détenus dans le contexte de l'Enquête suisse sur la santé

II. Enquête auprès des ménages	II. Enquête auprès des institutions
- Population: population de 15 ans et plus résidant en Suisse (y compris les étrangers avec permis B ou C vivant en ménage privé)	**- Population:** population de 15 ans et plus résidant en Suisse et vivant dans une institution de manière continue pendant plus de 3 mois (y compris les étrangers avec permis B ou C)
- Echantillon net: - 15'300 personnes	**- Echantillon net:** - 134 institutions, 1303 entretiens en tout, dont - 24 prisons (préventive et exécution des peines) - 201 détenus

(suite)

II. Enquête auprès des ménages	II. Enquête auprès des institutions
- Plan d'échantillonnage:	**- Plan d'échantillonnage:**
- échantillon stratifié, sondage aléatoire à 2 degrés	- échantillon stratifié, sondage aléatoire à 2 degrés
- sélection des adresses à partir du registre téléphonique des PTT (TERCO)	- tirage des institutions à partir d'une pré-enquête
- tirage au hasard d' une personne par ménage privé	- tirage au hasard de plusieurs personnes par institution
- Méthode de collecte:	**- Méthode de collecte:**
- interviews téléphoniques (de 30-40 mn) suivies de l'envoi de questionnaires (pour les 15 à 74 ans)	- entretiens face à face (30-40 mn)
- Périodicité:	**- Périodicité:**
- en 4 vagues (printemps, été , automne, hiver) de mai 1992 à avril 1993	- de juillet à novembre 1993
	- Taux de participation:
	- 87% (toutes institutions)
	- 90% (prisons)
	- 94% (des personnes en institution)
	- 94% (détenus)

2.2 Le choix des indicateurs

Dans une enquête, le choix des questions à poser lors des interviews et la construction des indicateurs revêt une grande importance. Ces questions et ces indicateurs doivent répondre à des critères de validation (tests sur la validité des résultats), de reliabilité (possibilité de reconstruction à des temps différents) et de comparabilité (comparaison avec d'autres enquêtes).

Dans le cadre de la problématique de la consommation de drogue en milieu carcéral, nous avons décidé de retenir certaines variables ou indicateurs relatifs au thème de la drogue prise au sens large et disponibles sur la base de notre enquête. Ainsi, au niveau des drogues légales, il s'agit de la consommation de médicaments (sans distinction), de deux types de médicaments à propriétés psychoactives (somnifères et calmants). La consommation de tabac fait également l'objet d'une attention particulière tout comme la consommation d'alcool.

Consommation de drogues licites
- Médicaments, somnifères, calmants (dans les 7 derniers jours et fréquence)
- Tabac (fumeurs, ex-fumeurs, non-fumeurs et nombre de cigarettes par jour)
- Consommation habituelle d'alcool

Au niveau des drogues illicites, il importe de cerner le type de drogues consommées ainsi que la répartition et le mode de consommation. Le haschich ne peut pas être assimilé à une drogue dure et seules certaines substances sont utilisées par voie intraveineuse comportant un risque épidémiologique (héroïne en particuliers). La toxicodépendance ne touche qu'une petite partie des consommateurs, c'est pourquoi il faut définir les populations à risque selon le degré de consommation et le mode d'utilisation. Pour ce faire, nous distinguerons *les utilisateurs ponctuels* (consommation en vue de faire une expérience)*, les utilisateurs occasionnels* et *les personnes dépendantes* (toxicomanes*)* (Rehm, 1995). Pour chaque «utilisateur» correspondra trois types d'indicateurs pouvant indiquer un gradient de niveau et de fréquence de consommation reconnus et acceptés dans la littérature scientifique. Il s'agit de la prévalence de vie (réponse à la question: «*avez–vous consommé une fois dans votre vie?*»), de la consommation actuelle (réponse à la question: «*consommez–vous encore à l'heure actuelle?*») et de la consommation régulière (au moins une fois par semaine; réponse à la question: «*avez–vous consommé de manière régulière dans les 12 derniers mois?*»). Les personnes représentées dans cette dernière catégorie correspondent à notre définition des toxicomanes.

D'autre part, l'Enquête suisse sur la santé permet de faire une distinction entre une dizaine de catégories de drogues (après regroupement: toutes drogues, drogues dures, opiacés) ou de drogues spécifiques dont

nous ne mentionnerons que les plus fréquentes: héroïne, cocaïne, méthadone.

Consommation de drogues illégales

Différencier trois types d'indicateurs:
- Lifetime–prevalence (une fois dans la vie)
- Consommation actuelle («Consommez–vous encore?»)
- Consommation régulière (une fois par semaine ou plus)
  [=> toxicodépendants]

Et trois catégories de drogues illicites:
1. Toutes «drogues illégales»
2. «Drogues douces» (haschich/marijuana)
3. «Drogues dures»:
   • Toutes «drogues dures» (héroïne, cocaïne, crack–freebase,
     méthadone, amphétamines, hallucinogènes, autres stupéfiants)
   • Opiacés (héroïne, crack–freebase, méthadone) et cocaïne
     (TRENDS 1975–auj.)
   ou séparément:
   • Héroïne
   • Cocaïne
   • Méthadone
   • Crack – freebase
   • Amphétamines (ecstasy, MDM)
   • Hallucinogènes (LSD, mescaline etc.)
   • Autres stupéfiants (morphine, codéine)

2.3 Situer la population carcérale étudiée

2.3.1 Par rapport à la population auprès des ménages

La structure de la population résidente dans les prisons suisses est fort
distincte de la population vivant auprès des ménages privés, ce qui explique une partie des différences observées au niveau de l'analyse. Sur la
base de notre échantillon de résidents en milieu carcéral, l'on constate en
effet que la part des hommes est supérieur à 90% et qu'il s'agit d'une
population très jeune: 26% des personnes interrogées ont moins de 25 ans

et 85% moins de 39 ans (contre 15% et 56% auprès de la population vivant hors institution). La jeunesse explique aussi que 57% des détenus soient célibataires (contre 29% hors institution).

D'autre part, l'inégalité sociale se lit à travers les résultats du niveau de formation avec 41% des détenus n'affichant pas de formation supérieure à la scolarité obligatoire, contre seulement 19% de la population des 18 à 60 ans vivant auprès des ménages.

Par contre, la part de la population étrangère interviewée correspond à la part de la population étrangère auprès des ménages (20%). Il faut rappeler à ce propos que la part réelle des étrangers se situe à environ 50% dans le milieu carcéral suisse (47% en 1993, selon l'OFS).

2.3.2 Différences entre concordats pénitentiaires et types de prisons

Le système pénitentiaire suisse peut être différencié à plusieurs points de vue. Tout d'abord, au niveau géographique, il est divisé en trois grands concordats, celui de la Suisse orientale (regroupant 8 cantons et demi–cantons: ZH, SH, SG, GR, GL, AP, AI, TG), de la Suisse centrale (11 cantons et demi–cantons: BE, BS, BL, ZG, AG, SO, LU, SZ, UR, NW,OW) et de la Suisse latine (7 cantons: TI, GE, VD, FR, NE, VS, JU). Près de 50% des entretiens de notre enquête ont été réalisés dans les prisons de la Suisse orientale (dont une bonne partie dans le canton de Zürich), un peu moins d'un tiers dans la Suisse centrale et 24% dans la Suisse latine.

L'autre différence tient au type d'établissement. Environ 1/3 des entretiens ont eu lieu dans de petits établissements (comptant moins de 50 détenus et correspondant grosso modo aux prisons préventives), moins d'un cinquième dans des établissements de taille moyenne et plus de la moitié dans de grandes prisons de plus de 100 détenus. Ces derniers établissements se caractérisent surtout par l'exécution de peines d'une durée souvent supérieure à un an et sont soumis à un régime strict et limi-

Tableau 1: Situer la population carcérale par rapport à la
population générale (18–60 ans), en pour cent

Population carcérale	Population générale
- Sexe 92% des détenus sont des hommes	49%
- Age 26% des détenus ont moins de 25 ans	15%
85% des détenus ont moins de 39 ans	56%
- Etat-civil 57% des détenus sont célibataires	29%
- Formation 41% des détenus n'ont pas achevé un niveau de formation supérieur au niveau «scolarité obligatoire»	19%
- Nationalité 81% des détenus interrogés sont de nationalité suisse	80%

© Office fédéral de la statistique, Enquête suisse sur la santé 1992/1993

Remarques concernant les tableaux, explication des signes:
En général, nous avons arrondi à la valeur supérieure ou à la valeur inférieure sans tenir compte de la somme totale. Par conséquent, il se peut que les totaux s'écartent très légèrement de la somme des différentes valeurs les constituant.

Trois points (...) mis à la place d'un nombre désignent une valeur inférieure à la moitié de la plus petite unité ou zéro.

Les chiffres mis entre parenthèses signifient que le nombre d'observations de l'échantillon est plus petit que 30. Les pour cent se réfèrent à la population (résultats pondérés) alors que les seuils se basent sur les résultats non pondérés.

tant les contacts des détenus avec le monde extérieur. Le type de régime varie en fonction de la gravité du délit, de la conduite du détenu ou encore selon la durée de la peine déjà effectuée. A l'inverse, les prisons de petite taille, souvent situées au niveau des districts, font purger généralement des peines de courte durée pouvant, dans certains cas, dépasser trois mois. Certaines de ces prisons se caractérisent par le double statut d'établissements d'exécution des peines et de détention préventive.

Il est plus difficile de dresser un portrait des établissements de taille intermédiaire, lesquels se situent le plus souvent à cheval entre la détention préventive et l'exécution des peines, offrant toutefois de large possibilités de régimes de semi–libertés pour les détenus arrivés en fin de peine et augmentant par la même les possibilités de contacts avec la population générale.

L'Office fédéral de la statistique estime «qu'il y a chaque année environ 14'000 entrées et sorties dans les prisons suisses, dont 3'500 (soit 25%) concernent des personnes avec un comportement à risque pour la transmission du VIH» (cité dans «Le sida en milieu carcéral», Harding, Manghi et Sanchez, 1990).

Tableau 2: Population carcérale (3 mois et plus) selon le concordat pénitentiaire

Concordat pénitentiaire	Population carcérale	Pour cent	Age moyen*
Suisse centrale (BE, BS, BL, ZG, AG, SO, LU, SZ, UR, NW, OW)	793	28.3	33
Suisse orientale (ZH, SH, SG, GR, GL, AP, AI, TG)	1'342	47.9	30
Suisse romande et Tessin	665	23.8	35
Total	**2'800**	**100.0**	**32**

Taux de sondage=7.1%   * de la population carcérale (arrondi à l'unité)
© Office fédéral de la statistique, Enquête suisse sur la santé 1992/1993

2.3.3 Autres variables permettant de mieux situer la population carcérale

En tenant compte de la date d'entrée dans l'institution, plus de 50% des personnes interviewées déclarent avoir séjourné dans l'établissement moins d'une année, 77% depuis moins de 2 ans, les 23% restant y séjournant depuis plus de deux ans.

Tableau 3: Date d'entrée dans la prison, en pour cent
(Depuis quand êtes-vous ici?)

Année d'entrée	Pour cent	Estimation de la durée du séjour*
1983-1990	(14.3)	3 ans et plus
1991	(8.5)	de 2 à moins de 3 ans
1992	26.3	de 1 à moins de 2 ans
1993	50.9	moins d'un an
Total	100.0	

* N.B. Ne fournit aucune indication sur la durée réelle de la peine.
© Office fédéral de la statistique, Enquête suisse sur la santé 1992/1993

Le lieu de résidence avant l'entrée dans l'institution démontre que près de la moitié des détenus résidaient dans leur propre ménage ou chez des parents avant de pénétrer en prison. L'autre moitié provenant dans la majeure partie des cas d'autres institutions. Dans ce cas de figure, il faut tenir compte du fait que la grande majorité des prisonniers sont transférés au moins une fois d'un établissement à l'autre, entre autre après que le verdict du jugement ait été prononcé. Cette forte proportion de détenus provenant d'une autre institution ne peut dès lors pas être interprété comme un signe de récidive ou de mauvaise intégration sociale avant l'incarcération.

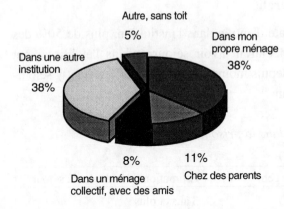

Autre, sans toit

5%

Dans une autre
institution

38%

Dans mon
propre ménage

38%

8%   11%

Dans un ménage   Chez des parents
collectif, avec des amis

Figure 1:
Lieu de résidence
avant l'entrée dans la
prison, en pour cent
(comment viviez-vous
avant d'entrer ici?)

A ce propos, tout laisse à penser que les détenus souffrent de l'isolement, autant en préventive qu'en exécution des peines, et qu'ils ont besoin d'être soutenus par des personnes extérieur à la prison (parents ou amis). A la question, «*avec quelle fréquence recevez–vous des visites de personnes venant de l'extérieur*», plus d'un quart a répondu «*au moins une fois par semaine*», 45% «*au moins une fois par mois*», les autres ne recevant pratiquement jamais de visites, soit un tiers. Le *tableau 4* montre que les relations avec l'extérieur sont limitées et pratiquement inexistentes pour certains. Cet isolement peut avoir des conséquences au niveau de la solitude endurée ainsi qu'au niveau de la réinsertion des détenus une fois libérés.

Tableau 4: Visites de personnes venant de l'extérieur, en pour cent
(Avec quelle fréquence recevez-vous de la visite de personnes venant de l'extérieur?)

Fréquence des visites	Pour cent
Au moins 1 fois par jour	...
Au moins 1 fois par semaine	26.0
Au moins 1 fois par mois	44.7
Au moins 1 fois par année	(7.5)
Moins d'une fois par année	11.9
Visites pas permises	(8.1)
«Ne sais pas»	(1.7)
Total	100.0

© Office fédéral de la statistique, Enquête suisse sur la santé 1992/1993

3 Les résultats

Précisions quant aux méthodes utilisées
Nous avons retenu principalement l'approche comparative pour l'analyse des résultats. Ainsi, nous comparerons les résultats obtenus pour les institutions pénales avec la population correspondante auprès des ménages âgée de plus de 17 ans. Cette limite d'âge s'explique par des raisons légales. Ainsi, il est possible que nos chiffres ne correspondent pas à d'autres résultats déjà publiés pour la population générale sur la base de notre enquête.
Les questions relatives aux drogues illicites n'ont été posées qu'aux personnes âgées de moins de 40 ans.

3.1 L'état de santé

Pour présenter l'état de santé de la population, nous avons décidé de retenir l'état de santé psychique et les symptômes de maladie. A ce propos, l'état de santé psychique de la population carcérale apparaît comme bien moins bon que celui de la population hors institution. En effet, 58%

des détenus déclarent un état de santé psychique mauvais (respectivement 30% de la population générale du même âge). D'autre part, cette population est deux fois plus touchées par des symptômes de maladies tels que mal de dos, maux de tête, mal à l'estomac, fièvre etc. que le reste de la population.

En tenant compte de la dimension sociodémographique, plus de 70% des jeunes détenus (18–24 ans) affichent un mauvais état de santé psychique contre 40% de la population générale du même âge. Tout comme pour la population générale, la santé psychique semble s'améliorer avec l'âge. Le niveau de formation semble également jouer un rôle important puisque 62% des prisonniers n'ayant pas achevé d'étude supérieure au niveau école obligatoire déclarent se sentir mal psychiquement contre 56%

Tableau 5: Santé psychique et symptômes de maladies dans les prisons, comparaison avec les mêmes caractéristiques de la population vivant dans les ménages, en pour cent

Santé psychique et symptômes de maladies (18-39 ans)	Prisons	Population générale
1. Santé psychique: mauvaise (1)		
Selon l'âge		
18-24 ans	69.7	40.0
25-39 ans	53.6	33.4
Selon le sexe		
hommes	59.1	32.4
femmes	(53.3)	37.7
Selon le niveau de formation achevé		
Ecole primaire	61.9	43.3
Ecole secondaire	55.5	33.3
Selon la nationalité		
Suisse	55.3	33.5
Etrangers	(74.3)	41.4
Total «mauvaise santé psychique» (18-39 ans)	**58.5**	**35.1**

Tabelau 5 (suite)

	Prisons	Population générale
2. Symptômes de maladies: forts symptômes physiques (2)		
Selon l'âge		
18-24 ans	50.4	24.7
25-39 ans	49.0	23.9
Selon le sexe		
hommes	47.1	18.8
femmes	(71.1)	29.4
Selon le niveau de formation achevé		
Ecole primaire	41.2	29.3
Ecole secondaire	56.8	22.9
Selon la nationalité		
Suisses	46.7	22.3
Etrangers	(61.2)	31.0
Total «forts symptômes» (18-39 ans)	**49.4**	**24.1**

© Office fédéral de la statistique, Enquête suisse sur la santé 1992/1993

(1) «Etat de santé psychique» (gradient sur la base de questions portant sur la dépression, la sérénité, la nervosité, l'optimisme).

(2) «Symptômes de maladies» (gradient sur la base de questions portant sur le mal de dos, le sentiment de faiblesse, le mal au ventre, la diarrhée, l'insomnie, les maux de tête, l'irrégularité cardiaque, la douleur, la fièvre (source: IGIP/ PROMES, 1990).

des personnes mieux formées (cette différence est encore plus marquée pour les ménages privés).

Pour les symptômes de maladies, l'âge ne semble pas être déterminant alors que le niveau de formation, la nationalité et surtout le sexe apparaissent comme plus importants. Ainsi, les femmes, les étrangers ainsi que les personnes peu formées déclarent davantage des symptômes de maladies autant dans les prisons qu'au sein des ménages privés.

3.2   La consommation de drogues au sens large

La consommation de tabac est très répandue parmi les détenus: 84% d'entre eux fument (contre un tiers du reste de la population du même âge). Le pourcentage de grands fumeurs (plus de 20 cigarettes par jour) est particulièrement élevé: il atteint 62% chez les détenus, contre 10% du reste de la population du même âge. Dans le domaine du tabagisme, la prévention ne semble pas de mise puisque le «Quit rate» (proportion des ex–fumeurs par rapport aux fumeurs et ex–fumeurs) est égal à 5% alors qu'il dépasse les 36% auprès de la population générale.

Les médicaments sont également davantage consommés dans les institutions pénales. En effet, la moitié des détenus en consomme régulièrement alors que cela ne touche qu'un tiers des 18 à 60 ans de la population générale. Cette consommation augmente avec l'âge tant dans les prisons que pour les ménages privés. Deux types de médicaments sont particulièrement prisés en milieu carcéral, il s'agit des somnifères et des calmants. Un tiers des détenus déclarent avoir consommé des somnifères au cours des sept derniers jours (1/5 des calmants) alors que ce taux est nettement plus faible pour la population (4% et 6%). Avec l'âge, cette consommation reste stable pour les somnifères alors qu'elle diminue fortement pour les calmants dans les institutions pénales. Auprès des ménages, la consommation augmente avec l'âge pour les deux types de médicaments. En tenant compte de la culture, contrairement à ce que l'on remarque pour la population générale, la consommation de tabac et de médicaments dans les institutions pénales n'est pas supérieure en Suisse latine par rapport à la Suisse alémanique.

La *consommation d'alcool* est relativement faible en milieu carcéral. Seulement 10% des détenus déclarent boire de l'alcool, plus d'un tiers sont abstinents et plus de la moitié n'ont soit pas l'occasion, soit pas l'autorisation d'en boire.

Tableau 6: Consommation d'alcool, de tabac et de médicaments dans les institutions pénales, comparaison avec la même tranche d'âge de la population vivant dans les ménages, en pour cent

Drogues licites (18-60 ans)	Prisons	Population générale
Consommation d'alcool en prison (1)		
Oui	(10.5)	...
Non, abstinents	35.5	...
Pas l'occasion, pas autorisés	54.0	...
Consommation d'alcool habituelle (2)		
Au moins 1 fois par jour	28.5	18.5
Au moins 1 fois par semaine	21.3	41.0
Moins d'une fois par semaine	(14.0)	25.7
Jamais, abstinents	36.2	14.8
Consommation de tabac		
Non-fumeurs (jamais fumé)	(11.1)	45.8
Ex-fumeurs	(4.5)	19.7
Fumeurs	84.4	34.5
Total	100.0	100.0
Consommation de tabac selon l'âge		
Fumeurs (18-39 ans)	88.3	37.3
Fumeurs (40-60 ans)	69.0	(31.1)
«Quit rate» (3)	5.1	36.3
Nombre de cigarettes consommées par jour	25	16

Tableau 6 (suite)

Drogues licites (18-60 ans)	Prisons	Population générale
Consommation de médicaments dans les 7 derniers jours		
Oui (18-39 ans)	50.6	25.4
Oui (40-60 ans)	63.7	(38.3)
Consommation de somnifères dans les 7 derniers jours		
Quotidiennement (18-39 ans)	33.1	(1.1)
Quotidiennement (40-60 ans)	(30.2)	5.6
Consommation de calmants dans les 7 derniers jours		
Quotidiennement (18-39 ans)	(22.9)	4.9
Quotidiennement (40-60 ans)	(6.2)	7.3

(1) Réponse à la question «Consommez-vous de l'alcool?»
(2) Personnes de 18 à 64 ans pour les ménages privés.
(3) Taux des ex-fumeurs / ex-fumeurs + fumeurs.
© Office fédéral de la statistique, Enquête suisse sur la santé 1992/1993

3.3   La consommation de drogues illégales

Avec l'enquête complémentaire menée dans les prisons en 1993, l'Enquête suisse sur la santé permet d'obtenir une meilleure image de la population dépendante de la drogue en Suisse âgée de moins de 40 ans.

Liens entre «expérience durant la vie» et «consommation régulière»

Sur la base des indicateurs proposés, la consommation passée est supérieure à la consommation actuelle et cette dernière supérieure à la consommation régulière. Ainsi, si 83% des détenus et 17% de la population générale déclarent avoir consommé au moins une fois dans leur vie des drogues illicites, la consommation régulière est pratiquement dix fois plus faible auprès de la population mais ne diminue que d'un facteur 2 en milieu carcéral. La consommation régulière de drogues illicites touche

36% des personnes interrogées en milieu carcéral et 2% de la population générale du même âge.

«Drogues douces» et «drogues dures»

Parmi les utilisateurs réguliers, *22% des détenus* (et environ 2% de la population) *déclarent consommer des «drogues douces»*.

Le nombre de personnes consommant uniquement et régulièrement des «drogues dures» (essentiellement des opiacés et de la cocaïne) atteint environ 20% dans les institutions pénales et 1% de la population auprès des ménages. *En prison, 11% des détenus consomment régulièrement de l'héroïne et 4% de la cocaïne.* D'autre part, *20% du total de la consommation s'effectue par voie intraveineuse,* alors que cette manière de consommer est inférieure à 1% pour la population générale.

Les consommateurs de méthadone

Dans le domaine des prescriptions médicales, la méthadone est géné-ralement utilisée comme drogue de substitution en vue du sevrage des toxicomanes, en particulier dans certaines prisons situées en Suisse alé-manique. Sur la base de l'Enquête sur la santé, nous constatons que *32% des prisonniers ont déjà consommé de la méthadone et que 10% en utilisent de manière régulière en prison.*

Tableau 7: Consommation de drogues illicites dans les prisons, comparaison avec la même tranche d'âge de la population vivant dans les ménages

	en pour cent		Echantillon	
Drogues illicites (18-39 ans)	Prisons	Population générale	N Prisons	N Population générale
Toutes les drogues				
Lifetime-prevalence [1]	82.6	17.4	141	1166
Consommation actuelle [2]	52.7	4.6	83	312
Consommation régulière [3]	36.4	1.8	58	125
Hachisch-marijuana				
Lifetime-prevalence	79.4	16.9	136	1135
Consommation actuelle	44.1	4.3	74	299
Consommation régulière	22.0	1.6	43	117
Drogues dures				
Lifetime-prevalence	73.0	4.5	127	304
Consommation actuelle	29.7	0.6	46	45
Consommation régulière	(19.9)	env. 1% [4]	(26)	(11)
Opiacés + cocaïne				
Lifetime-prevalence	73.0	4.4	127	299
Consommation actuelle	29.2	0.5	46	33
Consommation régulière	(19.8)	env. 1% [4]	(26)	(9)
Héroïne				
Lifetime-prevalence	62.1	1.4	113	86
Consommation actuelle	(19.2)	(0.1)	(28)	(7)
Consommation régulière	(10.9)	…	(13)	(2)
Cocaïne				
Lifetime-prevalence	60.2	2.9	106	199
Consommation actuelle	(11.0)	(0.4)	(22)	(25)
Consommation régulière	(4.0)	…	(7)	(2)
Méthadone				
Lifetime-prevalence	31.7	(0.5)	57	(25)
Consommation actuelle	(11.0)	(0.1)	(19)	(7)
Consommation régulière	(10.4)	(0.1)	(17)	(6)

Tableau 7 (suite)

	Prisons	Population générale	N Prisons	N Population générale
Crack, freebase				
Lifetime-prevalence	15.4	(0.1)	32	(7)
Amphétamines (Ecstasy, MDM)				
Lifetime-prevalence	17.8	1.1	34	78
Hallucinogènes (LSD, mescaline etc.)				
Lifetime-prevalence	42.9	2.2	77	161
Autres stupéfiants (morphine, codeine)				
Lifetime-prevalence	19.6	0.5	34	37

© Office fédéral de la statistique, Enquête suisse sur la santé 1992/1993

[1] A consommé une fois dans la vie (réponse à la question: «Avez-vous déjà consommé?»).

[2] Réponse à la question: «Consommez-vous encore?».

[3] A consommé une fois par semaine ou plus durant les 12 derniers mois (réponse à la question: «A quelle fréquence avez-vous consommé?»).

[4] Le pourcentage estimé a été corrigé à cause du fort taux de non-réponses parmi les consommateurs de drogues dures.

N.B (1) Plusieurs réponses possibles;

N.B (2) Le N indiqué se réfère aux personnes ayant répondu «oui» à la question. Dès lors, le N se rapportant aux «non» peut varier selon les catégories de drogues prises en compte.

L'analyse sur la base des concordats pénitentiaires fait apparaître des différences régionales quant à la consommation de drogues illicites. Une surreprésentation de la consommation régulière est observée dans la Suisse centrale (60% des détenus interviewés déclarent utiliser régulièrement des drogues illicites), alors que la Suisse latine affiche des taux moins élevés (27%) mais avec une prévalence identique (environ 80%). Cette constatation est valable pour toutes les catégories de drogues douces ou dures, y compris la méthadone.

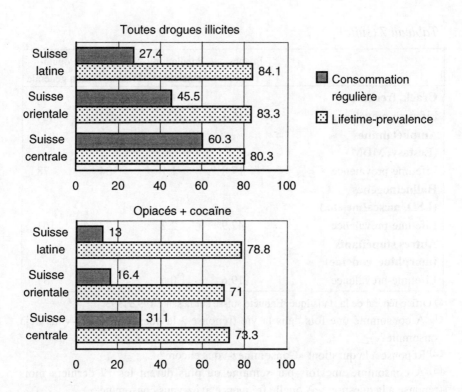

Figure 2: Consommation de drogues selon la région concordataire, en pour cent

3.4. Consommation de drogues, état de santé et polytoxicomanies

L'influence négative du tabac semble particulièrement marquée en milieu carcéral. En effet, 50% des détenus présentant de forts symptômes de maladies fument (25% pour la population auprès des ménages). La relation entre l'utilisation de médicaments et un mauvais état de santé est également claire. Ainsi, 62% des prisonniers ayant de forts symptômes de maladie consomment des médicaments alors que 37% se trouvent dans cette situation s'ils n'en consomment pas (42% et 18% pour la population générale).

L'influence néfaste des drogues illicites est tout aussi marquée. En milieu carcéral, 56% des personnes ayant déjà consommé des drogues dures présentent de forts symptômes de maladies alors que cela ne touche que 38% des non consommateurs. Des différences un peu moins nettes sont observées pour les consommateurs de drogues «douces» bien que celles–ci restent significatives.

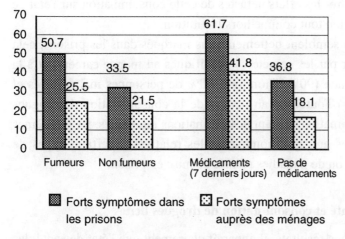

Figure 3: Relation entre consommation de drogues licites et forts symptômes de maladies selon le type de l'enquête, en pour cent

L'analyse de l'état de santé psychique présente les mêmes résultats avec, toutefois, des écarts moins grands entre utilisateurs et non utilisateurs autant pour la population incarcérée que pour la population générale.

Un autre problème bien visible sur la base de l'enquête suisse sur la santé est celui des polytoxicomanes. En effet, les consommateurs de médicaments ont plus largement tendance à consommer du tabac ou des drogues «dures» (cette constatation est surtout valable pour les somnifè-res). Les fumeurs quant à eux s'adonnent plus volontiers au haschich, voire aux drogues «dures», le haschich étant également fumé par la majo-rité des héroïnomanes. En milieu carcéral, la majeure partie des utilisa-teurs de drogues «dures» sont des héroïnomanes.

4 Discussion et conclusion

Avec l'enquête complémentaire dans les prisons, l'Enquête suisse sur la santé permet, entre autre, de mieux connaître la santé physique et psychique des détenus ainsi que les comportements ayant une influence sur cet état de santé. Elle fournit des données uniques relatives à la question lancinante de la consommation de drogue au niveau suisse. Elle permet aussi de démontrer les effets néfastes de cette consommation sur l'état de santé en institution tout comme hors institution.

Si ces effets semblent nettement plus marqués dans les prisons, cela peut s'expliquer par les caractères spécifiques au monde carcéral et à la population retenue (90% d'hommes, 40% de personnes mal formées et 80% de suisses).Toutefois, au niveau de la consommation de drogues illicites, nos estimations restent des estimations minimales, les problèmes de non réponses aux questions sensibles relatives à certains types de comportements ou de maladies restant de mise en prison.

4.1 Etat de santé et consommation de drogues licites

Sur la base de nos résultats, il apparaît clairement que l'état de santé des détenus est mauvais si on le compare à celui de la population générale. Or, il nous est impossible de connaître l'état de santé avant l'entrée dans l'institution. A ce propos, nous pensons comme Müller et Fahrenkrug (Fahrenkrug et al.,1995) que la prise en charge médicale et hygiénique dans les prisons peut contribuer à améliorer l'état de santé des prisonniers, en particulier pour les toxicomanes. Dans ce contexte, il importe de rappeler que *les activités physiques sont au programme des institutions carcérales*: en effet, seuls 19% des détenus déclarent ne faire aucune activité dans la semaine ayant précédé l'enquête (contre 33% de la population générale du même âge). Au niveau de la consommation de drogues, il faut bien distinguer les drogues licites des drogues illicites. Parmi les drogues licites, *la tabagisme en milieu carcéral touche pratiquement tous les détenus (84%) et 62% déclarent fumer plus d'un paquet par jour*. D'autre part, le «quit rate» est sept fois plus élevé hors institution par rapport à la population qui réside en prison. Dans ce contexte, la prévention en matière de consommation de tabac devrait être améliorée.

La consommation de médicament, en particulier de psychopharmacas (somnifères et calmants), est aussi très répandue dans les prisons. Elle est à mettre en relation avec les pressions psychologiques dues à l'isolement et à la privation de liberté mais aussi avec la surpopulation (effet de la concentration en milieu institutionnalisé) et les relations avec une population largement marquée par la délinquance et la criminalité. A ce propos, nous remarquons une relation entre le mauvais état de santé des détenus et la consommation de psychopharmacas. Les calmants sont particulièrement prisés des personnes se déclarant déprimées.

Si *l'alcool ne pose pas de problème au milieu cercéral,* du fait de son interdiction, il est important de rappeler que 6 des 36 buts établis pour la région européenne par l'Organisation mondiale de la santé (1985) font explicitement mention du problème de l'alcool. Les sous–chapitres «Actes et violences» et «Alcoolisme et toxicomanies» considèrent la consommation d'alcool comme un des facteurs essentiels de problèmes sociaux et de santé.

Dans le contexte des préjudices pour la santé subits en milieu carcéral, il peut être formulé l'hypothèse d'une augmentation de la consommation de tabac et de médicaments pendant la période de privation de liberté. Les cigarettes sont souvent utilisées comme moyen d'intégration mais également comme une monnaie d'échange. Quant aux médicaments, ils peuvent être prescrits par le médecin pour atténuer les maux dont souffrent le patient en cas de comportement dépressif ou névrotique.

4.2 Les différences observées au niveau de la consommation des drogues illicites

En ce qui concerne les drogues illicites, l'appréciation semble plus difficile. A ce propos, il nous semble important de rappeler que la consommation régulière est nettement inférieure dans les prisons de la Suisse latine par rapport à la Suisse alémanique. Cette situation semble bien refléter la politique plus répressive en matière de consommation de drogues menée dans le milieu carcéral relevant du concordat de la Suisse romande et du Tessin. Cette politique est à l'image d'un courant dominant (prévalant également dans l'ensemble des pays francophones) tant au niveau de l'opinion publique, que des professionnels de la branche ou des autorités politiques de la Suisse latine.

D'autre part, la consommation de drogues, et surtout des «drogues dures», a nettement augmenté ces dernières années. Dès lors, il est difficile d'imaginer que les toxicomanes incarcérés excluent certaines drogues (par exemple l'héroïne) plutôt que d'autres une fois entrés en prison. Quant à l'utilisation en milieu carcéral, il n'est pas inutile de rappeler que la drogue reste plus facile à introduire que l'alcool, par exemple, et que la consommation peut toujours avoir lieu avant l'entrée dans la prison.

En comparant la consommation de drogues licites et illicites, il est important de distinguer les drogues qui ne posent pas de problèmes majeurs à court terme, celles dont l'abus pose un problème (le plus souvent limité dans le temps) et la consommation provoquant une dépendance (dans notre cas, les consommateurs réguliers de drogues). Or, à ce niveau, les deux types de populations prises en compte dans notre enquête doivent faire l'objet d'une approche séparée. En effet, avec l'enquête auprès des ménages, les consommateurs ont accès plus ou moins librement («drogues dures» excepté) à toutes les drogues disponibles sur le marché. Les possibilités de substitution sont multiples et évoluent en fonction des modes ainsi que de la politique de répression à l'égard des consommateurs. Auprès de cette population, les cas de polytoxicomanies sont fréquents mais très peu de personnes s'y adonnant deviennent un jour des toxicos–dépendants.

Dans les prisons, la situation est différente. Seul le tabac est en vente libre, les autres drogues étant interdites. Or, la consommation de ces drogues (illicites ou alcool) ne peut pas être soumise à un contrôle permanent au sein de l'institution pénale car celles–ci peuvent être consommées en congé ou introduites frauduleusement avec l'accord plus ou moins tacite du personnel et/ou de l'autorité compétente. Dans ce contexte, de grandes différences de stratégies existent entre les prisons suisses et donnent lieu régulièrement à des débats passionnés.

4.3 Comparaisons avec d'autres statistiques

La comparaison avec d'autres statistiques disponibles au niveau international, relative à la consommation de drogues, fournit des informations intéressantes. En comparant les résultats de l'enquête menée dans les prisons suisses avec ceux d'une enquête semblable menée dans les prisons anglaises en 1994 (Bridgwood et Malborn, 1995), nous remarquons que l'utilisation de certaines drogues tels que les médicaments ou les drogues illicites est supérieure dans le milieu pénitentiaire suisse par rapport aux prisons anglaises (51% en Suisse contre 30% au Royaume–Uni pour la consommation de médicaments et 83% contre 63% pour la consommation passée de drogues illicites). La consommation de tabac est pratiquement identique (84% contre 81%).

Pour la population générale, le taux d'utilisateurs est à peu près égal pour le tabac entre la Suisse et l'Angleterre (35% contre 38%) alors qu'une enquête menée pour le compte du gouvernement américain en 1992 (Survey on drug abuse, Public Health Service, 1994) fournit des résultats nettement moins élevés (26%). A ce propos, les campagnes anti–tabacs menées Outre–Atlantique semblent avoir porté leurs fruits.

Pour les drogues illicites, tenant compte que la Suisse est un pays à prévalence forte, les Etats–Unis comptent davantage de personnes consommant des drogues tels que le haschich (prévalence: 33% contre 17% en Suisse) et surtout de drogues dures (prévalence de 20% Outre–Atlantique et 4,4% en Suisse). La part des utilisateurs occasionnels de cocaïne semble supérieure aux consommateurs d'héroïne aux Etats–Unis (prévalence: 11% contre environ 1% pour l'héroïne). Des résultats similaires sont observés en Suisse mais avec des taux nettement moins élevés pour la cocaïne (environ 3% pour la cocaïne et environ 1% pour l'héroïne).

Tableau 8: Consommation de drogues licites et illicites, comparaison avec d'autres statistiques au niveau international, en pour cent

Type d'enquête	Enquête suisse sur la santé (18-39 ans)		Enquête anglaise sur la santé (hommes de 16-49 ans)		Enquête américaine sur les abus de drogues (12 ans et plus)
Type de consommation	Prisons 1993 (CH)	Ménages privés 1992/93 (CH)	Prisons 1994 (UK)	Ménages privés 1992 (UK)	Ménages privés 1993 (USA)
Consommation de tabac					
Fumeurs	84	35	81	38	26
Consommation régulière de médicaments					
Oui (1)	51	25	30	19	…
Consommation de toutes drogues illicites					
Lifetime prevalence (2)	83	17	63	…	36
Consommation de haschich / marijuana					
Lifetime prevalence	79	17	…	…	33
Consommation de drogues «dures»					
Lifetime prevalence	73	5	…	…	20
Consommation d'héroïne					
Lifetime prevalence	62	1	…	…	1
Consommation de cocaïne					
Lifetime prevalence	60	3	…	…	11

(1) Pour la Suisse, dans les 7 derniers jours; pour l'Angleterre, déclarant avoir pris au moins un médicament (sans précision).

(2) Consommation au moins une fois dans la vie.

Sources: pour l'enquête anglaise cf. Bridgwood et Malbom, 1995; pour l'enquête américaine. Public Health Service, 1994.

N.B. Tous les pourcentages ont été arrondis à l'unité.

4.4 Que faudrait–il faire pour améliorer l'état de santé des détenus?

Partant du constat que l'état de santé en milieu carcéral est mauvais, que la consommation de drogues y est largement répandue et que celle–ci influence négativement l'état de santé, il nous apparaît important de poser certaines questions telles que: *les services sanitaires sont–ils efficaces?* ou *les conditions de vie des prisonniers étaient–elles déjà mauvaises avant l'entrée dans la prison?*

A ce propos, le rôle des autorités pénitentiaires devrait être celui d'assurer le maintien d'un bon état de santé aux détenus afin de garantir des conditions de détentions acceptables (au niveau des droits de l'homme, des conditions sanitaires et de la prévention) et ainsi de fournir les meilleures chances de réintégration et de resocialisation lors de la libération. Du point de vue épidémiologique, différents projets menés récemment en Suisse sous les auspices de l'Office fédéral de la santé publique ont montrés leur efficacité. Des mesures telles que la mise à disposition de matériel de désinfection, la distribution de seringues, de préservatifs ou encore le sevrage par la méthadone sont de plus en plus reconnues et acceptées autant par les autorités pénitentiaires que par l'opinion publique.

D'autre part, vu le caractère atypique de la population carcérale, nous pensons également que «*les pénitenciers ne sont pas des institutions de réhabilitation pour toxicomanes*» (Baechtold, 1993), et que la meilleure solution consisterait à placer ces derniers, dans la mesure du possible, dans des sections spécialement aménagées au sein des prisons ou alors dans des centres spécialisés dans le traitement de ce type de patients. Ces mesures apparaissent comme appropriées afin de limiter les risques de contamination de la population «in muros» et surtout hors de la prison lorsqu'interviennent la libération ou les congés. Ainsi, les risques de voir certaines épidémies (sida, hépatite, tuberculose) se développer en milieu carcéral devraient–ils diminuer.

4.5 Bilan de l'Enquête suisse sur la santé

Pour terminer, il importe de rappeler, premièrement, que l'Enquête suisse sur la santé permet pour la première fois de tenir compte de l'ensemble de la population résidant en Suisse. Deuxièmement, la méthodologie utilisée pour les interviews réalisées auprès des ménages et les entretiens menés auprès des détenus est pratiquement la même, ce qui autorise des comparaisons directes entre la population résident en prison et la population générale. Troisièmement, que les établissements carcéraux sélectionnés dans l'échantillon, tout comme les détenus correspondants aux critères de sélection, sont représentatifs de l'ensemble des prisons suisses, alors que la plupart des études réalisées jusqu'à ce jour en Suisse ne concernaient qu'une seule prison, voire une partie des détenus incarcérés dans cette prison.

Pour terminer, nous rappellerons toutefois que sur la base actuelle de l'enquête, il nous reste impossible de connaître les causes des comportements «à risque» pour la santé, pourquoi les détenus se trouvent en prison et si la stratégie de l'Etat ou la formation du personnel des prisons sont bonnes.

Bibliographie

Baechtold, A., Principes de la politique en matière de drogue applicables à l'exécution des peines et mesures dans le canton de Berne, Berne: Office de la privation de liberté et des mesures d'encadrement, juillet 1993.

Bridgwood, A., Malborn, G., Survey of the physical health of the prisonners – preliminary findings, Office of Population Census and Survey (OPCS, UK), Social Survey division, 1995.

Estermann, J., Maag, V., Rônez, S., Drogues et droit pénal en Suisse. Dénonciations, jugements pénaux et exécutions de peines: comparaison dans le temps, Berne: OFS, 1994.

Estermann, J., Drogenepidemiologie: Schätzung von Gruppengrössein Dinamik, in: *Revue suisse de sociologie*, 20 (3), 1994, pp. 717–726

Estermann, J., Consommation et trafic de drogues: les coûts de la répression en 1991, Berne: OFS, 1995.

Facy, F., Toxicomanes incercérés vus dans les antennes-toxicomanie (Enquête épidemiologique 1989–1990), Paris: INSERM U.302.

Fahrenkrug, H. et al. Drogues illégales en Suisse 1990–1993 (La situation dans les cantons et en Suisse), Sur mandat de l'Office fédéral de la santé publique, Zürich: Seismo 1995.

Gmel, G. und Schmid, H. (ed.) [inédit], Alkoholkonsum and anderen Drogen, in: Alkoholkonsum in der Schweiz – Ergebnisse der Schweizerischen Gesund-heitsbefragung 1992/1993, Berne, Lausanne: OFS–ISPA, 1996.

Harding, T.W., Manghi R., Sanchez G., Le SIDA en milieu carcéral (Les stratégies de prévention dans les prisons en Suisse), Rapport mandaté par l'OFSP, Genève, 1990.

Harding, T.W., Manghi R., Sanchez G., HIV/AIDS and Prisons (A survey covering 54 prison systems in 45 countries for the WHO Global Programme on AIDS), Geneva: University Institute of Legal Medicine, 1990.

Juhani L., Ph. D., A socioecological approach to health in prison (A paper to be presented at the Quality Health Care Conference in Liverpool, 29 March 1994), Alcohol, Drugs and Tobacco Unit, WHO Regional Office for Europe, Copenhagen, 1994.

Nelles J., Waldvogel D., Maurer C., Aebischer C., Fuhrer A., Hirsbrunner H. P., Pilotprojekt Drogen– und HIV – Prävention in den Anstalten in Hindelbank (Schlussbericht der Evaluation), Bern: Psychiatrische Universitätsklinik, im Auftrag des BAG, 1995.

Nelles J., Fuhrer A., Drogen– und HIV– Prävention in der Anstalten in Hindelbank (Kurzbericht über die Evaluation), Bern: Psychiatrische Universitäts-klinik, im Auftrag des BAG, 1995.

Nelles J., Harding, Timothy., Preventing HIV transmission in prison: a tale of medical disobedience and Swiss pragmatism. The Lancet, vol. 346, no 8989, pp. 1507–1508

Office fédéral de la statistique – Communiqué de presse. Drogues et droit pénal, Berne: OFS, No 95 & 109, novembre 1994 & décembre 1995.

Office fédéral de la statistique – Communiqué de presse. Etrangers et exécution des peines: une analyse de la situation, Berne: OFS, 1994.

Office fédéral de la statistique – Actualités OFS Enquête suisse sur la santé 1992 / 93: La santé des personnes séjournant dans un hôpital, un établissement de santé non hospitalier ou un établissement d'exécution des peines, Berne: OFS, août 1995.

Office fédéral de la statistique – Officie fédéral de la justice, Catalogue des établissements destinés à l'exécution des peines, des mesures et de la détention préventive en Suisse, Berne, 1995.

Office fédéral de la santé publique, Rapport sur la méthadone (Utilisation d'un succédané opiacé dans le traitement des héroïnomanes en Suisse (troisième édition), Commission fédérale des stupéfiants, Groupe de travail Méthadone de la sous–commission «Drogues», Berne, décembre 1995.

Preliminary estimates from the 1993 national household survey on drug abuse, U.S. Department of Health and Human Services: Public Health Service, 1994.

Rehm, J., Mode de consommation et répartition des drogues en Suisse, in: Drogues illégales en Suisse 1990–1993, Zürich: Seismo, 1995, pp. 13–34.

Rehm, J., Situation sociale des consommateurs de drogues, in: Drogues illégales en Suisse 1990–1993, Zürich: Seismo, 1995, pp. 25–54.

Rotily M., Galinier–Pujol Anne, Obadia Y. et al., HIV testing, HIV infection and associated risk factors among inmates in south–eastern French prisons. AIDS, 8, 1994, pp. 1341–1344.

Schweizerische Fachstelle für Alkohol und andere Drogenprobleme (SFA), Zahlen und Fakten zu Alkohol und anderen Drogen, 1993.

Zeegers Paget, D., HIV– und Aidsprävention in Untersuchungsgefängnissen und Vollzugsanstalten, in: AIDS INFOTHEK, 5/96.

Zimmermann E., von Allmen, M., Rouge S., Evolution de la santé mentale pendant les 60 premiers jours de détention préventive à la prison de Champ–Dollon (Problématique et principaux enseignements d'une étude–pilote menée d'octobre 1982 à mars 1983), Genève: Institut de médecine légale, unité de recherche 1983.

HIV–Prävention und Spritzenabgabe in der Frauenvollzugsanstalt Hindelbank – Paradigma für die Nöte der Vollzugsbehörden?

Andrea Baechtold

1 Der Sachverhalt: Zwischen Banalität und Häresie

Im Juni des Jahres 1994 begann eine eigens dafür zusammengestellte Projektgruppe damit, in der Frauenvollzugsanstalt Hindelbank ein während zwei Jahren intensiv vorbereitetes Projekt für eine umfassende Drogen– und HIV–Prävention zu implementieren (Nelles und Bürki 1993; Bürki 1994). Die Projektgruppe stand unter der Leitung des Arztes Dr. Bernhard Bürki, dem vier Mitarbeiterinnen mit insgesamt 130 Stellenprozenten zur Seite standen, zwei Sozialarbeiterinnen, eine Psychatrieschwester, eine ehemalige Mitarbeiterin in Entwicklungshilfeprojekten. Diese Projektgruppe hatte den Auftrag übernommen, während der Dauer eines Jahres in der Bevölkerung bereits erprobte Präventionsmassnahmen gezielt auf die besondere Risikogruppe in Hindelbank anzuwenden.

Wie bei vergleichbaren, allgemeinen oder auf bestimmte Risikogruppen ausgerichteten Präventionsprogrammen bestand die Aufgabe der Projektgruppe darin, nachfrageseitig Einfluss auf den Konsum illegaler Drogen zu nehmen sowie negative Folgen des Drogenkonsums mindern zu helfen. Angesichts der Verbreitung des intravenösen Konsums bei der

Zielgruppe stand dabei die Infektionsprophylaxe naturgemäss im Vordergrund. Angestrebt wurden also entsprechende Verhaltensänderungen: Verzicht auf Drogenkonsum, risikoarmer Drogenkonsum, gezielte Infektionsverhütung in allen Lebensbereichen.

Dieses Ziel sollte durch «Beratung» erreicht werden, durch Vermittlung von Sachinformationen als notwendige Grundlage für rationale Entscheidungen also, durch die Befähigung der Adressaten, einsichtskonform zu handeln, was sowohl die Vermittlung von Resistenztechniken, das Angebot alternativer Verhaltensweisen sowie personale und soziale Fähigkeiten bei den Adressaten voraussetzt. Die konkreten Beratungsangebote waren durchaus traditionell: Für die Vermittlung präventionsrelevanter Sachinformationen wurde ein Veranstaltungsprogramm ausgearbeitet, Plenums– und Gruppenveranstaltungen zur Drogenprävention im allgemeinen, zum HI–Virus, zur Hepatitis, zu anderen Infektionskrankheiten, zu risikoarmem Sexualverhalten, zu Fragen der Gesundheitspflege und zur Ersten Hilfe. Im Projektverlauf wurden insgesamt 80 derartige Veranstaltungen durchgeführt, der Zielgruppe entsprechend in vier verschiedenen Sprachen und unter Einsatz verschiedener Hilfsmittel, welche die Attraktivität des Angebotes und die affektive Akzeptanz der vermittelten Botschaften stärken sollten. Das Informationsangebot wurde ergänzt durch die Bereitstellung von Informationsmaterial, wiederum in verschiedenen Sprachen, teilweise speziell für die Zielgruppe des Projektes erarbeitet, für alle Adressaten leicht zugänglich aufgelegt. Für eine vertiefte und persönliche Beratung wurde eine wöchentliche Sprechstunde eingerichtet, eine ärztliche und eine nicht–ärztliche Sprechstunde, ferner ein Sorgentelefon, welches den anonymen Zugang zum Projektteam sicherstellte. In der Folge wurden insgesamt 370 Sprechstundentermine realisiert, an welchen auch klinische Befunde erhoben und Blutuntersuchungen durchgeführt wurden. Zur Wahrnehmung dieser Beratungsaufgaben musste das Projektteam in den ersten Juniwochen des Jahres 1994 vorerst die materiellen und organisatorischen Voraussetzungen bereitstellen: Im Bereich des Gesundheitsdienstes wurde ein Büro– und Beratungszimmer eingerichtet, das

Sorgentelefon in Funktion gesetzt, das Informationsmaterial beschafft und ausgelegt, externe Referenten wurden für die Informationsveranstaltungen kontaktiert und – das wichtigste – die Angebote des Projektteams mussten der Zielgruppe bekannt und attraktiv gemacht werden. Weil sich die Präventionsprogramme ja nicht an eine unbestimmte Öffentlichkeit richteten, sondern – ähnlich wie bei Präventionsprogrammen in Schulen oder in der Armee – an eine institutionell definierte Zielgruppe, hatte das Projektteam bei der Planung und Durchführung seiner Beratungstätigkeit im übrigen auf spezielle institutionelle Rahmenbedingungen Rücksicht zu nehmen und entsprechende Absprachen zu treffen.

Mit Blick auf das Ziel, risikoärmere Verhaltensweisen zu fördern, wurden gleich bei Projektbeginn in den einzelnen Abteilungen Spritzenaustauschautomaten installiert. Wie wir dies aus unseren grösseren Städten kennen, wurden diese Automaten an allgemein leicht und möglichst anonym zugänglichen Orten angebracht – hier in Dusch- oder Putzräumen. Gegen eine gebrauchte Spritze oder eine Spritzenattrappe konnte an diesen Automaten eine sterile Spritze eingetauscht werden. Ferner wurden bei den Automaten die einschlägigen Präventionshilfsmittel aufgelegt: Alkohol- und Trockentupfer, Pflaster, Präservative, Fingerlinge, Ascorbinsäure. Zu Beginn des Projektes erwiesen sich die speziell entwickelten, mechanischen Austauschapparate noch als störungsanfällig. In der Folge wurden an diesen, nun gut funktionierenden Apparaten im Durchschnitt täglich 14 Spritzen ausgetauscht. Da die Projektgruppe während der ganzen Projektphase auch die Wartung der Spritzenaustauschautomaten besorgte, hatte sie unmittelbar spontane Kontakte zur Zielgruppe, ähnlich wie der «Gassenarbeiter», ein Umstand, der im Projektverlauf bewusst als Beratungselement eingesetzt wurde.

Ende Juni 1995 hat die Projektgruppe ihre Tätigkeit, wie vorgesehen, eingestellt. Da sich die Präventionsmassnahmen mit Blick auf die Projektziele im wesentlichen bewährt haben und keine nennenswerten negativen Nebenwirkungen festgestellt werden mussten (Baechtold 1995; Nelles et al. 1995), wurde für ein weiteres Jahr ein Anschlussprogramm festgelegt, das in beschränktem Masse eine Weiterführung der Beratungs– und Informationsangebote sicherstellt, natürlich auch die Fortsetzung der Spritzenabgabe mittels Austauschautomaten. Im Rahmen des Anschlussprogramms werden auch Mediatorinnen und Mediatoren aus dem Personal ausgebildet, womit die Präventionsaufgaben künftig im Rahmen des normalen institutionellen Leistungsangebotes wahrgenommen werden können.

Weshalb diese narrative Beschreibung der Projektgeschichte?

Diese Beschreibung soll deutlich machen, dass das Projekt, von dem hier berichtet wird, eigentlich nicht der Rede wert ist. Denn nichts ist im Rahmen des Projektes unternommen worden, was nicht bereits tausendmal erprobt worden wäre und mittlerweilen zum allgemeinen Standard geworden ist, nicht bloss im Ausland, sondern auch auf helvetischem Boden. Blosse Präventionsroutine also.

Die für die Durchführung des Pilotprojektes verantwortlichen Behörden haben dies allerdings völlig anders gesehen, ebenso die Strafvollzugsbehörden in anderen Kantonen, politische und fachliche Behörden im Ausland, ferner auch die Massenmedien. Diese kontroverse Beurteilung betrifft allerdings nur ein einziges Element des Pilotprojektes: die Abgabe von Spritzen mittels Austauschautomaten in einer Strafanstalt. Dazu nachstehend einige Präzisierungen.

Die politische Verantwortung für das Pilotprojekt trug die Polizei– und Militärdirektion des Kantons Bern (POM), der die Frauenvollzugsanstalt Hindelbank unterstellt ist, die fachliche Verantwortung das hierarchisch zwischen der POM und der Anstalt stehende Amt für Freiheitsentzug und Betreuung. Die POM hat einer Spritzenabgabe in Hindelbank vorerst nur zögerlich zugestimmt: Als im Jahre 1988 der Gesundheitsdienst der Anstalt Hindelbank eingewiesenen Frauen in eigener Kompetenz sterile Spritzen abgab, bekräftigte die POM das Abgabeverbot unter Androhung fristloser Entlassung. Erst vier Jahre später stellte sich die POM hinter eine Spritzenabgabe in Hindelbank und beantragte beim Bundesamt für Gesundheitswesen die Ausarbeitung eines entsprechenden Grobkonzeptes. Dieser Gesinnungswandel war allerdings an bestimmte Auflagen geknüpft. Für die POM war von vorneherein klar, dass eine Spritzenabgabe nur versuchsweise, auf beschränkte Zeit und in einer einzigen Anstalt in Frage kommen konnte, also im Rahmen eines reversiblen Pilotprojektes. Diese Prämisse hatte zur Konsequenz, dass das Projekt wissenschaftlich zu evaluieren war, wofür eine von allen Vollzugsbehörden unabhängige Evaluationsgruppe der Psychiatrischen Universitätsklinik Bern gewonnen werden konnte, welche unter der Leitung von Dr. Joachim Nelles stand. Trotz ihrer abschliessenden Zuständigkeit für den Entscheid zur Durchführung des Pilotprojektes war es für die POM undenkbar, ein solches Vorhaben ohne Abstimmung mit den anderen Kantonen durchzuführen, also ohne Zustimmung des Strafvollzugskonkordates der Nordwest– und Innerschweiz und des Neunerausschusses der Konferenz der kantonalen Justiz– und Polizeidirektoren (die 11 Kantone der Nordwest– und Innerschweiz haben sich im Strafvollzugskonkordat zu einer «Vollzugsgemeinschaft» zusammengeschlossen; der Neunerausschuss ist beratendes Organ der Konferenz für Fragen des Strafvollzugs und des Anstaltswesens, die Konferenz eine Vereinigung der für Justiz– und Polizeifragen zuständigen kantonalen «Minister»). Entscheidend für die – unter den erwähnten Voraussetzungen – schliesslich vorbehaltlose Unterstützung des Pilotprojektes durch die POM war sodann der Umstand, dass das Pilotprojekt vom Bundesamt für Gesundheitswesen nicht bloss mit allem Nachdruck verbal gefördert, sondern fachlich begleitet und fast umfassend finanziert wurde. Für den Entscheid der POM hilfreich waren wohl auch die vom Amt für Freiheitsentzug und Betreuung im Sommer 1993 veröffentlichten «Drogenpolitischen Grundsätze» (Baechtold 1993), welche im Kontext eines ausformulierten Konzeptes zur Drogenpolitik im Strafvollzug die Durchführung des Pilotprojektes in Hindelbank ausdrücklich befürworteten.

Bei den politisch und fachlich für den Strafvollzug verantwortlichen Behörden der anderen Kantone ist das Pilotprojekt zunächst – und teilweise bis heute – auf etliche Skepsis gestossen. Die Zustimmung des Strafvollzugskonkordates zum Pilotprojekt, diese dann allerdings einstimmig, konnte erst im April 1993 erlangt werden, jene des Neunerausschusses, gegen erheblichen Widerstand aus der französischsprachigen Schweiz, erst im September 1993.

Heftig reagiert auf das Pilotprojekt haben auch die Medien, allerdings kaum mit Vorbehalten, sondern mit Erstaunen. Bereits die Medienorientierung vom 16. Mai 1994, mit welcher der Projektbeginn angekündigt wurde, stiess bei den Medien auf grosses Interesse und fand fast vorbehaltlos Unterstützung, ebenso die Medienorientierung vom 27. November 1995, an welcher die Ergebnisse des Pilotversuches eingehend vorgestellt wurden. Während der Durchführung des Projektes selbst wurden die Medien lediglich mit zwei Pressemitteilungen vom 10. November 1994 und vom 2. Juni 1995 bedient, welche rege verbreitet wurden. Das grosse Interesse der Medien am Pilotprojekt belegt beispielhaft der Sachverhalt, dass während des Projektjahres beinahe ein Dutzend in– und ausländischer Fernsehanstalten um eine Drehbewilligung vor Ort nachgesucht haben. Für die Medien war das Pilotprojekt in Hindelbank also offensichtlich keine blosse Banalität.

Ebenfalls interessiertes Erstaunen zeigten etliche Behörden im Ausland: Für eine Gruppe hoher Justizbeamter aus deutschen Bundesländern und ein Beratergremium des Justizministeriums von Rheinland–Pfalz war das Pilotprojekt ebenso eine Reise nach Hindelbank wert wie für die Justizministerin aus Niedersachsen und die Justizsenatorin aus Berlin. Selbst der deutsche Bundestag zeigte Interesse am Pilotprojekt und lud den Evaluationsleiter zu einem Hearing ein.

Weitere Interessenten, auch aus Nordamerika und Australien, informierten sich persönlich, andere brieflich über das Pilotprojekt, welches überdies an internationalen Fachkongressen (Aids–Kongress in Yokohama 1994, Harm–Reduction–Konferenz in Florenz 1995 usw.) auf erhebliche Beachtung stiess.

Weshalb diese Aufgeregtheiten? Haben wir nicht eben festgestellt, dass das Pilotprojekt lediglich etablierte Präventionsroutine angeboten hat, die eigentlich nicht der Rede wert sein kann?

Die Antwort auf diese Frage findet sich in Artikel 37 Ziffer 1 des Schweizerischen Strafgesetzbuches – andere Staaten kennen analoge Vorschriften. Nach der erwähnten Gesetzesbestimmung sind die zuständigen Vollzugsbehörden angehalten, Eingewiesene auf ein straffreies Leben nach der Entlassung vorzubereiten. Da der Konsum illegaler Drogen strafbar ist, schliesst dieser Auftrag an den Vollzug auch die Vorbereitung der Eingewiesenen auf ein Leben ohne Konsum solcher Drogen ein. Zu diesem Abstinenzziel steht die Abgabe oder die Tolerierung von Spritzen im Vollzug offensichtlich insofern in Widerspruch, als damit ein risikoarmer Drogenkonsum erleichtert (und eben nicht verhindert) und das Verbot des Konsums illegaler Drogen im Vollzug möglicherweise bagatellisiert wird. Nach den bernischen Disziplinarvorschriften sind Spritzen «verbotene Gegenstände», analog anderen Gegenständen, deren Besitz verboten ist, weil sie unzulässigem Verhalten dienlich sind, etwa Funkgeräte, Ausbruchwerkzeuge, Waffen. Wird die Drogenabstinenz somit als eine hier und jetzt zu realisierende Aufgabe des Vollzugs und nicht prozesshaft als Zielnorm verstanden, bedeutet eine Tolerierung oder gar Abgabe von Spritzen gewissermassen Beihilfe zur Fortsetzung des Drogenkonsums, zu illegalem Verhalten, also blanke Häresie.

Die Spritzenabgabe in Hindelbank: Banalität oder Häresie? Im nachfolgenden Abschnitt soll aufgezeigt werden, dass die Spritzenabgabe in Hindelbank nur vordergründig an einem Widerspruch zwischen gesundheits– und kriminalpolitischen Zielen festgemacht wird, dass die Kontroverse im Grunde genommen vielmehr vollzugsimmanent angelegt ist.

2 Das böse Erwachen aus dem Traum vom widerspruchsfreien Strafvollzug

Um ganz vorne anzufangen: Definitionsmerkmal des strafrechtlichen Freiheitsentzugs ist neben der Beschränkung der Freiheit in örtlicher und zeitlicher Hinsicht die Unterordnung der Eingewiesenen unter eine für das gesamte Anstaltskollektiv einheitliche, alle Bereiche des Anstaltsalltags umfassende, verbindliche und deshalb sanktionsbewehrte Anstaltsordnung. Diese Anstaltsordnung ist als Gesamtheit der anwendbaren generell–abstrakten Normen zu verstehen, seien diese auf Gesetzesstufe verankert, in Verordnungen, in Hausordnungen oder durch konkretisierende Weisungen der Anstaltsleitung.

Diese Anstaltsordnung legt die Rechte und Pflichten sowie die Handlungsspielräume aller Anstaltsakteure fest, der Eingewiesenen also, aber auch der Mitarbeitenden. Die Anstaltsordnung ist für die Eingewiesenen – und weitgehend auch für die Mitarbeitenden – nicht verhandelbar. Auch wo Mitwirkungsmöglichkeiten für Eingewiesene vorliegen – das Petitionsrecht, vielleicht ein Gefangenenrat – stehen dem Eingewiesenen keine Instrumente zur Verfügung, um Mehrheiten für eine Änderung der Anstaltsordnung zu beschaffen; in der Strafanstalt werden die Eingewiesenen zwar vergesellschaftet, diese Gesellschaft ist aber keine demokratisch verfasste. Abgesehen von der Flucht aus der Anstalt, aus dem Leben oder von Versetzungen in eine andere Anstalt hat der Eingewiesene im Gegensatz zum freien Bürger ferner auch nicht die Möglichkeit, sich für eine ihm besser entsprechende Anstaltsordnung zu entscheiden, wie wir dies durch einen Umzug in eine andere Gemeinde, einen anderen Kanton oder in einen anderen Staat an sich jederzeit tun können. Aus der geltenden Anstaltsordnung gibt es für den Eingewiesenen prinzipiell kein Entrinnen.

Die Anstaltsordnung regelt überdies das ganze Leben für ein zahlenmässig begrenztes, sich auf einem überschaubaren Territorium aufhaltenden Personenkollektiv. Das hat zur Folge, dass Verletzungen der Anstaltsordnung nicht leicht übersehen werden und nicht leicht übersehen werden können. Umso weniger kann auf eine Sanktionierung erkannter Verletzungen der Anstaltsordnung verzichtet werden. Dazu kommt, dass die Kleinräumigkeit und die Totalität des Anstaltslebens den Eingewiesenen eine Emigration ins Private weitgehend verwehrt. Die Anstaltsordnung ist omnipräsent.

Diese umfassende und dominante Stellung der Anstaltsordnung ist gewollt. Denn nach heutigem Rechtsverständnis geht der zu einer Freiheitsstrafe Verurteilte des Schutzes der Rechtsordnung nicht verlustig, namentlich behält er seine verfassungsmässigen Grundrechte. Er verliert seine Freiheit nur soweit, als dies der Freiheitsentzug und das Leben im Anstaltskollektiv notwendigerweise zur Folge haben. Deshalb müssen die Einschränkungen dieser Grundrechte bzw. die Rechte und Pflichten der Eingewiesenen und der Anstaltsmitarbeiter so klar und detailliert geregelt sein, dass über verbotenes und gebotenes Verhalten aller Anstaltsakteure sicher entschieden werden kann, nötigenfalls auch durch eine Aufsichtsbehörde oder ein Gericht. In der Diktion unseres Bundesgerichts: «Aus rechtsstaatlichen Gründen erscheint es unerlässlich, die wichtigsten mit Untersuchungshaft und Strafvollzug verbundenen Freiheitsbeschränkungen in einem allgemeinen Erlass zu regeln, um den Gefangenen vor Willkür zu schützen» (BGE 99 Ia 268). Wem die Rechtmässigkeit des Strafvollzugs ein Anliegen ist, sorgt dafür, dass diese «durch eine ausreichende Regelungsdichte und eine klare Fassung selber eine erhöhte Gewähr für die Vermeidung verfassungswidriger Anordnungen bietet» (BGE 106 Ia 139) und säubert die Anstaltsordnung von jedweden Widersprüchen und Ambiguitäten.

Vielfach werden solche Ansprüche auch aus dem sog. Erziehungsauftrag des Strafvollzugs hergeleitet, also aus der Aufgabe, während dem Strafvollzug derart auf die Eingewiesenen einzuwirken, dass sie nach der Entlassung in der Lage sind, ein Leben ohne weitere Straftaten zu führen. Danach bieten die klaren Regeln des Strafvollzugs und die konsequente Überprüfung der Einhaltung dieser Regeln, gefolgt von positiven oder negativen Sanktionen, ein gutes Lernfeld für die Bewährung in Freiheit. Diese Begründung ist allerdings umstritten. Denn das Leben in Freiheit ist ja keineswegs frei von Unsicherheiten und Widersprüchen. Deshalb hat schon *Gustav Radbruch* davon gesprochen, der Vollzug bessere allenfalls für die Anstalt, nicht aber für das Leben (Radbruch 1911/1994). Über die Berechtigung dieser unterschiedlichen Auffassungen muss hier nicht entschieden werden. Die Einsicht reicht aus, dass bereits aus rechtsstaatlichen Gründen eine umfassende, hinreichend detaillierte, klare und widerspruchsfreie Anstaltsordnung erforderlich ist.

Wir wissen allerdings, dass sich dieser Anspruch in der Praxis nicht integral umsetzen lässt: Das Leben ist mehr als die Summe von Rechtsnormen. Schon das Schweizerische Bundesgericht hat deshalb anerkannt, dass die Grundrechte Strafgefangener unter bestimmten Voraussetzungen auch ohne ausdrückliche gesetzliche Grundlage eingeschränkt werden können («besonderes Rechtsverhältnis»; BGE 68 I 78, 98 Ib 305). Aber auch im Vollzugsalltag ist es für Mitarbeitende ein Ding der Unmöglichkeit, allen Vorschriften jederzeit und minutiös Nachachtung zu verschaffen: Der Anstaltsbetrieb wäre schlechthin nicht aufrecht zu erhalten, wenn nicht gelegentlich eine Vorschrift oder ein Fehlverhalten übersehen, ein Auge zugedrückt würde.

Dazu kommt, dass Strafanstalten heute keine völlig isolierten, autarken Inseln darstellen, sondern in mannigfachen Beziehungen zur übrigen Gesellschaft stehen: Die Strafanstalt kann sich der Pluralität unserer Gesellschaftsordnung deshalb nicht entziehen, gesellschaftliche Brüche und Widersprüche dringen in den Anstaltsalltag ein. Und weil nach dem Vollzugsgrundsatz der «Normalisierung» des Anstaltsalltags (im deutschen Recht als «Angleichungsgrundsatz» bekannt) diese Ausseneinflüsse nicht abgewiesen werden, sondern aktiv ins Anstaltsleben einfliessen sollen, ist keine Anstaltsordnung in der Lage, im Vollzugsalltag jene gewissermassen mechanistisch funktionierende, widerspruchsfreie, heile Welt zu schaffen, von der wir oben geträumt haben.

Diese Unmöglichkeit ist aber auch bereits im Strafvollzug selbst angelegt. Die nach schweizerischem Recht gleichermassen massgeblichen Vollzugsaufgaben der Förderung der Lebenstüchtigkeit der Eingewiesenen (Art. 37 Ziff. 1 StGB) und der Gewährleistung der besonderen Fürsorgepflicht (Art. 46 Ziff. 2 StGB) gegenüber den Eingewiesenen bedingen in der Praxis immer wieder Abwägungen, welche nicht durch binäre Entscheide zwischen «richtig» und «falsch» getroffen werden können, sondern Optimierungsaufgaben darstellen. Das gilt beispielsweise auch, wenn über einen Gefangenenurlaub zu entscheiden ist und abgewogen werden muss, ob ein gewisses Sicherheitsrisiko während der Urlaubszeit verantwortet werden kann bzw. muss, um Sicherheitsrisiken nach der Entlassung des Betreffenden zu minimieren. Entscheide in Situationen, in welchen nicht alle Vollzugsaufgaben vollständig erfüllt werden können, wo abgewogen und optimiert werden muss und Ermessen zum Tragen kommt, gehören zum Vollzugsalltag der Vollzugsbehörden und jedes bzw. jeder einzelnen Mitarbeitenden.

Die Strafvollzugsbehörden und die Direktionen der Strafanstalten haben natürlich gelernt, mit dem «überdeterminierten» System Strafvollzug, seinen Dilemmatas und Widersprüchen umzugehen. Gewissermassen als «kollektives Über–Ich» haben sie aber auch die Überzeugung verinnerlicht, dass dies eigentlich so nicht sein sollte, dass die im Vollzug zu treffenden individuellen Massnahmen allein schon aus rechtsstaatlichen Gründen deduktiv eindeutig aus dem Vollzugsauftrag abzuleiten wären. Diese Diskrepanz zwischen «Sollen» und «Sein» ist ein Problem, das in aller Regel allenfalls innerhalb des Strafvollzugssystems als solches erkannt wird, wie ein schwelender Brand, der zuwenig Rauch erzeugt, um in einem breiteren Umfeld zur Kenntnis genommen zu werden.

Aufgrund der im Zusammenhang mit der Abgabe steriler Spritzen in der Frauenvollzugsanstalt Hindelbank geführten Diskussionen habe ich die Überzeugung gewonnen, dass die diesbezüglich unterschiedlichen Wertungen auch – aber eben nicht nur – etwas mit unterschiedlichen drogenpolitischen Optionen zu tun haben, dass an diesem Beispiel vielmehr die Überdeterminiertheit des Leistungsauftrags an den Strafvollzug so offensichtlich erkennbar geworden ist, dass Irritation über die zu treffenden Massnahmen herrscht – für überdeterminierte Systeme gibt es keine oder keine eindeutigen Lösungen:

• Spritzen dürfen nicht abgegeben werden, weil der Konsum von Drogen mit allen verfügbaren Mitteln verhindert werden muss.
• Spritzen müssen abgegeben werden, weil die Gesundheit der Eingewiesenen und der Bevölkerung mit allen verfügbaren Mitteln geschützt werden muss.

• Und: Diesen beiden Aufträgen kann nicht derart Rechnung getragen werden, wie in der Strafvollzugspraxis vergleichbare Probleme häufig gelöst werden (etwa bei der Gewährung von Urlauben), dass ein bisschen gar keine Spritzen und ein bisschen dennoch Spritzen abgegeben werden.

Ich vermute deshalb, dass die überdies in aller Öffentlichkeit ausgetragene Diskussion über die Spritzenabgabe im Strafvollzug gewissermassen den Vorhang geöffnet hat, welcher inhärente Grunddilemmatas des Strafvollzugs normalerweise vor neugierigen Blicken schützt. Und ich verstehe deshalb, dass viele im Strafvollzug tätige oder dafür verantwortliche Mitarbeitende die Spritzenabgabe im Strafvollzug nicht oder nicht bloss aus drogenpolitischen Überlegungen in Frage stellen, sondern als Bedrohung ihrer beruflichen Identität empfinden.

Das Beispiel der Spritzenabgabe im Strafvollzug macht deutlich, dass der Traum vom widerspruchsfreien Strafvollzug ausgeträumt ist und damit auch die Erwartung, dass zumindest im Strafvollzug jene eindeutigen und stabilen Strukturen und Prozesse des gesellschaftlichen Zusammenlebens konstruiert werden können, welche wir so sehr vermissen, in unserem Alltag und vermehrt noch mit Blick auf unseren ganzen Planeten.

3 Glanz und Elend des Vollzugsföderalismus

Die im ersten Abschnitt knapp zusammengefasste, bewegte Vorgeschichte des Pilotprojektes in Hindelbank verweist auf eine zweite, über den Anlass der Spritzenabgabe hinausreichende, diesmal spezifisch helvetische Grundproblematik: das föderalistische Strafvollzugssystem. Auch hierzu muss ich etwas weiter ausholen: Wir Schweizer sind nicht nur stolz darauf, die schönsten Alpen geschaffen, sondern auch darauf, den Föderalismus erfunden zu haben. Dass in beiden Fällen die Urheberrechte nicht so ganz für unser Land reklamiert werden können, wissen wir natürlich, möchten dies aber eher doch übersehen dürfen. Abgesehen von der unser gesamtes Staatswesen umfassenden föderalistischen Tradition sind zwei spezifische inhaltliche Argumente hervorzuheben, welche dem föderalistisches Strafvollzugssystem besonderen Glanz verleihen.

Erstens: Der Strafvollzug kann – als Teil der gesellschaftlichen Realität verstanden – nicht unabhängig von dieser Realität – der wirtschaftlichen, sozialen, kulturellen – ausgestaltet werden. Auch wenn ich nicht übersehen möchte, dass sich die Unterschiede zwischen den Kantonen in den letzten Jahrzehnten nivelliert haben und dass die traditionell regional geprägte gesellschaftliche Heterogenität durch andere Dichotomien überlagert worden ist (städtische und ländliche Bevölkerung, alte und junge Bürger, Arbeitende und Arbeitslose), dass ferner zwei von fünf Inhaftierten über einen ausländischen Pass verfügen (einer von fünf ohne Wohnsitz in der Schweiz), bleiben doch deutliche regionale Mentalitätsunterschiede unübersehbar, sowohl in der Bevölkerung als auch in der poenologischen Lehre. Die französischsprachigen Kantone sind auch im Strafvollzug nach wie vor stark von den frankophonen Staaten – Frankreich, Belgien, zunehmend auch Kanada – beeinflusst, während die deutschsprachigen Kantone die Gesetzgebung und Rechtsprechung in Deutschland als – allerdings überzogenen – Massstab grundsätzlich anerkennen. Die verhältnismässig rigide Strafvollzugspolitik in den meisten französischsprechenden Kantonen wird von der Bevölkerung offensichtlich ebenso mitgetragen wie die mehr pragmatischen Strategien der übrigen Kantone. Deshalb ist beispielsweise auch unmittelbar einsehbar, dass es in weitaus den meisten Kantonen unvorstellbar erschiene, den Insassen ein Glas Wein auszuschenken, dass es aber auch Kantone gibt, in welchen das Gegenteil kaum vorstellbar wäre. Wenn der Strafvollzug von der Bevölkerung – in deren Namen die Strafen ja vollzogen werden – als glaubhafte und sinnvolle Reaktion auf Straftaten anerkannt werden soll, dann müssen kulturell oder situativ begründete Unterschiede im Vollzug möglich bleiben.

Zweitens: Die föderalistische Organisationsstruktur des Strafvollzugs hat zur Folge, dass die Strafen nicht von einer zentralen, anonymen, tausende von Mitarbeitern umfassenden Vollzugsbehörde vollstreckt und vollzogen werden. Unsere 26 Vollzugsbehörden sind klein, bürgernah, stehen in einem kompetitiven Verhältnis zueinander und sind deshalb auch verhältnismässig flexibel. Veränderungen müssen nicht flächendeckend eingeführt werden. Wo ein günstiges Umfeld vorhanden ist, namentlich motivierte Mitarbeitende, können so Neuerungen mit geringem Risiko rasch nach der Methode des «try and error» pragmatisch ausgetestet werden. Dass sich diese gleichermassen umsichtige und reformfreudige Strategie in der Schweiz insgesamt bewährt hat, illustrieren die vorerst in einzelnen Kantonen erprobten und später ganz oder weitgehend verallgemeinerten Vollzugsformen der Halbfreiheit, der Halbgefangenschaft, des tageweisen Vollzugs, die gemeinnützige Arbeit, aber auch die Klassifikation der gemeingefährlichen Eingewiesenen oder die Einrichtung kleiner Hochsicherheitsabteilungen.

Der föderalistische Strafvollzug weist natürlich auch eine Kehrseite auf: Die Vollzugsbedingungen in der Schweiz sind verhältnismässig heterogen. Dies ist unter dem Gesichtspunkt der Rechtsgleichheit dann stossend, wenn die mit dem Freiheitsentzug verbundenen Eingriffe in die persönliche Freiheit der Inhaftierten in einem Kanton wesentlich weiter gehen als in einem anderen. In der Praxis kann Inhaftierten letztlich auch nicht plausibel gemacht werden, dass ihnen diese oder jene Rechte bloss deshalb nicht zustehen, weil sie von einer Vollzugsbehörde eines anderen Kantons eingewiesen oder in einer in einem anderen Kanton gelegenen Anstalt untergebracht sind.

Das hat in den letzten Jahren dazu geführt, dass im Rahmen der Strafvollzugskonkordate (der drei regionalen «Vollzugsgemeinschaften» der Kantone) vermehrt eine Vereinheitlichung des Vollzugs durch gemeinsame Richtlinien angestrebt wird. Diese Entwicklung ist prinzipiell gewiss zu begrüssen.

Aber auch sie hat wiederum eine Kehrseite, welche bei der Einführung des HIV–Präventionsprojektes in Hindelbank deutlich zu Tage getreten ist: Der Vereinheitlichungsdruck kann dazu führen, dass die Vorteile des kompetitiven und flexiblen föderalistischen Systems verloren gehen und

Anpassungen des Vollzugs an neue Gegebenheiten verhindert oder nurmehr mit erheblichem Zeitverzug realisiert werden können. Beim Projekt in Hindelbank lag die Zuständigkeit für die Einführung des Projektes zweifelsfrei einzig bei der bernischen Polizei– und Militärdirektion. Aus Rücksichtnahme auf die interkantonale Zusammenarbeit war diese aber faktisch gezwungen, sowohl die Zustimmung des Strafvollzugskonkordates als auch jene der Konferenz der kantonalen Justiz– und Polizeidirektoren einzuholen. Damit wurde der Projektbeginn um rund ein Jahr verzögert. Dazu kommt, dass eine Ablehnung des Projektes durch das Bundesamt für Gesundheitswesen oder das Bundesamt für Justiz ebenfalls das «Aus» für das Vorhaben bedeutet hätte. Im vorliegenden Fall wären somit nicht weniger als vier Behörden oder behördenähnliche Organisationen in der Lage gewesen, das Projekt zu Fall zu bringen.

Wer Veränderungen im schweizerischen Strafvollzug verhindern will, besitzt deshalb derzeit faktisch die besseren Karten; die diffusen Machtkonstellationen lassen sich zur Verhinderung oder Verzögerung von Reformen leicht ausnützen oder führen auch ohne jeden «bösen Willen» leicht von sich aus zu diesem Ergebnis. Wir stehen deshalb derzeit an einem heiklen und für den künftigen Strafvollzug entscheidenden Wendepunkt: Noch ist das föderalistische Strafvollzugssystem weitgehend unbestritten, doch droht es zur blossen Ideologie zu verkommen, weil die Kantone im Begriff sind, sich die Vorteile des gepriesenen Systems zu verbauen. Dies im an sich legitimen Interesse, keine übermässige Heterogenität der Vollzugsbedingungen aufkommen zu lassen und dem Bundesgesetzgeber die Versuchung zu ersparen, als übergeordnete Ordnungsmacht in den traditionellen Zuständigkeitsbereich der Kantone einzugreifen. Schliesslich sei auch nicht verschwiegen, dass die kantonalen Behörden versucht sein könnten, heikle Entscheide gewissermassen an die Konkordate oder gar an die Konferenz der Kantonalen Justiz– und Polizeidirektoren zu «delegieren», um sich nicht direkt der Kritik und der demokratischen Kontrolle stellen zu müssen.

Diese Wertungen mögen einigen Kennern des schweizerischen Strafvollzugs als düstere Prophezeiungen erscheinen. Wenn wir uns aber die Geschichte des Pilotprojektes in Hindelbank vergegenwärtigen, ferner die Einführung anderer Neuerungen im Strafvollzug, etwa die erweiterte Abgabe von Methadon an drogenabhängige Inhaftierte, die versuchsweise in der Anstalt Oberschöngrün eingeführte kontrollierte Heroinabgabe, die zeitliche Erweiterung des Anwendungsbereiches der gemeinnützigen Arbeit und der Vollzugsform der Halbgefangenschaft, dann wird klar: der föderalistische Strafvollzug droht, seinen Glanz zu verlieren.

4 Die Konsequenz: De quoi s'agit–il?

Im abschliessenden Abschnitt meines Beitrages möchte ich versuchen, einige Konsequenzen aus den bisherigen Ausführungen zu ziehen. Dieser Abschnitt steht unter dem Titel «De quoi s'agit–il?». Ich widme diese Überlegungen Max Rentsch, dem verstorbenen ehemaligen Direktor der im Kanton Freiburg gelegenen Strafanstalt Bellechasse, der sich in auswegslos scheinenden Kontroversen jeweils mit erhobenem Zeigefinger und eben dieser Frage zu Wort zu melden pflegte: De quoi s'agit–il?

Wenn ich zunächst an den Ausführungen im vorangehenden Abschnitt anknüpfen darf: Es geht darum, die Vorzüge des föderalistischen Strafvollzugssystems zu erhalten und optimal auszuschöpfen, seine Nachteile aber bestmöglich einzugrenzen. Dabei ist nüchtern anzuerkennen, dass der Entscheid für ein föderalistisches System zwingend auch einen Verzicht auf Vorteile eines zentralistischen Systems in sich schliesst: Im föderalistischen System ist Einheitlichkeit nicht oberstes Gebot, es lässt nicht zu, dass strafvollzugspolitische Optionen durch eine einzige Behörde flächendeckend umgesetzt werden. Wenn wir aber die Vorteile des föderalistischen Systems ausschöpfen wollen, dann müssten die Zuständigkeiten des Bundes, der Konkordate und der Kantone anders als heute festgelegt werden, nämlich verbindlich, systematisch und klar. Das heisst auch, dass alle drei Ebenen Selbstbeschränkungen in Kauf nehmen müssten. Erhebliche Eingriffe in die Rechte der im Freiheitsentzug stehenden Personen, also Eingriffe, welche gewissermassen den Inhalt des Freiheitsentzugs ausmachen, müssten einheitlich bestimmt und stufengerecht im Bundesrecht verankert werden. Der Expertenentwurf für eine Gesamtrevision des Allgemeinen Teils des StGB zielt bekanntlich in diese Richtung. Wo auch eine Einheitlichkeit bei der Konkretisierung von Bundesvorschriften erforderlich erscheint, bietet sich das Konkordatsrecht an, weshalb die Konkordate in diesen Bereichen unmittelbar rechtssetzend tätig sein müssten. Dieses Postulat ist derzeit ebensowenig erfüllt wie das folgende: Wo das Bundesrecht keine einheitlichen Vollzugsregeln als erforderlich erachtet, haben die Konkordate auf einheitliche Vorschriften konsequenterweise ebenfalls zu verzichten. Damit erhielten die Kantone von Bund und Konkordaten klare und abgegrenzte Vorgaben, in deren Rahmen sie die Vorteile des Föderalismus frei zum Tragen bringen könnten.

Für die Drogen–, HIV– und Infektionsprävention würde dies bedeuten, dass jedenfalls rein operationelle Fragen wie die Abgabe von Spritzen an Drogenabhängige durch die Kantone für ihre einzelnen Anstalten abschliessend zu regeln wären. Denn der Entscheid, ob eine Abgabe von sterilen Spritzen geeignet und notwendig ist, hängt von einer Vielzahl auch anstaltsbezogener Faktoren ab. In einer «überdeterminierten Entscheidsituation» kann angesichts der teils widersprüchlichen Anforderungen an den Strafvollzug auf der Makroebene dagegen keine zureichende Optimierung erzielt werden.

Damit möchte ich natürlich keineswegs unter dem Schlagwort des anstaltsbezogenen Pragmatismus enggestrickten, minimalistischen Präventionsprogrammen das Wort reden. Denn als Richtschnur wäre immer die eingangs gestellte Frage im Auge zu behalten: De quoi s'agit–il? Die grundlegende Antwort auf diese Frage ist eigentlich simpel: Im Strafvollzug geht es letztlich immer darum, die Bevölkerung vor künftiger Kriminalität und anderen vitalen Sicherheitsrisiken zu schützen.

Zur Bewältigung dieser Aufgabe stehen endliche, beschränkte Ressourcen zur Verfügung. Deshalb kommen wir auch im Strafvollzug nicht darum herum, besonders wichtige von ziemlich wichtigen und diese wiederum von weniger wichtigen Leistungen zu unterscheiden. Die Strafvollzugsbehörden müssen sich somit noch konsequenter auf jene Leistungen konzentrieren können, welche für den Schutz der Bevölkerung entscheidend sind; sie müssen deshalb auch bereit und in der Lage sein, geringere Sicherheitsrisiken bewusst in Kauf zu nehmen. Das heisst namentlich, dass künftig weniger Menschen inhaftiert werden sollten als heute, damit zusätzliche Ressourcen frei werden, um erhebliche Sicherheitsrisiken besser ausschliessen zu können als bisher. Der von der Expertenkommission des Eidgenössischen Departements des Innern für die Revision des Betäubungsmittelgesetzes am 22. Februar 1996 veröffentlichte Antrag, die Strafbarkeit des Drogenkonsums aufzuheben, ist deshalb ebenso als zwar bescheidener, aber wichtiger Schritt in die richtige Richtung zu werten wie der vom Bundesrat auf den Beginn dieses Jahres erweiterte Anwendungsbereich der gemeinnützigen Arbeit als Alternative zum kurzfristigen Freiheitsentzug. Im weiteren bleibt zu hoffen, dass der Bundesrat mit der Revision des Allgemeinen Teils des Strafgesetzbuches entschieden zu grösseren Schritten ansetzen wird, dass er den längst überfälligen Revisionsentwurf endlich der parlamentarischen Beratung zuleitet und dass sich schliesslich unsere Parlamentarier nicht von populistischem Kleinmut, sondern von der nüchternen Frage «De quoi s'agit-il?» werden leiten lassen.

Unter diesem Gesichtspunkt sind auch die Massnahmen zur Drogen- und HIV–Prävention zu werten: Denn dass die Verhinderung der Übertragung von im Ergebnis tödlichen Infektionskrankheiten vitale Sicherheitsinteressen der ganzen Bevölkerung trifft, darf ernstlich nicht bezweifelt werden.

Literatur

Andrea Baechtold: Drogenpolitische Grundsätze für den Straf– und Massnahmenvollzug im Kanton Bern. Bern, Juli 1993

Andrea Baechtold: Pilotprojekt HIV–Prävention in den Anstalten in Hindelbank. Schlussbericht zu Handen des Bundesamtes für Gesundheitswesen. Bern, September 1995

Bernhard Bürki: Pilotprojekt HIV–Prävention in den Anstalten in Hindelbank. Feinkonzept. Bern, 9. März 1994.

Joachim Nelles und Bernhard Bürki: Pilotprojekt in den Anstalten in Hindelbank. Projektentwurf für das Bundesamt für Gesundheitswesen. Bern, 1. März 1993

Joachim Nelles, Doris Waldvogel, Christine Maurer et al.: Pilotprojekt Drogen– und HIV–Prävention in den Anstalten in Hindelbank. Evaluationsbericht. Bern, September 1995

Gustav Radbruch: Die Psychologie der Gefangenschaft (1911). Gesamtausgabe Band 10, Strafvollzug. Heidelberg 1994.

Die kontrollierte Opiatabgabe in der Strafanstalt Oberschöngrün – Forschungsplan und erste Zwischenergebnisse

Beat Kaufmann
Anja Dobler–Mikola

1 Einleitung

Zu Beginn der 90er Jahre wurde in der Schweiz mit der Entwicklung von wissenschaftlichen Versuchen für die ärztliche Verschreibung von Betäubungsmitteln an Opiatabhängige begonnen. Die ersten Versuche der Opiatverschreibung begannen im Januar 1994. Das Gesamtprojekt der ärztlichen Betäubungsmittelverschreibung stützt sich auf das bundesrätliche Massnahmenpaket zur Verminderung der Drogenprobleme vom 20. Februar 1991 und auf die bundesrätliche Verordnung über die «Förderung der wissenschaftlichen Begleitforschung zur Drogenprävention und Verbesserung der Lebensbedingungen Drogenabhängiger» vom 21. Oktober 1992. Die Versuche für eine ärztliche Verschreibung von Betäubungsmitteln an Drogenabhängige sind definiert als wissenschaftliche Versuche mit dem Ziel, den Erfolg der vorgesehenen Therapie als Schritt auf dem Weg zur Drogenabstinenz zu überprüfen. Dabei stehen die Verbesserung des körperlichen und/oder psychischen Gesundheitszustandes, die Verbesserung der sozialen Integration sowie die Erhöhung des Verantwortungsbewusstseins bei den Versuchspersonen betreffend des HIV–Infektionsrisikos im Vordergrund. Wie mit dem Begriff «wissenschaftliche Versuche» ausgedrückt wird, ist die Begleitforschung ein integraler Bestandteil der Abgabeversuche, und jeder Einzelversuch muss sowohl therapeutisch–betreuerischen Anforderungen genügen als auch die Voraussetzungen für eine wissenschaftliche Auswertung erfüllen. Um diesen Anforderungen gerecht zu werden, wurden für den Gesamtversuchsplan klare Rahmenbedingungen festgelegt, die für jeden einzelnen Versuch verbindlich sind.

Der ursprüngliche Forschungsplan sieht fünf Gruppen von Verschreibungsversuchen vor:

- In der ersten Gruppe werden spezifische Heroineffekte im Vergleich zum Morphin geprüft. Das Untersuchungsdesign für die eine Hälfte dieser Gruppe ist doppelblind (weder die Betroffenen noch die Therapeuten wissen, welche Teilnehmer/innen welche Substanzen erhalten). Für die andere Hälfte erfolgt die Zuordnung nach Zufall.

- In der zweiten Gruppe werden substanzspezifische Unterschiede zwischen Heroin, Methadon und Morphin im Rahmen eines randomisierten Modells geprüft. Die Zuordnung in dieser Gruppe erfolgt nach Zufall.

- In der dritten Gruppe kommen die regionalen Unterschiede neben den substanzspezifischen Unterschieden zum Tragen.

- In der vierten Gruppe stehen die substanzspezifischen Unterschiede bei einer individuellen Indikation im Zentrum.

- Schliesslich gibt es einen Versuch nur für Frauen, in dem analysiert werden soll, inwiefern ein frauenspezifisches Angebot besondere Vorteile für die betroffenen Frauen mit sich bringt.

Dieser Versuchsplan wurde einmal angepasst und einmal ergänzt.

Aufgrund der Erfahrungen mit der Verschreibung von intravenösem Morphin (häufige und deutliche Nebenwirkungen, schlechte Akzeptanz) wurde die Zahl der vorgesehenen Behandlungen mit Morphin reduziert; dasselbe gilt für intravenöses Methadon. Die Anzahl der Heroinverschreibungen wurde durch Beschluss des Bundesrates vom 30. Januar 1995 von höchstens 250 auf höchstens 500 heraufgesetzt.

Im Mai 1995 beschloss der Bundesrat eine Ausweitung der Versuche mit zusätzlichen Fragestellungen und zusätzlichen Pilotversuchen. Damit wurde die Zahl der Plätze für Heroinverschreibungen auf höchstens 800 erhöht, die Gesamtzahl der Verschreibungsplätze auf höchstens 1000.

Die Auswertung der Ergebnisse orientiert sich an klar formulierten Forschungsfragen. Überprüft werden soll, inwiefern die Verschreibungsversuche:

• Heroinabhängige, die von den bisher verfügbaren Behandlungsmöglichkeiten nicht oder nicht mit ausreichendem Erfolg erreicht wurden, einer Behandlung zugeführt werden können;

• Verbesserungen der gesundheitlichen und sozialen Lage der Versuchsteilnehmer/innen ermöglichen, einschliesslich Verminderung des Risikoverhaltens und einschliesslich eines möglichen Ausstiegs aus der Sucht;

• zusätzliche Erkenntnisse und Grundlagen über die Wirkungsweise von Betäubungsmitteln und über deren Eignung zu Substitutionszwecken liefern.

Die Teilnahme an den Versuchen muss aufgrund eindeutiger Eintrittskriterien dokumentiert werden können. Aus therapeutischen und wissenschaftlichen Gründen kommen für die Verschreibungsversuche nur heroinabhängige Personen in Frage, bei denen negative gesundheitliche und/oder soziale Folgen drohen oder vorliegen und für die eine andere Behandlung versagt hat oder aus indizierbaren Gründen nicht in Frage kommt.

Im Rahmen dieses umgewandelten und ausgeweiteten Versuchsplanes für eine ärztliche Verschreibung von Betäubungsmitteln bildet die kontrollierte Opiatabgabe in der Strafanstalt Oberschöngrün ein Teilprojekt.

Dementsprechend basiert das grundsätzliche Erkenntnisinteresse einerseits auf den gleichen Fragestellungen wie sie im Gesamtprojekt formuliert wurden. Da sich aber die Lebensbedingungen im Strafvollzug erheblich von denjenigen ausserhalb der Gefängnismauern unterscheiden, sind die Erhebungsmethoden und die konkreten Fragestellungen andererseits für dieses spezifische Forschungsobjekt eigens angepasst worden. Infolgedessen beschäftigt sich diese Studie hauptsächlich mit der Frage nach der Machbarkeit und Durchführbarkeit einer kontrollierten Opiatabgabe in einer Strafvollzugsanstalt.

2 Forschungsplan

2.1 Fragestellung

Die Evaluation des Projekts KOST geht der Frage der Machbarkeit der kontrollierten Opiatabgabe im Strafvollzug nach. Sie beschäftigt sich mit jenen Prozessen, von denen die Durchführbarkeit eines solchen Projektes abhängt. Das Ziel dieser Untersuchung ist es, den Verlauf des Projektes zu dokumentieren und zu illustrieren, Antworten auf die formulierten Forschungsfragen zu finden und daraus schlussfolgernd Empfehlungen abzuleiten, die – zwingendermassen – primär auf die Partikularität des Projekts KOST und seiner Rahmenbedingungen bezogen sind, sekundär jedoch – wo möglich – zu Aussagen führen, die generelle Machbarkeitsaspekte einer kontrollierten Opiatabgabe im Strafvollzug klären.

Untersucht wird die Strafanstalt Oberschöngrün, die den Versuch KOST durchführt als Ganze und spezifisch die verschiedenen Organisationsgruppen innerhalb der Gesamtorganisation in ihren spezifischen Funktionen und ihrem eigenen Erfahrungsbereich. Diesem Untersuchungsfeld gehören auch die Versuchs–Probanden als einzelne und als Gruppe an.

Innerhalb der Evaluation lassen sich zwei Hauptfragestellungen bestimmen: Fragen bezüglich der *Organisation und Durchführung* sowie Fragen, die auf die *Versuchsteilnehmer* bezogen sind (*Abbildung 1*):

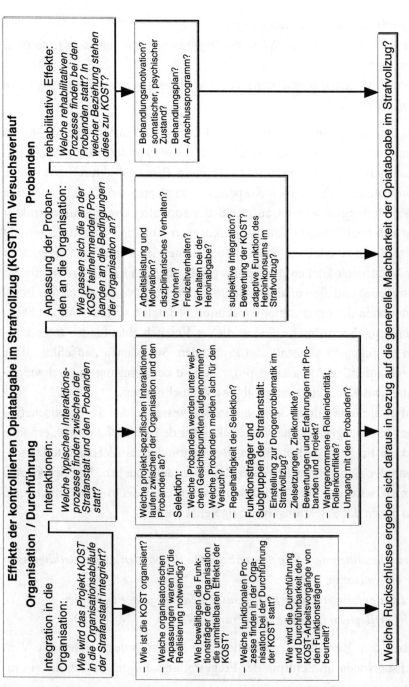

Abbildung 1: Effekte der kontrollierten Opiatabgabe im Strafvollzug (KOST) im Versuchsverlauf

Organisation und Durchführung:
Wie wird das Projekt KOST in die Organisationsabläufe der Strafanstalt
integriert?
Welche typischen Interaktionsprozesse finden zwischen Strafanstalt und
Probanden statt?

Um den Platz, den das Projekt KOST in der Strafanstalt Oberschöngrün
einnimmt, adäquat zu erfassen, wird es notwendig sein, die Organisationsstruktur der Strafanstalt mit ihren Binnenstrukturen sowie den
Schnittstellen mit externen Körperschaften zu erfassen. Die Organisation
einer Vollzugsanstalt ist aufgrund der formalen Organisationsstruktur
und den beobachteten vollzugspraktischen Abläufen jedoch noch nicht
ausreichend zu erklären (Wenzel 1979). Interviews und Fragebogendaten
der Mitarbeiter können Aufschluss geben über das Rollenverständnis der
Mitarbeiter und die von den handelnden Personen vorgenommenen Inter-
pretationen der organisationsstrukturell bedingten sozialen Wirklichkeit.
Von besonderem Interesse sind die im Versuch ablaufenden Interaktionen zwischen Strafanstalt und Probanden. Sie können Aufschluss über
die ablaufenden Anpassungsprozesse und den Umgang mit Schwierig-
keiten und Konflikten innerhalb des Versuchs geben.

Für die Beurteilung der Selektionsprozesse werden die Eigenschaften
jener Insassengruppe, die sich effektiv für den Versuch bewirbt, erhoben
und die Frage gestellt nach den Beweggründen, am Versuch teilzunehmen oder sich eventuell wieder davon zurückzuziehen. Der Selektions-
prozess wird mit dem Ziel dokumentiert, die Regeln herauszuarbeiten,
von denen der Selektionsvorgang geleitet wird.

Versuchsteilnehmer: Wie passen sich die Probanden an die Bedingungen
der Organisation an?
Welche rehabilitativen Prozesse finden bei den Probanden statt? In
welcher Beziehung stehen diese zur KOST?

Neben dem Bereich «Organisation und Durchführung» stehen die Versuchspersonen im Zentrum der Fragestellung. Es stellen sich dabei Fra-

gen nach dem Anpassungsverhalten der Probanden und dessen subjektiver und objektiver Wahrnehmung sowie nach rehabilitativen Effekten, die eventuell bei den Probanden beobachtet werden können.

Schlussfolgerungen für die Machbarkeit: Welche Schlussfolgerungen ergeben sich aus den Ergebnissen der Evaluation des Projekts KOST bezüglich der generellen Machbarkeit der kontrollierten Opiatabgabe im Strafvollzug?

Ziel der Auswertung ist es, Zusammenhänge, Verhaltens– und Interaktionsmuster sowie strukturelle Bedingungen der kontrollierten Opiatabgabe im Strafvollzug zu identifizieren, die Aussagen darüber ermöglichen, von welchen Faktoren die Machbarkeit einer solchen Opiatabgabe im Strafvollzug abhängt.

2.2 Methodik

Forschungs–Approach

Für die Evaluation des Projektes KOST und die beschriebene Fragestellung wird der Forschungsansatz einer Einzelfallstudie (auch Fallstudie oder engl. case study) gewählt.

In der Fallstudie versucht man, ein umfassendes Verständnis über einen komplexen Sachverhalt zu gewinnen. Dieses Verständnis wird durch umfangreiche Beschreibung und Analyse des Sachverhalts gewonnen, der zu diesem Zweck als ein Ganzes in seinem Kontext betrachtet wird. Diese Vorgehensweise ist dann besonders indiziert, wenn die einen Sachverhalt bestimmenden Wirkungszusammenhänge unbekannt oder unklar sind. So stellen sich im Projekt KOST insbesondere Fragen nach den Anpassungsprozessen, die zwischen der Organisation Strafanstalt, den Probanden im Versuch und den Rahmenbedingungen des Projekts KOST stattfinden: Ein umfassendes Verständnis der Abläufe und Interaktionen wird gewonnen, indem ein möglichst vollständiges Bild dessen erarbeitet wird, was innerhalb des Sachverhaltes aufgrund bestimmter und noch zu bestimmender Wirkungszusammenhänge abläuft (U.S. General Accounting Office 1990).

Die prospektive Perspektive, die bei der Evaluation des Projekts KOST eingenommen wird, ermöglicht ein vertieftes Verständnis dafür, warum bestimmte Ereignisse eintreten und welche Faktoren in Zukunft in einem derartigen Projekt der Heroinabgabe relevant werden können. Ziel ist es in diesem Prozess, typische Verhaltens– und Verarbeitungsmuster der am Versuch Teilnehmenden zu erkennen und zu beschreiben. Die untersuchten Reaktionsmuster werden dabei in ihrer Partikularität und in ihrer gesamten Varianz zu verstehen versucht. Aufgrund dieser Analyse werden Hypothesen generiert, die in enger Verbindung mit den vorhandenen Daten stehen.

Die Einzelfallanalyse ist prinzipiell offen für vielfältige Methoden und Techniken der empirischen Sozialforschung. Innerhalb des qualitativen Paradigmas nimmt sie eine eigenständige Position ein, indem sie eine «wissenschaftliche Rekonstruktion von Handlungsmustern auf der Grundlage von alltagsweltlichen realen Handlungsmustern anstrebt» (Lamnek 1993, S. 16). In der Falluntersuchung der KOST sind qualitative Forschungsmethoden von zentraler Bedeutung, da davon ausgegangen wird, dass sie den untersuchten Prozessen, die sie möglichst in ihrer Komplexität und Partikularität verstehen will, angemessen sind.

Datenerhebung

Bei der Datenerhebung – wie auch bei der Datenauswertung – wird ein multimethodischer Ansatz gewählt. Eine einseitige Methodenwahl widerspräche der Komplexität des Sachverhalts. Eine Methodentriangulation erlaubt einerseits, die vielfältigen Aspekte des Falles wahrzunehmen und verringert gleichzeitig die Gefahr von Methodenfehlern im Sinne von Methodenartefakten (Mayring 1990).

Interviewdaten werden mittels *fokussierter, halbstrukturierter Interviews* einzeln mit den Probanden bzw. in Form von Kollektivinterviews mit verschiedenen «natürlichen» Anstalts–Gruppen der Strafanstalt er-

hoben. Die Interviews und Diskussionen werden anhand von Gesprächs-
leitfäden geführt, die aufgrund der Forschungsfragen entwickelt werden.
Die Fragen, die in den angesprochenen Interviews gestellt werden, sind
mehrheitlich halbstrukturiert, d.h. entweder der Stimulus oder die Reaktion ist in der Frage strukturiert, während jeweils der andere Teil völlig
offen ist (Hron 1982).

Standardisierte Interviews aus der PROVE–Evaluation werden – in
einer den Verhältnissen im Strafvollzug angepassten Form – mit den Probanden zu Beginn des Versuchs und dann in halbjährlichem Abstand
durchgeführt.

Anhand eines *standardisierten Verlaufsjournals* werden Ereignisse
aus dem Vollzugsalltag – Arbeit, Wohnen, disziplinarisches Verhalten,
die Häufigkeit der Teilnahme an Freizeitaktivitäten, die Benützung des
Betreuungsangebots sowie die Anzahl Besuche von extern – dokumentiert. Zudem wird die Arbeitsleistung durch die Vorgesetzten und die
Zimmerordnung durch einen Vollzugsbeamten eingeschätzt.

Das *Verhalten der Probanden im zweiwöchentlichen Gruppenge-
spräch* wird von den Gesprächsleitern in bezug auf folgende Kategorien
beurteilt und protokolliert: Gesprächsverlauf, Kooperation, Häufigkeit
der Wortmeldungen, Nüchternheit, emotionale Beteiligung, Konfliktbe-
wältigung, Integration in die Gruppe, verantwortliches Verhalten, Fru-
strationstoleranz und Lebensperspektiven.

Alle *Mitarbeiter der Strafanstalt* werden schriftlich durch einen standardisierten Fragebogen zu ihrer Einstellung zum Projekt KOST und den
Erfahrungen, die sie in Zusammenhang damit machen, zu Beginn des
Versuchs befragt. Diese Befragung wird vor Versuchsende noch einmal
wiederholt.

Die fokussierten Interviews und die Gruppendiskussionen werden zusammenfassend protokolliert oder auf Tonband aufgenommen und dann
transkribiert. Das qualitative Datenmaterial wird reduktiv weiterverarbei-
tet, indem der Text paraphrasiert wird. Durch Codieren im Sinne der
Grounded Theory (Strauss und Corbin 1990, Strauss 1991) bzw. inhalts-

analytischen Methoden (Mayring 1985) werden Verhaltenskategorien gebildet, die miteinander in Beziehung gesetzt werden können.

Alle quantitativen Daten, die im Rahmen der standardisierten PRO-VE–Evaluation erhoben werden, werden innerhalb derselben ausgewertet und allenfalls beschreibend in die Evaluation des Projekts KOST integriert. Die Mitarbeiter–Daten werden bivariat und – wo es die Stichprobengrösse ermöglicht – multivariat im Verlauf analysiert. Bei den wöchentlich ermittelten Journal–Daten und den zweiwöchentlich erhobenen Gesprächsprotokollen werden Zeitreihenanalysen durchgeführt.

3 Das Projekt KOST

3.1 Ausgangslage

In der Strafanstalt Solothurn Oberschöngrün (OSG) findet seit September 1995 im Rahmen der vom Schweizerischen Bundesrat bewilligten Versuche für eine diversifizierte Suchtmittelabgabe ein Versuch der kontrollierten Opiatabgabe im Strafvollzug (KOST) in Form einer Machbarkeitsstudie statt.

Die Verantwortlichen der Strafanstalt OSG ergriffen die Initiative für dieses Projekt angesichts einer grossen Anzahl von Sucht–Delinquenten, die auch im Strafvollzug entgegen aller repressiven Massnahmen als Händler oder Konsumenten den Suchtkreislauf weiterführten (Schaefer et al 1995). Aufgrund der Beobachtung, dass die meisten dieser Insassen nach Entlassung erneut delinquieren, kam man zur Schlussfolgerung, dass der gesetzliche Resozialisierungsauftrag bei dieser Gruppe von der Strafanstalt nicht erfüllt werden kann. Mit Hilfe der kontrollierte Opiatabgabe im Strafvollzug (KOST) wollte die Strafanstalt eine aktive Rolle ergreifen, um den gesetzlichen Resozialisierungsauftrag auch gegenüber opiatabhängigen Straftätern besser zu erfüllen und ihnen die Möglichkeit zu verschaffen, sich ohne Beschaffungsstress psychisch und physisch zu stabilisieren.

3.2 Die Strafanstalt Solothurn Oberschöngrün

Die Strafanstalt Solothurn ist eine kantonale Strafvollzugsinstitution, die die Insassen dabei unterstützen soll, sich in der rechtsstaatlichen Ordnung zurechtzufinden (Regierungsrat des Kantons Solothurn, 1976). Gemäss Art. 37 des StGB soll sie ihre Insassen erziehen, sie auf den Wiedereinstieg ins Leben vorbereiten, ihnen eine Arbeit verfügbar machen, die ihnen entspricht, und zur Wiedergutmachung an Leib und Leben beitragen.

Aufgrund dieses Auftrags praktiziert die Anstalt OSG einen halboffenen Vollzug. Es stehen in der Anstalt Plätze für 75 männliche Insassen zur Verfügung, die nicht gemeingefährlich oder fluchtgefährdet sind. Unter den Insassen sind alle Deliktgruppen vertreten. Das Strafmass geht von mindestens drei Monaten bis zu lebenslänglich.

Die Strafanstalt besteht aus dem Kernkomplex in Oberschöngrün und dem Aussenhof Bleichenberg.

Die Strafanstalt betreibt einen umfangreichen Landwirtschaftsbetrieb, eine Gemüsegärtnerei, eine Landschaftsgärtnerei, eine Schreinerei, eine mechanische Werkstatt, eine Lingerie, eine Baugruppe, eine Hausindustrie und den Hausdienst. Die Insassen werden in diesen Betrieben eingesetzt. In einzelnen Fällen besteht die Möglichkeit, dass Insassen extern arbeiten oder Berufsausbildungen intern oder extern absolvieren.

In der Anstalt sind insgesamt 40 Personen auf 36.5 Stellen angestellt, wovon der grössere Teil in den genannten Produktionsbetrieben beschäftigt ist.

3.3 Aufnahmeverfahren

Als Zielgruppe werden im Feinkonzept des Projekts KOST (Schaefer et al 1995) opiatabhängige Insassen angesprochen, deren deliktisches Verhalten in Zusammenhang mit ihrer Suchtproblematik steht. Aufgrund ihres fortbestehenden devianten Verhaltens sind sie kaum in den ordentlichen Strafvollzug integrierbar und können daher auch nicht die sozialintegrativen Angebote der Strafanstalt in Anspruch nehmen.

Die Teilnahme am Versuch ist für alle Probanden freiwillig, d.h. sie werden nicht durch Mitarbeiter zur Teilnahme aufgefordert oder angehalten. Es wurden Probanden aus der Strafanstalt Solothurn sowie aus Anstalten des Nordwest– und Innerschweizer Gefängniskonkordats, dem die Strafanstalt OSG ebenfalls angehört ,rekrutiert.

3.4   Organisation

Für die Durchführung des Projekts wurde ein Organisationsmodul konzipiert, das als eigene Organisationsform in das Projekt integriert werden sollte (Schaefer et al 1995). Dieses Modul wurde im Verlauf des Versuchs frühzeitig an die Organisation des Normalvollzugs angepasst. Die Trägerschaft des Projekts hat der Kanton Solothurn. Als Mitglied des Projektausschusses ist die Direktion der Strafanstalt OSG dem Kanton Solothurn gegenüber verantwortlich für die Projektrealisation. Der Projektausschuss wird vom Projektleiter (Leiter Vollzug) geleitet, der für die Durchführung des Versuchs verantwortlich ist. Dem Projektausschuss gehören mittlerweile zwölf Mitarbeiter und Mitarbeiterinnen an, die in den verschiedenen Abteilungen (Medizin, Betreuung und Freizeit, Arbeit, Sozialdienst, Sicherheit), die vom Projekt betroffen sind, Verantwortung übernehmen und wichtige Funktionen ausführen. Der Einbezug einer grossen Anzahl von Mitarbeitern in den Projektausschuss hat sich bewährt und die Integration des Projekts KOST in die Strafanstalt gefördert.

3.5   Die Durchführung der kontrollierten Opiatabgabe

Heroinabgabe

In der Aussenstation der Strafanstalt OSG, Bleichenberg, in der der Versuch durchgeführt wird, wurden ein Abgaberaum und ein Pikettzimmer – zur Vorbereitung und Lagerung des Heroins und Methadons – sicherheitstechnisch und sanitarisch eingerichtet. Das Heroin wird den Probanden im Abgaberaum dreimal täglich zur Selbstinjektion abgegeben. Die Abgabe findet morgens um 7.30 Uhr, mittags um 13.30 Uhr und abends um 19.30 Uhr statt. Anwesend bei der Abgabe ist eine medizinische Mitarbeiterin des Abgabe–Teams sowie ein Mitarbeiter aus dem Innendienst, der für die Gewährleistung der Sicherheit zuständig ist. Die erforderliche Heroinmenge wird für die Abgabe vom Medizinalpersonal bereitgestellt. Die Probanden erscheinen zur vereinbarten Zeit im Abgaberaum, erhalten die vorbereitete Spritze und applizieren sich das Heroin – bis auf medizinisch indizierte Ausnahmen – selbst. Für die Heroinabgabe ist pro Abgabe für alle Probanden insgesamt ein Zeitraum von einer Stunde vorgesehen.

Wohnen

Die Probanden sind während des Versuchs im Aussenhof Bleichenberg der Strafanstalt untergebracht, der drei Kilometer von der Strafanstalt Oberschöngrün entfernt liegt und Platz für acht Insassen bietet. Der Bleichenberg umfasst neben den Stallungen und der landwirtschaftlichen Nutzfläche den Wohntrakt der Insassen. Der Hof ist nicht umzäunt und auch sonst äusserlich nur durch die Gitter an den Fenstern des Wohngebäudes als eine Strafvollzugsanstalt identifizierbar.

Arbeit

Die Probanden werden im Landwirtschaftsbetrieb beschäftigt. Sie werden in den Ställen (Kuhstall, Kälberstall, Pferdestall), im Obstbau, im Hausdienst und bei allgemeinen Arbeiten im Bleichenberg eingesetzt. In diesen Bereichen werden sie von den Arbeitsvorgesetzten fachlich angeleitet und beaufsichtigt. Die Arbeitszeiten im Bleichenberg richten sich nach einem für einen Landwirtschaftsbetrieb typischen 7–Tage–Rhythmus, der ensprechend mit Urlaub kompensiert wird. Folgende Arbeitszeiten gelten für die Probanden: Montag bis Freitag: 5.30 – 7.30, 8.30 – 11.45, 15.00 – 18.30; Samstag und Sonntag: 5.30 – 7.30, 16.00 – 18.30.

Psychosoziale Betreuung und Beratung

Für die Probanden des Projekts KOST werden neben den allen Insassen offenstehenden Betreuungsangeboten durch den Sozialdienst und den Psychologen weitere Fördermassnahmen angeboten. Im Rahmen der Vollzugsplanung legt jeder Proband nach einem Monat im Projekt seine persönlichen Entwicklungsziele schriftlich fest. Im Lauf des Versuchs werden diese Ziele mit der zuständigen Betreuungsperson immer wieder thematisiert. Bis Ende 1995 ein– bis zweiwöchentlich, seit Beginn 1996 wöchentlich finden obligatorische Gruppengespräche mit allen Insassen im Bleichenberg statt, die von einem Sozialarbeiter und dem Psychologen geleitet werden.

Versuchsbeginn

Es stehen Plätze für acht opiatabhängige Insassen zur Verfügung. Am 8. September wurde der Versuch mit drei Probanden gestartet. Eine dreimonatige Pilotphase von September bis November wurde mit vier Probanden durchgeführt. Im Dezember wurden zwei weitere Versuchspersonen aufgenommen. Anfang 1996 wurde ein Proband aus der Haft entlassen, was zu Versuchsbeginn noch nicht absehbar war, und trat in eine stationäre sozialpädagogische Institution und gleichzeitig in ein ambulantes Heroinverschreibungsprojekt über. Im Januar trat ein weiterer Proband in den Versuch ein, im Februar zwei weitere, so dass Anfang März 1996 sieben der acht Versuchsplätze belegt sind.

In den ersten 10 Tagen traten Injektionsprobleme auf, die in Verbindung zu bringen sind mit der für die Probanden ungewohnten Injektionssituation und dem z.T. sehr schlechten Zustand der Venen. Nach einer Angewöhnungszeit, in der die Venenpflege und die Anpassung an die Abgabesituation vom Abgabeteam aktiv gefördert wurden, verlief die Abgabe im untersuchten Zeitraum bis Dezember 1995 ohne gravierende Störungen und ohne Zwischenfälle wie Überdosierungen, Gewaltanwendung oder Entwendung von Heroin.

Die Herointagesdosierungen haben sich nach anfänglichen Schwankungen innerhalb der ersten Monate auf 250 bis 600 mg eingependelt.

Die Arbeitsleistungen waren bei zwei der vier Probanden bei Versuchsbeginn ungenügend, was Qualität und Arbeitsgeschwindigkeit betraf. Nach Ablauf der ersten Versuchswochen haben sich die Leistungen merklich verbessert und erreichten ein durchschnittliches Niveau.

4 Erste Ergebnisse

Die im folgenden dargestellten Ergebnisse gehen auf Befragungen in der *Startphase* des Projekts, also den Monaten September bis November zurück. Sie basieren auf verbalen Daten, die in fokussierten Interviews mit den Probanden, mit Anstaltsmitarbeitern und Insassen erhoben und dann paraphrasiert und systematisch kategorisiert wurden. Die beschriebenen Kategorien gehen auf verbale Äusserungen dieser Anstaltsangehörigen zurück. Die daraus gezogenen Schlussfolgerungen werden von den Ergebnissen im folgenden Text explizit abgehoben.

Bezeichnend für die Phase des Versuchsbeginns war, dass alle Beteiligten absolutes Neuland miteinander betraten und dass daher wenig festgefügte Erlebnis– und Bewertungsmodi vorhanden waren. Dementsprechend vorläufig fallen auch die Ergebnisse der ersten Analyse aus, die noch nicht abgeschlossen ist. Der im folgenden beschriebene Bereich «Verhältnis zwischen den Probanden und der Organisation der Strafanstalt Oberschöngrün» repräsentiert nur einen Teilbereich der gesamten qualitativen Auswertung. Aufgrund dieses Kontextes vermögen die folgenden Resultate nichts anderes als ein erstes Schlaglicht auf die Prozesse zu werfen, die im Projekt KOST ablaufen.

Das Verhältnis zwischen den Probanden und der Organisation der Strafanstalt Oberschöngrün

Der im folgenden beschriebene Bereich «Verhältnis zwischen den Probanden und der Organisation der Strafanstalt Oberschöngrün» gibt eine Antwort auf die Frage, unter welchen Gesichtspunkten *die Beteiligten* dieses Verhältnis beschreiben. Es umfasst die Kategorien – «Behandlungsspezifische Interaktionen», «Abhängigkeitsverhältnis» und «Widersprüchlichkeit» der Heroinabgabe im Strafvollzug – die im folgenden mit ihren Unterkategorien beschrieben werden.

A Behandlungsspezifische Interaktionen

Dieser Bereich betrifft die Interaktionen, die zwischen den Probanden und den anderen Institutionsangehörigen stattfinden. Behandlungsspezifische Interaktionen in einer Strafanstalt sind deshalb von besonderem Interesse, weil sie im Normalfall mit kustodialen Interaktionen konkurrieren. Wie ein roter Faden zieht sich durch etliche Forschungsarbeiten im Bereich Strafvollzug (Friedrichs 1979, Kette 1991, Klär 1987, Leehr 1988, Molitor 1989, Wenzel 1979) dieser festgestellte Konflikt zwischen rehabilitativen und kustodialen Zielen in Vollzugskonzepten. Man kann deshalb davon ausgehen, dass dieser Interaktionsform im Versuch eine wesentliche Bedeutung zukommt.

Im einzelnen sind dies Interaktionen, die sich qualitativ und quantitativ von der üblichen Anstaltsroutine unterscheiden und eine Spezifizität des Projekts KOST ausmachen. Dazu gehören die Subkategorien «intensive Betreuung und Zuwendung»,»Heroin abgegeben bekommen» und «Kontrolle des Heroinkonsums durch die Strafanstalt OSG».

A.a intensivierte Betreuung und Zuwendung

Die Probanden werden im Vergleich mit dem Normalvollzug intensiver und teilweise in einer anderen Form betreut. Diese Betreuung ist gekennzeichnet durch:

– von den Probanden positiv empfundene, verstärkt unterstützende Zuwendung. *Der Proband nimmt wahr, nach Jahren der Verfolgung und des «Fertig-gemacht-Werdens» erstmals von der «Justiz» unterstützt zu werden.*

– Umgang mit weiblichem Betreuungspersonal im Rahmen der Heroinabgabe. *Der Kontakt mit weiblichem Pflegepersonal ist für Insassen im Strafvollzug aussergewöhnlich. In Betreuungsaufgaben sind sonst nur männliche Mitarbeiter in der Anstalt tätig.*

– Häufigeren Kontakt mit Medizinalpersonal. *Der Projektarzt ist viermal wöchentlich bei der Abgabe anwesend. Die Probanden interagieren mit ihm bezüglich Dosisfestlegung und eventueller Zusatzmedikation. Der Arzt ist verpflichtet, für die wissenschaftliche Auswertung regelmässig Untersuchungen mit den Probanden durchzuführen. Die Probanden lassen sich diverse Wunden von den Krankenschwestern laufend behandeln.*

– Die zweiwöchentlichen Gruppengespräche. *Mindestens in zweiwöchentlichem Abstand finden Gruppengespräche mit den Insassen des Bleichenbergs statt, die von einem Sozialarbeiter und dem Psychologen geleitet werden.*

– Den Mehraufwand an Betreuung seitens des Sozialdienstes. *Der Sozialdienst ist bei der Abgabe regelmässig anwesend, begleitet die Probanden auf Sachurlaub, steht für telefonische Anfragen ständig zur Verfügung und ist für die Probanden generell ansprechbarer.*

– Regelmässige, mindestens halbjährliche Interviews mit externen Befragern. *Im Rahmen der Begleitforschung werden die Probanden in fokussierten und standardisierten Interviews regelmässig von zwei verschiedenen Interviewern zu ihrer Situation befragt.*

A.b Heroin abgegeben bekommen

«Heroin abgegeben bekommen» ist jene Interaktionsform, die vollumfänglich versuchsspezifisch ist und dadurch den Kern der behandlungsspezifischen Interaktionen bildet. Sie beinhaltet:

... dass die Probanden die Substanz, von der sie abhängig sind, privilegiert – im Gegensatz zu anderen suchtmittelabhängigen Insassen – im Gefängnis erhalten.

... dass sie für den Konsum von Heroin – im Gegensatz zu den anderen suchtmittelabhängigen Insassen – nicht mehr bestraft werden.

... dass die Heroinabgabe auch bei Disziplinarstrafen – wie Arrest ausserhalb des Versuchsbetriebs – aufrechterhalten wird.

A.c Kontrolle des Heroinkonsums durch die Strafanstalt

Die Abgabe und Einnahme des Opiats steht unter der Kontrolle der Strafanstalt:

– Die Probanden sind an regelmässige Abgabezeiten und einen bestimmten Abgabekontext gebunden. *Die Probanden sind verpflichtet, sich an die vorgegebenen Abgabezeiten zu halten, im Gegensatz zu anderen Heroinabhängigen, die den Zeitpunkt und Kontext der Drogeneinnahme – sofern Drogen verfügbar sind – selbst bestimmen können.*

– Bei der Dosisfestlegung wird nach einem bestimmten Dosierungskonzept vorgegangen. *Die Probanden sind – anders als andere drogenabhängige Insassen – bei der Dosisfestlegung abhängig von einer Dosisabsprache mit dem Projektarzt. Dagegen sind sie nicht abhängig von der aktuell vorherrschenden Angebotssituation illegalen Heroins und sind nicht den Mechanismen der Drogenbeschaffung im Gefängnis unterworfen, wie ihre nicht an der KOST teilnehmenden Kollegen.*

– Bei disziplinarischen Vergehen bei der Heroinabgabe können vom Leiter Vollzug (Projekleiter) Heroin–Sperrtage ausgesprochen werden.

– Die Probanden werden verplichtet, im Hafturlaub täglich in einer zuvor vereinbarten Abgabestelle Methadon zu beziehen.

*A.d Spezifischer Verhandlungsspielraum der Probanden in der Inter-
aktion mit Instanzen der Strafanstalt*

Durch die Teilnahme am Projekt KOST können die Probanden direkt
oder indirekt Einfluss nehmen auf die Dosisfestlegung, die Abgabe-
reihenfolge, die Spritzenhilfe und allfällige Zusatzmedikationen. Die
Probanden erhalten einen Verhandlungsspielraum mit den Instanzen der
Strafanstalt, über den die Insassen im Normalvollzug nicht verfügen. Der
KOST–spezifische Verhandlungsspielraum betrifft:

– Dosisfestlegung. *Die Probanden legen in Absprache mit dem Projektarzt die Heroindosis fest. Es besteht die Tendenz, bei Anwesenheit des
Projektarztes über die Dosis zu verhandeln.*

– Abgabereihenfolge. *Die Abgabereihenfolge wurde aufgrund der viru-
lenten Konflikte zwischen verschiedenen Probanden immer wieder
den Bedürfnissen der Probanden angepasst, indem «Streithähne» bei
der Abgabe getrennt wurden.*

– Spritzenhilfe. *Spritzenhilfe wurde – entgegen der anfänglichen Hal-
tung – im Fall von Injektionsproblemen vom Abgabepersonal ebenfalls geleistet, da dies bei bestimmten Probanden aus medizinischen
Gründen erforderlich wurde und von diesen auch gewünscht wurde.*

– Zusatzmedikation. *Durch den häufigen Kontakt mit dem Arzt und den
Krankenschwestern versuchen die Probanden immer wieder, zu Zusatzmedikationen zu gelangen.*

Folgerungen «Behandlungsspezifische Interaktionen»

Die Interaktionen zwischen den Probanden und den Mitarbeitern der
Strafanstalt sind teilweise qualitativ und quantitativ verschieden von jenen ihrer Mitinsassen im Normalvollzug. Dieser Effekt wird sowohl von
den Mitarbeitern als auch von den Probanden wahrgenommen. Die Strafanstalt steigert den Betreuungsaufwand in den beschriebenen Bereichen
im Versuch deutlich. Dieser Aspekt des Sich–Kümmerns zeigt sich als
zentrale Dimension in der Heroinabgabe selbst. Davon ausgehend, dass

die Versorgung mit Opiaten diesen opiatabhängigen Insassen ein primäres Bedürfnis ist, übernimmt die Strafanstalt in diesem Fall die Verantwortung für die Sättigung des Opiathungers und erkennt dadurch auch dessen Legitimität an.

Die Heroinabgabe als Interaktionsform ist jedoch nicht nur durch die Sättigung des Opiathungers der Probanden durch die Strafanstalt geprägt, sondern ebenso durch die Kontrolle ihres Heroinkonsums durch die Anstalt. Und gerade in denjenigen Bereichen der Heroinabgabe, die der Kontrolle der Anstalt unterstehen, versuchen die Probanden ihrerseits, Einfluss zu nehmen und Kontrolle über die Interaktion zu gewinnen.

Den Probanden gibt das Angebot der Strafanstalt in Form der spezifischen Interaktionsformen und der Kontrolle einen Anreiz, in Interaktionsbereichen, die sich um die Abgabe drehen, mit Anstaltsangehörigen zu verhandeln, um eigenen Bedürfnissen Nachdruck zu verschaffen. Es bildet sich ein eigentlicher Verhandlungsspielraum zwischen Anstalt und Probanden.

B Abhängigkeitsverhältnis

Immer wieder werden von den Befragten verschiedener Seiten Aussagen gemacht, die im Verhältnis zwischen Anstalt und Probanden den Aspekt der Abhängigkeit zur Sprache bringen. Das gegenseitige Abhängigkeitsverhältnis zwischen Probanden und Strafanstalt wird von den Befragten in bezug auf die folgenden Bereiche erlebt und beschrieben:

B.a Abhängigkeit der Probanden von der kontrollierten Opiatabgabe
    Die Abhängigkeit von der Heroinabgabe wird Probanden deutlich in Zusammenhang mit ...

... Angst vor Abbruch der KOST. *Befürchtet wird von den Probanden ein gegebenenfalls drohender Versuchsabbruch bzw. die Versetzung aus dem Projekt bei Disziplinarvergehen.*

... Angst, «abhängiger» (gemacht) zu werden. *Probanden befürchten, durch die Einnahme reinen Heroins dosisbedingt stärker abhängig zu werden als dies bei illegalem «gestrecktem» Heroin der Fall wäre. Ein Proband hat Angst, durch den Methadonbezug im Vollzugsurlaub von dieser Substanz abhängig zu werden, die er mit einem extrem schweren Entzugssyndrom in Verbindung bringt.*

... Substitution des Suchtmitteldistributors. *Die Strafvollzugsinstitution tritt aus Sicht von Probanden und Mitarbeitern an die Stelle des Drogen–Dealers, d.h. in die Funktion desjenigen, der das begehrte Suchtmittel kontrolliert.*

B.b Abhängigkeit des Projekts KOST von den Probanden im Versuch

– Probanden nicht verlegen können. *Das Verlegen von unangepassten – insbesondere disziplinarisch auffälligen – Insassen in andere Strafanstalten oder anstaltsintern in andere Abteilungen gehört zum Sanktions– und Konfliktlösungssystems einer Strafanstalt. Insassen und Personal wissen um diese Mechanismen, die von allen Beteiligten in unterschiedlichem Ausmass beeinflusst werden können. «Verlegen» als Sanktion von grob unangepasstem Verhalten – in bezug auf Arbeit und Disziplin – wird bei Versuchsbeginn von der Anstalt vermieden.*

– Machtzuwachs bei den Probanden. *Die verstärkte Zuwendung, die die Probanden erhalten und der Umstand, dass dieser Versuch von grossem öffentlichem Interesse ist und ohne sie nicht stattfinden kann, kann bei Probanden ein Gefühl von Machtzuwachs erzeugen. Von einem Probanden wird dieses Argument gezielt ausgespielt. Die Projektverantwortlichen verwahren sich explizit gegen diese Ansprüche.*

B.c Ablehnung der Teilnahme am Versuch aus Angst vor Abhängigkeit

Ein opiatabhängiger Insasse, der nicht am Projekt KOST teilnehmen wollte, begründet dies dadurch, dass er Einnahmezeitpunkt, Appli-

kationsform und die gewünschte Menge und Wirkung selbst kon-
trollieren wolle. Bei einer Teilnahme am Projekt KOST wird eine
Abhängigkeit vom «Staat» befürchtet.

Folgerungen «Abhängigkeitsverhältnis»

Die Probanden fühlen sich, was die Suchtmittelkontrolle betrifft, der
Strafvollzugsinstitution gegenüber ausgeliefert. Die Angst vor einem
Versuchsabbruch wird noch gestärkt durch die subjektive Wahrnehmung
stärkerer Abhängigkeit. Der Wille, die Kontrolle nicht an die Vollzugs-
instanz abzugeben, kann opiatabhängige Insassen dazu veranlassen, nicht
am Projekt KOST teilzunehmen.

In dieser ersten Versuchsphase thematisieren verschiedene Probanden
den Aspekt der «Abhängigkeit». Er steht aber nicht im Vordergrund der
Versuchswahrnehmung der Probanden, sondern bleibt gegenüber verschiedenen anderen als positiv bewerteten, aber auch einzelnen eindeutig
als negativ empfundenen Erfahrungen mit der KOST im Hintergrund.

C Widersprüchlichkeit der Heroinabgabe im Strafvollzug

Widersprüche bei der Heroinabgabe im Strafvollzug werden von Probanden, anderen Insassen und Mitarbeitern angesprochen. Sie beziehen sich
auf die folgenden Bereiche:

C.a Irritation über die Heroinabgabe nach vorheriger Verfolgung

Der Umstand, wegen Betäubungsmitteldelikten strafrechtlich verfolgt
und inhaftiert worden zu sein und jetzt das Suchtmittel zu bekommen,
provoziert teilweise Irritation bei Probanden und Mitarbeitern.

C.b Neid wegen zweierlei Rechts

Insassen beschweren sich, dass sie in der Strafanstalt für den
Heroinkonsum bestraft werden, z.B. durch Urlaubsaufschub, während
die Probanden trotz Heroinkonsums in den Urlaub dürfen. Alkohol-

abhängige Insassen beschweren sich über das «Unrecht», dass das Suchtmittel, von dem sie abhängig sind, nicht abgegeben wird.

Folgerungen «Widersprüchlichkeit der Heroinabgabe im Strafvollzug»
Von Seiten der Mitarbeiter, Insassen und Probanden wird wahrgenommen, dass die Strategie, den Heroinkonsum strafrechtlich und innerhalb der Anstalt disziplinarisch zu verfolgen, im Widerspruch dazu steht, dass Heroin im Gefängnis abgegeben wird. Dieser Widerspruch ist bei bei den angesprochenen Gruppen unaufgelöst da, wird jedoch verschieden bewertet: Der Umstand, dass «zweierlei Recht» gilt bzw. dass von den traditionellen Anstaltszielen der Repression und Prohibition abgewichen wird, wird von jenen, die der Heroinabgabe kritisch oder ablehnend gegenüberstehen, negativ bewertet. Die Probanden begrüssen diese radikale Kursänderung, können sie jedoch kaum einordnen.

Erste Schlussfolgerungen

Das Verhältnis der Strafanstalt zu den Probanden in dieser ersten Versuchsphase ist gekennzeichnet durch eine stärkere Verzahnung und Interdependenz zwischen der Organisation und den Probanden: Die Anstalt trägt Sorge zu diesen Insassen, indem sie die Verantwortung für die Opiatversorgung und die Durchführung der Abgabe übernimmt. Die Probanden werden im Verhältnis zu ihren Mitinsassen intensiver und umfangreicher betreut. Dieses Betreuungs– und Versorgungsprivileg ist für die Probanden aber auch damit verbunden, dass sie an Autarkie verlieren und sich der heteronomen Kontrolle ihres Opiatkonsums durch die Versuchsbedingungen unterwerfen müssen. In der «totalen Institution Strafanstalt», in der die Insassen stark heteronom bestimmt werden, sind alle autonomen Bereiche von besonderem Wert. Dies führt hier letztlich dazu, dass auch die Probanden sich intensiver mit den MitarbeiterInnen, mit denen sie innerhalb des Projekts KOST interagieren, auseinanderzusetzen beginnen. Innerhalb dieser Interaktionen ringen sie um Mit-

kontrolle der Bedingungen der Heroinabgabe und versuchen, das Angebot, das ihnen die Strafanstalt macht, optimal zu nutzen.

Zusammenfassend ist die stattfindende gegenseitige Verzahnung und
Interdependenz im Verhältnis von Strafanstalt und Probanden gekennzeichnet durch:

– die eingegangenen gegenseitigen Verpflichtungen und Abhängigkeiten
– die gesteigerte gegenseitige Involvierung
– das gewachsene Engagement der Strafanstalt für die Probanden
– die intensivierten Interaktionen innerhalb der Organisation

Die Strafanstalt und die Probanden haben sich durch den Entscheid der
Durchführung bzw. der Teilnahme am Projekt KOST darauf eingelassen,
sich intensiv miteinander auseinanderzusetzen: die Probanden mit dem
vorrangigen Ziel, dass sie mit Opiaten versorgt werden; die Strafanstalt
auf der Suche nach einer adäquaten Form, bei opiatabhängigen Insassen
ihre Zielsetzungen besser zu erreichen. Es wird daher im Versuchsverlauf
von besonderem Interesse sein, zu beobachten, wie sich dieses Verhältnis
entwickelt und welche Rückschlüsse dies auf die Machbarkeit der kontrollierten Opiatabgabe im Strafvollzug zulässt.

Zusammenfassung

Seit Januar 1994 finden in der Schweiz – sich stützend auf das bundesrätliche Massnahmenpaket zur Verminderung der Drogenprobleme vom 20.
Februar 1991 – wissenschaftliche Versuche für die ärztliche Verschreibung von Betäubungsmitteln an Opiatabhängige statt. Innerhalb eines
erweiterten Versuchsplans bildet die kontrollierte Opiatabgabe im Strafvollzug ein Teilprojekt. Aufgrund der spezifischen Rahmenbedingungen
im Strafvollzug beziehen sich die Forschungsfragen einerseits auf Aspekte der Organisation und Durchführung und andererseits auf Aspekte
der Versuchsteilnehmer. Beide Aspekte werden abschliessend reflektiert
bezüglich der generellen Machbarkeit der Opiatabgabe im Strafvollzug.

Die Evaluation wird in Form einer Fallstudie durchgeführt. Bei der Datenerhebung und –auswertung werden innerhalb einer qualitativen Vorgehensweise multimethodische Ansätze verwendet.

Die Strafanstalt Solothurn Oberschöngrün praktiziert einen halboffenen Strafvollzug mit insgesamt männlichen 75 Insassen. Der Versuch wurde im September 1995 mit drei Probanden aufgenommen. Bis Ende März 1996 nahmen, bei acht verfügbaren Plätzen, sieben Probanden am Versuch teil. Nach anfänglichen Anpassungsschwierigkeiten lief der Versuch ohne grössere Komplikationen ab. Erste Ergebnisse der qualitativen Analyse zeigen auf, welche versuchsspezifischen Interdependenzen sich zwischen Strafanstalt und Probanden bilden.

Literatur

Friedrichs J, Dehm G, Giegler H, Schäfer K, Wurm W (1979) Resozialisierungsziele und Organisationsstruktur. Teilnehmende Beobachtung in einer Strafanstalt. Kriminologisches Journal 3:204

Hron A (1982) Interview. In: Huber GL, Mandl H (Hg), Verbale Daten. Beltz, Weinheim, Basel

Kette G (1991) Haft. Eine sozialpsychologische Analyse. Hogrefe Göttingen

Klär (1985/87) Organisationsentwicklung in einem sozialtherapeutischen Modellversuch der Jugendstrafanstalt Plötzensee. Magisterarbeit. Philosophische Fakultät der Albert–Ludwigs–Universität, Freiburg i. Br.

Lamnek S (1993) Qualitative Sozialforschung. Methoden und Techniken Bd 2. Beltz, Psychologie Verlags Union, Weinheim

Leehr D (1988) Opfer oder Täter. Angemessene Hilfe für inhaftierte Drogenabhängige. In: Brakhoff J, Drogenarbeit im Justizvollzug. Lambertug V, Freiburg i.B.

Mayring PH (1985) Qualitative Inhaltsanalyse. In: Jüttemann G (Hrsg), Qualitative Sozialforschung in der Psychologie. Weinheim

Mayring Ph (1990) Einführung in die qualitative Sozialforschung. Psychologie Verlags Union, München

Molitor A (1989) Rollenkonflikte des Personals im Strafvollzug. Eine organisationspsychologische Untersuchung. C.F. Müller Juristischer Verlag, Heidelberg

Schaefer Ch, Fäh P, Weibel U, Probst F (1995) Feinkonzept für die Strafanstalt Kanton Solothurn. KOST: Kontrollierte Opiatabgabe im Strafvollzug. Strafanstalt Solothurn, Projektunterlage, unpubliziert

Strauss AL, Corbin J (1990) Basics of Qualitative Research: Grounded Theory Procedures und Techniques. Sage Publications, Inc, Newbury Park, Ca

Strauss AL (1991) Grundlagen qualitativer Sozialforschung: Datenanalyse und Theoriebildung in der empirischen und soziologischen Forschung. Fink, München

U.S. General Accounting Office (1990) Case Study Evaluations. Transfer Paper 10.1.9, Gaithersburg M.D.

Wenzel C (1979) Organisationsstruktur und Behandlungsauftrag im Strafvollzug. Darstellung und Analyse am Beispiel der Teilanstalt IV der Justizvollzugsanstalt Berlin Tegel. Minerva–Publikation, München

Do prisons need special health policies and programmes?

Timothy W. Harding

1 Introduction

Prison medicine has a strange identity, stranded in a no-man's land between two major social systems, that of health delivery and that of criminal justice.

The uncomfortable and marginal status of the discipline is not the result of choices or orientations of prison health care staff themselves. It is due to pressures created by criminal justice policy, and especially prisons policy, and decades of neglect by the «health establishment»: Ministries of Health, medical associations, faculties of medicine regarded prisons as extra–territorial, as far as health care was concerned. Until the AIDS epidemic, the World Health Organisation had devoted not one single activity, consultation or study to the prison environment. Until ten years ago, major medical journals almost never carried articles about health or medical care in prisons.

Statistics from the French penitentiary authorities on mortality and morbidity exist since 1828. In 19th century France, mortality rates in prisons varied from 40 to 400 per 1'000 prisoners/year, depending on whether deaths were due mainly to the almost continuous presence of tuberculosis or to additional factors such as cholera epidemics. Prison administrators soon demonstrated that adequate food, preventing overcrowding and basic hygiene could reduce mortality dramatically. However, for the first half of this century, most large prisons continued to have special units for tuberculous prisoners – the «mouroirs» of French penitentiaries.

How have advances in medical care and preventive medicine been applied to the prison environment? This paper starts with a critical appraisal of the identity of the prison physician. It then outlines the failure to analyse the dangers created by the association of multiple risk factors both in the incoming population of prisoners and in the environment itself. The great public health disaster of the U.S. prison system is analysed (in many ways the disaster had been predicted by Jessica Mitford in her book with its tragically ironic title «Kind and Usual Punishment» published in 1971). This disaster is enormous in scale, affecting nearly 1,5 million detainees. Concentrating on this one striking example is, of course, an arbitrary choice but reminds us of the scale of health problems that can be created within prisons and allows a number of conclusions to be drawn. For example, the availability of sensible and authoritative sets of recommendations has little effect in the face of criminal justice policy dictated by other interests. The U.S. example is then compared with other settings and, in particular, Europe. A number of factors suggest that a similar disaster could be avoided in Europe provided that pragmatic and courageous policies are pursued which correspond to public health principles. It is argued that human rights law and enforcement mechanisms can play a significant role in influencing positively health policy in prisons.

The paper closes in suggesting that prison medicine might be a false and misleading concept. Places of detention present such a degree of diversity in terms of population, length of stay, regimen and factors affecting health that «prison medicine» could usefully be subdivided into a number of component parts: health care for marginal groups; health provision in situations of rupture; combating environments conducive to transmission of air born diseases; psychiatric care under conditions of security, etc. Prison medicine should wither away and be replaced by the pervasive presence of appropriate elements of public health, preventive measures and health care delivery.

2 The strange identity of prison medicine: an orphan of two systems

Physicians and nurses working in prison medical services have an unusual professional identity. Within prisons they are often seen by prison personnel and administrations as foreign bodies, creating rather than solving problems, suspect in their motives in an environment dominated by values of discipline, security and repression. Prisoners themselves usually perceive health personnel as part of the system with at best divided loyalties between the medical needs of inmates and institutional needs for order and smooth running. At worst they are experienced as traitors to the Hippocratic tradition of medical ethics, denying basic health needs, refusing to make independent medical assessments, for example after violent incidents, accepting the administration's vetos on preventive measures, such as access to condoms, and remaining silent about the risks to health created by overcrowding, poor ventilation and inadequate care. The medical profession views prison doctors as a strange category of outsiders working in hidden places where the relationships between delinquency, deviance, marginality and ill health are complex and troubling (Lancet, 1991).

Health administrations have largely ignored the needs of prisons and have been more than willing to leave the thorny problems of health in prisons to prison administrations. Medical schools, professional associations and scientific journals have until recently paid scant attention to prison health. As a result prison medicine has developed largely as a marginal and poorly defined discipline (Harding, 1991).

The professional identity of prison doctors is characterised by the particularities of health problems in detention and by the impact of the criminal justice system. They encounter extraordinary patients, in terms of notoriety, public condemnation and punishment. They deal with automutilation, body pack syndrome, swallowing of strange objects, prolonged voluntary fasting (or «hunger striking») or prisoners refusing medical care. But in concentrating on the extraordinariness of the prison environment and such unusual problems, the prison doctor often fails to assess the epidemiological realities of overall health status, that is to say the morbidity and mortality of the prison population. Prison doctors also tend to see health problems as existing within the closed environment and to underestimate the amount of flow of health problems into and out of prisons. Prisons are part of the community, both in terms of the dynamics and spread of transmissible diseases but also in terms of institutional care for marginal and deprived populations.

3 The ingredients of disaster

In 1974, the medical director of the U.S. Bureau of prisons, responsible for health care provision in all U.S. federal prisons, spoke at the Annual Meeting of the Medical Society of the State of New York on «Problems of Health Care Delivery in Penal Institutions» (Brutsche, 1975). He spoke of the «great frustration» in attempting to deliver health care and of how the «attitude and behaviour of a very large segment of an inmate population tends to militate against a satisfactory interface between the offender and the health services delivery system». Prisoners have «already demonstrated a difficulty with integrity, impulsive and devious behaviour and a variable disregard for society, its members and its rules of contact». Thus, according to Dr. Brutsche, prisoner patients tend to seek medical attention for «secondary gain»: to pass the time of day with other inmates or staff, to avoid work or other undesirable activity, to seek various advantages by the fabrication or exaggeration of complaints, to seek tranquillising medication to sell to other inmates, to thieve drugs or other hospital items, to harass health services staff, to prepare an escape plot. Prisoners, Dr. Brutsche laments, manipulate prescribed treatment to distort the expected result and falsify their objective medical signs. The picture painted by Dr. Brutsche is clear: prisoners knowingly and deviously distort the doctor–patient relationship; health care staff spend most of their time «ferreting out real health problems»; communication between staff and prisoners breaks down; few health services staff remain to work under such conditions. The word «frustration» or «frustrating» occurs ten times in Dr. Brutsche's text. However, what is frustrating in his analysis of health care delivery in penal institutions is the complete absence of any reference to actual health problems in prisons.

At roughly the same time Novick (1977) provided good epidemiological data on the health status of prisoners entering New York state prisons. Despite the fact that the prison population is made up largely of young adults, Novick found strikingly high prevalence rates of infectious diseases and a wide variety of morbidity from non–communicable diseases. Only 40% of prisoners were found to be in good health. The most frequently occurring problem at entry was substance abuse and dependence (41% to illicit drugs and 18% to alcohol) – other significant health problems identified were recent trauma, eye abnormalities, dermatological disorders and serious dental problems. 13% of the sample suffered from an active psychiatric disorder. Other, more general observations about health status were a poor nutritional state and a lack of information about preventive care. A comparison of Brutsche's lament with Novick's epidemiological data leads directly to the conclusion that health care in U.S. prisons in the 1970s was inadequate and unresponsive to health needs of prisoners. The frustration experienced by prison doctors, including the most senior administrators, as being a product of devious, manipulating and antisocial prisoner/patients was in fact a product of their own failure to see the public health realities, the need for appropriate preventive care and to be responsive to the whole range of health problems. Prison health care was based on the notion of a «sick call» integrated into the daily routine of prison life, much as in the army. In this context, it is hardly surprising that in 1976, the U.S. Supreme Court delivered a seminal decision in the case of *Estelle v. Gamble*. The Court held that «the deliberate indifference to the serious medical needs of prisoners» constitutes «unnecessary and wanton infliction of pain» and therefore violates the Eighth Amendment of the U.S. Constitution. This important decision has often been said to create a substantive «right to treatment» for prisoners in the U.S.A. However it should be noted that the decision was clearly limited. The court indicated, for example, that «inadvertent failure to provide adequate medical care» or «negligent... diagnosis or treatment [of] a medical condition» would not constitute such a violation.

By the end of the decade of the 1970s, the situation in the U.S. was characterised by the triad of:

1) inappropriate health care provision for prisoners and failure to recognise the realities of health problems,

2) an epidemiological profile of morbidity corresponding to the health status of the urban poor, marginal populations and to the growing extent of substance abuse in these populations;

3) legal intervention recognising that authorities are not permitted to disregard the health needs of inmates but failing to define effective means of redress.

4 The unfolding of the public health disaster in U.S. prisons

Within a few years, the AIDS pandemic was to expose in a dramatic and tragic manner the structural weaknesses and management failures of health care provision in U.S. prisons. Ted Hammett's successive studies demonstrated the failure of U.S. prisons at local, state and federal levels to respond to the challenge of the AIDS epidemic. The high prevalence of HIV infection reflects, of course, the high proportion of intravenous drug users in the prison population (Hammet, 1992).

Thus, a major public health problem was effectively created by a series of political, legislative and administrative decisions: the U.S. National Commission on AIDS (1991) has stated succinctly: «By choosing mass imprisonment as the federal and state governments' response to the use of drugs, we have created a *de facto* policy of incarcerating more and more individuals with HIV infection».

The American College of Physicians went further in its position paper published in the Annals of Internal Medicine in 1992: they pointed out that the prison population in the U.S.A. had doubled in a decade; most inmates are male, young, poor, and from minority groups; the problems were rapidly being exacerbated by the National Drug Control Strategy, also known as the War on Drugs which started in 1989. The paper concluded that:

1) the national policy on drug control must be reconsidered;

2) prison health care budgets should reflect the growing mental and physical health needs of the inmate population – providing integrated care to treat substance abuse and associated conditions: HIV infection, hepatitis B and also responding to the needs of female inmates and mentally ill inmates;

3) prison health care must be recognised as an integral part of the public health sector;

4) prison facilities must implement and maintain standards of «minimally adequate health care delivery systems»;

5) health care delivery evolve from the present «reactive» sick call system into a «proactive» system that emphasises screening, early disease detection and treatment, health promotion, and disease prevention.

These are worthy and wise conclusions and could be widely applied both within and without the U.S.A. Unfortunately, the position paper came too late and had almost no political impact.

The most recent and alarming development in U.S. prisons is the emergence of tuberculosis as a major and widespread problem and, in particular, multi–drug resistant forms (MDRTB). The incidence of T.B. among New York State prisoners rose fivefold in the decade 1980–90 to 134 per 100'000 (Glaser et al, 1992) while outbreaks of MDRTB were reported in New York (Valvay et al, 1991) and then in California (Centre for Disease Control, 1993). By 1995, the U.S. Department of Justice acknowledged the extent of the tuberculosis epidemic in U.S. prisons and the need for widespread preventive measures both for inmates and for staff. In a report commissioned by the authorities Wilcock et al (1995) conclude: «The resurgence of tuberculosis in the United States, the occurrence of several major outbreaks of TB in prisons, and the concentration in prisons and jails of individuals at high risk for TB suggest the need for treatment and control measures at all phases of the system – from pretrial release to incarceration to parole ... This (prison) population at relatively high risk for TB ... tends to be poor and includes disproportionate numbers of racial and ethnic minorities, recent immigrants from high risk countries, injection drug users and individuals infected with HIV. In general, this population is characterised by poor access to health care».

Larry Gostin in a thorough review of the public health, legal and societal implications of the «resurgent tuberculosis epidemic in the era of AIDS» (Gostin, 1995) devotes a substantial portion of his study to prisons. His conclusions are even more alarming than those published under official auspices. «If a person were to set out to design facilities that efficiently transmit airborne diseases, then that person might well emulate the physical conditions found in congregate settings in America such as ... correctional facilities. ... residents live, eat, and sleep in small enclosed spaces; beds are inches or feet apart; buildings are dark and poorly ventilated. Moreover, the residents ... are impoverished, malnourished and overrepresented in populations that have disproportionately high rates of communicable diseases ... and have significantly impeded access to health care services». At the time Gostin prepared his study, 1.12 million persons were resident in correctional facilities, well over 400 persons per 100'000 population. Present policy on drug use, on tighter immigration controls and on crime in general means that the rate will rise to over 500 persons per 100'000 population and nearly 1.5 million persons over the coming years. 10–25% of people in correctional facilities are infected with tuberculosis – the incidence of active pulmonary infection is about 10 times that in the general population.

The prison TB epidemic is closely associated with the HIV/AIDS epidemic, but affects many prisoners and staff who are not HIV infected. The inadequate housing, with gross overcrowding and poor ventilation, are pressuring prison authorities to apply energetic control measures, screening for TB infection, isolation, compulsory treatment regimens and return of non–compliant parolees to prison. There is also an additional and renewed pressure to carry out systematic and obligatory screening for HIV infection. In this respect, the measures taken in the U.S. prison systems at local, state and federal levels in response to the HIV/AIDS epidemic can be summarised as follows:

(a) compulsory HIV antibody testing on entry and during detention in about 25% of systems;

(b) special housing (segregation) for HIV infected prisoners in about 40% of systems;

(c) restricted access for HIV infected prisoners to work and leisure activities in about 80% of systems;

(d) information on HIV transmission and prevention provided to prisoners and staff in about 80% of systems;

(e) early release for prisoners with advanced AIDS in about 15% of systems;

(f) access to condoms in less than 5% of systems;

(g) access to disinfectant for needles and syringes in less than 1% of systems.

This is a telling indictment of the failure of internationally approved recommendations to have a significant impact at national level: the conclusions of the two WHO consultations HIV/AIDS in prison (WHO, 1993) are almost entirely ignored.

A further damaging element to health in U.S. prisons is their use for custodial care of the seriously mentally ill. «Quietly but steadily, jails and prisons are replacing public mental hospitals as the primary purveyors of public psychiatric services for individuals with serious mental illnesses in the United States» (Torrey, 1995). Torrey estimates (conservatively) that there are nearly 170'000 people with major, active psychiatric illnesses (schizophrenia, manic–depressive disorder, organic psychosis) in U.S. prisons. These individuals are subject to abuse and physical assaults and rarely receive any effective treatment. This is a consequence of de–institutionalisation of mentally ill – «the largest failed social experiment in twentieth–century America».

I have dwelt in some length and, I hope, not unfairly on the situation of health care provision in U.S. prisons because it provides a historical perspective of the making of a health disaster which should have been predictable and preventable. It is largely a government–made disaster, with the health authorities and the medical profession as bemused and passive bystanders. The excellence of the recommendations in the report on the *Crisis in Correctional Health Care* (1992) is matched only by its lack of significant impact.

5 Is the U.S. experience predictive of disaster elsewhere?

It is more difficult to analyse the diverse and sometimes rapidly evolving situation in other countries. But the U.S. situation has great relevance for many other parts of the world. The prevalence of tuberculosis is increasing rapidly in Asian and African prison populations and is by no means always associated with HIV infection. Coninx and his colleagues from the medical division of the International Committee of the Red Cross have described the tuberculosis problem in the prisons of the former Soviet republics in the Caucasus and Central Asia: they point out that successful interventions are possible but require careful planning and adequate resources (Coninx et al, 1995). HIV infection and AIDS are major problems in prisons of Thailand and Brazil, where «preventive» policies are similar to those adopted in the U.S. and equally ineffective and inappropriate. The prisons in the great lakes region of Africa provide the most extreme examples of the combination of overcrowding, malnutrition, high rates of tuberculosis and mortality rates which, expressed in terms of one week, exceed those in most other countries expressed in terms of one year.

The seriously mentally ill frequently end up in police stations and prisons of many countries. In India, an investigation ordered by the Supreme Court revealed that in many Indian States, the Courts ordered the mentally ill to be confined in prison, even when they had committed no offence. Tens of thousands of mentally ill men and women were found to be detained for periods sometimes over 10 years, with no adequate mental health care.

Australia is grappling with a similar set of problems as in U.S. prisons with varied responses by State authorities. However, good epidemiological research has been carried out, including on the spread of bloodborne viruses (Crofts et al, 1995) and on hepatitis C prevalence. Public health oriented policies are more widely adopted and the prison population has not increased in such a dramatic fashion. The State of Victoria is one of the best and largest scale examples of health authorities taking over responsibility for health in prisons: prevention, health promotion, screening, health care provision, substance abuse, psychiatric care.

6 The situation in Europe: is guarded optimism justified?

In Europe, many of the ingredients of the U.S. situation are present: prison populations are rising, tuberculosis incidence is increasing. In at least one country (Spain) multi–drug resistant tuberculosis is a major problem in prisons. Many psychotic patients end up in prison after committing minor offences (Gunn and Maden, 1994). About 30% of prisoners in Europe were illicit drug users prior to imprisonment and drug use is widespread within prison. Overcrowding and inadequate accommodation are major problems in Italy, Spain, France, United Kingdom, Belgium and most East and Central European countries. Some of the highest rates of HIV prevalence have been recorded in European countries: Spain (28% in 1987; 20% in 1992); Italy (17%) (Harding, 1987). In the Republic of Ireland 17% of all known cases of HIV infection were reported among prisoners in Dublin's main prison (168 known cases). An outbreak of HIV infection clearly related to sharing of injection equipment has been documented in a Scottish prison (Taylor et al, 1995).

However, despite these alarming indicators, there are good reasons to believe that a public health disaster on the scale of the U.S. can be avoided in European prisons, provided that adequate policies are adopted, strengthened and carried out rapidly, energetically and with sufficient resources.

What are the factors which justify some guarded optimism?

(a) *Prison populations*, although rising, do not seem likely to rise to U.S. levels. Overall, among the members of the Council of Europe (but excluding the newest member, Russia) rates of detention are well under 1/3 of that recorded in the U.S. There is also considerable variation in detention rates. Most governments, with the possible exception of the United Kingdom and Poland, seem intent on avoiding penal policies, especially in the area of drug control, which will lead to further rapid rises in prison population.

(b) The *basis in human rights* law for adequate health care is stronger and more actively enforced than the *Estelle v. Gamble* decision in the U.S. The European Commission of Human Rights has clearly established that failure to provide adequate health care to a prisoner would constitute «inhuman and degrading treatment» and thus violate article 3 of the European Convention of Human Rights. In a series of decisions involving Switzerland (the Bonnechaux case 1979), France (the De Varga Hirsch case, 1983) and Italy (the Chartier case 1982 and the Patanye case 1986) the need to provide «appropriate health care» has been spelled out.

The work of the European Committee for the Prevention of Torture and Inhuman or Degrading Treatment or Punishment (CPT) has further strengthened the human rights approach to health care in European prisons. The CPT, through its visits to prisons and other places of detention, has identified health care as one of the priorities in ensuring the rights of prisoners. The CPT in its Third General Report (Council of Europe, 1993) devoted a chapter to health care services, providing a de facto set of guidelines. The essential elements are strikingly similar to the recommendations of the American College of Physicians, but come from an official intergovernmental committee. These are the elements: access to a doctor with the direct support of a fully equipped hospital service; equivalence of care to that available in the community; respect of principles of confidentiality and patient's consent to treatment; adequate preventive care; and the need for professional medical independence (Bertrand and Harding, 1993).

At the end of the first cycle of periodic visits, the overall impression is that governments are responsive to the CPT's recommendations in the field of prison health care and are prepared to make more resources available. The CPT's work has certained promoted awareness of the relationship between detaining drug users, problems of HIV/AIDS and tuberculosis as well as recognition of the extent of psychiatric problems. The published reports demonstrate many inadequacies in health care provision but also a willingness by the authorities to make substantive reforms (Harding and Bertrand, 1995).

(c) The response of prison authorities in European countries to the *HIV/AIDS epidemic* has been notably more constructive and denotes a significantly greater adherence to WHO directives (WHO 1987, 1993), backed up by the Council of Europe's own recommendation (Council of Europe, 1993). Thus, when the policies of 32 prison systems in 17 European countries were reviewed, it was found that: information was provided to prisoners in 30/32 systems (92%); compulsory HIV testing in only 2/32 systems (6%), segregation in special units in 4/32 systems (12%), restricted access to workshops 7/32 systems (19%) and early release procedures for prisoners with AIDS in nearly all countries (30/32 systems, 92%). Condoms were available in 24/32 systems (75%) and disinfectant for needles and syringes in 9/32 systems (28%) (Schaller and Harding, 1995). The differences with the situation in the U.S. are striking.

(d) In Europe, *health authorities at national* or regional levels (e.g. Länder in Germany, Cantons in Switzerland, autonomous regions elsewhere) *have become more directly involved in prison health*. This may be through a joint venture financed both by the health and the criminal justice sectors, according the model already cited of the Australian state of Victoria. This is the case for example in the Spanish region of Catalonia. Other countries have well resourced health facilities within the prison system, e.g. in Holland and Finland. But the most striking examples are the countries in which health care has come entirely under the responsibility of the health ministry, as in Norway since 1993 and France since 1994 (psychiatric services were already a health ministry activity for over ten years previously). In the Canton of Geneva, prison health care has developed within the health and social services department over the past 30 years as an independent, university based service. Thus there appears to be a growing realisation by the health authorities of the importance of health care in prisons and the need for policy formulation, training and, above all, resources. Of course there are major deficiencies and even sordid scandals. The descriptions of Brixton prison's F Wing (CPT report on visit to UK, 1991) or of the Lantin prison psychiatric annexe (CPT report on visit to Belgium 1993) make harrowing reading; while news about women giving birth while shackled to their beds (in Marseilles, 1991 and in London, 1995) raised storms of indignation. More generally, primary health care in most prisons remains unsatisfactory, characterised by lack of intimacy and confidentiality, inadequate response to immediate symptoms, overprescribing of tranquillisers because of lack of alternatives, and failure to provide any preventive measures. Nevertheless, the authorities no longer seem blind to these deficiencies and there are signs that politically and socially, prisons are no longer seen as a hidden world where ordinary criteria of health and hygiene can be ignored.

7 Re–thinking prison medicine

Police stations, remand prisons, jails, lock–ups, penitentiaries, half–way hostels, closed juvenile centres... the semantics of places of detention shows great variety. In human rights law, all such places can be con-ceptualised in a singular fashion – deprivation of liberty (in terms of article 5 of the European Convention of Human Rights). Yet, the diversity of places of detention has important implications for health; «prison» is a loose concept for which a single epidemiological model simply does not exist. The length of stay, the age, sex and social pa-rameters of inmates, the detention environment itself: all these factors and many others vary so that the health profile of places of detention can have almost infinite forms. A detention centre for asylum seekers at a major international airport; a closed hostel for disturbed, delin-quent adolescents; a remand prison with over 2'500 inmates serving a large urban area with up to 100 entries and discharges or transfers every day; a maximum security prison with 200 inmates in solitary confinement, most of whom have been in the same facility for at least five years; a detoxification centre for remand prisoners with heroin dependence; a large penitentiary hospital; a medium security penitentiary with a 300 acre dairy farm; a sociotherapy unit for prisoners with severe personality disorders. All these can be called «prisons» but their dissimilarities in terms of morbidity and health needs are greater than their similarities.

That is why we should re–analyse the prison experience in public health terms and re–design health interventions in relation to needs.

This also helps us to understand that the results of the study by Clavel et al (1987) showing decreased mortality among male prisoners was misleading, since it was limited to the population of condemned prisoners serving sentences in penitentiaries. The study therefore overlooked excess morbidity and mortality in remand prisoners and, in particular, the risk of suicide. The study was also carried out at an usual time of falling population of condemned prisoners and in the years before the AIDS epidemic.

First of all prisons should be seen as an integral part of the community, with a constant flow in both directions. The dynamic relationship between inside and outside means that walls are not epidemiological barriers. Inadequate health care in prisons will have adverse consequences on public health in the community, for example in terms of transmissible diseases and the consequences of severe, untreated mental disorders. A telling illustration of an effect of the prison environment following release is the striking excess in mortality during the early weeks of liberty, persisting for up to a year: four times the age and sex adjusted rate in the general population (Harding–Pink, 1990).

The health problems of marginal groups, of poverty, of foreigners, of drug users and alcohol dependent persons tend to congregate in prisons. But the same problems are seen in other institutions, on the streets and in health facilities serving the indigent or poor, underprivileged areas.

The same individuals pass from prisons to municipal health clinics, to hostels for the homeless and back to prison. Health delivery services should follow the clients and provide linkages, continuous care and social support across the institutional barriers.

Psychiatric care should be integrated between the community, mental health facilities and prisons. This would avoid the phenomenon of passing the «difficult patient» down through a spiral of decreasingly resourced services to end up in a remand prison.

Thus we can understand why two studies on diabetes control in prison come to completely different conclusions. «Good diabetic metabolic control is usual in prison» (MacFarlane et al, 1992); or, alternatively that inadequate access to care gives rise to frequent diabetic ketoacidosis (Keller et al, 1993). The first observation was of men serving sentences in a large prison in Britain, the second was in jail «holding» facilities in New York city. The authors of the second paper point out that inadequate care in the early weeks of detention frequently gives rise to acute exacerbation of asthma, hypertension, seizure disorders, as well as creating risks of infections disease transmission. What is needed, therefore is one model of medical care adapted to social discontinuity, rupture and crisis and a completely different model for long term institutional care. Neither need be specific to the prison environment.

«Prison medicine» as an identity in public health terms also risks to condone or normalise unacceptable aspects of the prison environment. Prison medicine might be seen as necessary to counteract the harmful effects of overcrowding, lack of ventilation, promiscuity, lack of physical activity and violence. Gostin describes such unhealthy environments in «congregate settings» ranging from nursing homes, mental institutions, homeless shelters, Indian reservations, migrant worker camps etc. Grossly unhealthy environments are unacceptable in any of these situations and no medical speciality should be identified with them. There should be concerted pressure by all public health bodies to proscribe all such environments; indeed they should be construed as a form of inhuman and degrading treatment and therefore as collective forms of human rights violation.

It is therefore proposed that *prison medicine* may be a dangerous and counterproductive concept. There should be a coalition of health delivery services operating in prisons, with a blend of interventions adapted to needs. Continuity of care, by the same carers, should be ensured on entry and on discharge, if possible. In this context, prisoners should not been seen as passive recipients of care, but actively involved in health promotion and preventive measures, with a right of access to appropriate forms of care available in the community.

References

American College of Physicians (1992): The crisis in correctional health care. *Annals of Internal Medicine*, 117:71–77.

Bertrand D. and Harding T.W. (1993): European guidelines on health care in prisons. *Lancet*, 342:253–254.

Brutsche R.L. (1975): Problems of health care delivery in penal institutions. *New York State Journal of Medicine*, 75:1082–1084.

Centre for Disease Control (1993): Probable transmission of a multi–drug resistant tuberculosis in a correctional facility – California. *Morbidity and Mortality Weekly Report*, 48:50.

Clavel F., Benhamou S. and Flamant R. (1987): Decreased mortality among male prisoners. *Lancet*, 2:1012–1014.

Coninx R., Eshaya–Chauvin B. and Reyes H. (1995): Tuberculosis in prisons. *Lancet*, 346:1238–1239.

Council of Europe (1993a): Recommendation N° R(93)6 of the Council of Ministers of Member States. Strasbourg: Council of Europe.

Council of Europe (1993b) CPT: third annual general report. Chapter 3. Strasbourg: Council of Europe.

Crofts N., Stewart T., Hearne P., Xin YP., Breschkin AM. and Locarini SA. (1995): Spread of bloodborne viruses among Australian prison entrants. *British Medical Journal*, 310:285–288.

Editorial (1991): Health care for prisoners: implications of Kalk's refusal. *Lancet*, 337:647–648.

Glaser J.B., Aboujaoude J.K. and Greifinger R. (1992): Tuberculin skin test conversion among HIV–infected prison inmates. *Journal of AIDS*, 5:430–431.

Gostin L.O. (1995): The resurgent tuberculosis epidemic in the era of AIDS. *Maryland Law Review*, 64:1–131.

Gunn J., Maden A. and Swinon M. (1991): Treatment needs of prisoners with psychiatric disorders. *British Medical Journal*, 303:338–341.

Hammet T.M. (1994): HIV/AIDS in correctional facilities: 1992 update. National Institute of Justice, Washington D.C.

Harding T.W. (1991): Can prison medicine be ethical? *Journal of the Irish Colleges of Physicians and Surgeons.* 20:262–265.

Harding T.W. (1987): AIDS in prison. *Lancet*, ii:1260–1663.

Harding T.W. and Bertrand D. (1995): Preventing human rights violations in places of detention: a European initiative. *Health and Human Rights*. 1:234–242.

Harding–Pink D. (1990): Mortality following release from prison. *Medicine, Science and the Law*. 30:12–16.

Keller A.S., Link N., Bickell N.A., Mitchell H.C., Kalet A.L. and Schwartz M.D. (1993): Diabetic ketoacidosis in prisoners without access to insulin. *Journal of the American Medical Association*. 269:619–621

MacFarlane I.A., Gill G.V., Masson E. and Pucker N.H. (1992): Diabetes in prison: can good diabetic care be achieved? *British Medical Journal*. 304:152–155.

Mitford J. (1974): *Kind and usual punishment*. Vintage Books: New York.

Novick L.F. (1977): Health status of the New York prison population. *Medical Care*, 15:205–216.

Schaller S. and Harding T.W. (1995): La prévention du SIDA dans les prisons. *Médecine Sociale et Préventive*. 40:298–301.

Taylor A., Goldberg D., Emslie J. (1995): Outbreak of HIV infection in a Scottish prison. *British Medical Journal*. 310:289–292.

Torrey E.F. (1995): Jails and prisons – America's new mental hospitals. *American Journal of Public Health*. 85:1611–1613.

U.S. National Commission on AIDS (1991): *HIV disease in correctional facilities*. Washington.

U.S. Supreme Court (1976): *Estelle v. Gamble*. 429 U.S. 97.

Valvay SE, Richards SB, Kovacovich J, Greifinger RB, Crawford JT, Dooley SW. (1994): Outbreak of multi–drug–resistant tuberculosis in a New York state prison, 1991. *American Journal of Epidemiology*. 140:113–122.

Wilcock K., Hammett T.M., and Parent D.G. (1995): *Controlling tuberculosis in community corrections*. National Institute of Justice, Washington D.C.

WHO (1993): World Health Organization guidelines on HIV infection and AIDS in prison. Geneva: WHO.

Ban on drugs or health care:
The dilemma of a repressive drug policy

Monika Frommel

**Legal–theoretical reflections on the limits of prohibitive norms
which do not have any impact on the external behaviour
but on internal attitudes**

I   Is it possible to criminalize the consumption of certain «illegal» drugs within the framework of a liberal criminal law?

The concept of liberal criminal law – conceived in the 19th century – is a normative construction, which has never been put into practice completely. The debate in the 20th century shows that this concept can be reconstructed under the conditions of a democratic society (Holmes, 1993; Honneth, 1993). Liberal criminal law distinguishes between *external behaviour* which may be *detrimental to society* and *moral convictions* which ought to be free and unregulated.

Habits of consumption are a matter concerning the individual's personality and thus the identity of those who are subject to norms. They are thus closely associated to the spheres of moral conviction and therefore should not, according to the liberal model, be impeded by criminal law. However, since subcultural conduct leads to types of external behaviour which a prescriptive legislator may define as criminal offences, we find ourselves entangled in the contradictions of this controversial issue of liberal criminal law.

I do not think we should try to attain an unambiguous dissection of conduct (at an abstract level) into external behaviour and internal attitudes. Each criminal ban is morally charged and therefore not exclusive to external behaviour.

However, the concept of liberal law intends to deregulate habits of consumption whereas the preventive approach – the mainstream in the 20th century – tends to regulate habits of consumption, inasmuch as public interests exist – e. g. to restrict drug use because it is a prerequiste to drug dealing.

At the end of the 20th century we know that prevention by criminalization has failed. The consequence is a lack of legitimation: Neither the concept of liberal law nor the preventive approach can legitimate the criminalization of drug use or dealing with harmless drugs like cannabis.

We have to distinguish between drug use and dealing with drugs. Dealing affects external social spheres. It can be penalised following the logic of the concept of liberal criminal law if the drugs are capable to cause health damage (this is why, in the case of cannabis, conservatives claims – contrafactually to this drug's nature – that the health risk «can not be dismissed»).

Of course the dealer's customers act at their own risk, endangering themselves. However, with regard to a state's controlling policy, it can be justified to define – albeit vaguely – a legal concept of «public health» (as a public interest).

Matters are different when we turn to «consumption». Without doubt, «consumption» is associated with private conduct, subcultural orientation and therefore with the identity of the individual in question. In the case of drug addiction it may have consequences for the mental and physical health of the individual. However, following the logic of liberal criminal law, putting oneself at risk, whether through one's own fault or not, ought to be tolerated. Alternatively, the goals of public health policy apply.

Repressive drug policy follows the illiberal preventive approach which gained acceptance in the late sixties; it aimed at the «drug culture» of the anti authoritarian generation. The illiberal preventive approach explicitly addresses «dangerous» attitudes and tries to «combat» a criminogenic environment. This approach ignores the ineffectiveness of prevention by criminalization. In my opinion, the days of this strategy are over. As far as drug use is concerned, hard-liners are beating retreat. The principle of priority of care over punishment becomes more and more accepted.

Drug addiction is a condition which may once have been brought about through one's own fault. However, this «fault» might be seen as deriving from a kind of error of conduct. In fact, drug addiction reduces or even eliminates any guilt associated to a deed. Even if they wanted to, addicts are not able to comply with the ban of drug consumption at the present time nor in the near future without the fear of relapse. Any strict dogma of abstinence is therefore utterly unrealistic. Someone who has created a certain internal reality through drug abuse behaves at a psychologically deterministic level and is at best able to change this situation on a long term basis.

A ban of drug consumption by repression results logically and practically in a vicious circle. The strict enforcement of norms leads to pauperisation and degeneration of the overt drug scene. It renders any help impossible and leads to a dilemma. In the following, therefore, we will take a closer look at the goal of penal institutions for drug addicted prisoners.

II How can institutions involved in criminal prosecution and programmes against drug abuse deal professionally with the contradictions inherent in the criminal law of narcotics?

As long as the prevention of criminal offences constitutes a goal of the penal system, and as long as illegal consumption of drugs remains a criminal offence to be «fought», it is difficult to offer help at the same time. Prisoners are prevented from tackling their problem openly, if they consider their drug addiction as a problem at all. Thus their right to obtain medical care cannot be implemented. This kind of repressive approach which also focuses on drug use will in any case lead to irreconcilable contradictions within penal institutions at both, logical and practical levels.

Even outside prison walls, criminal policy on the one hand and the demands of an adequate medical care on the other lead to severe problems. In fact, the criminal law on narcotics does allow physicians to treat their drug addicted patients. It is not the criminal law on narcotics but its enforcement regulations which cause problems for physicians in Germany. These low–level–regulations limit the number of recognised treatments without any consideration of their individual effectiveness. Reluctant physicians are dismissed of their legal obligation to provide medical treatment, and those physicians who offer substitution therapy are burdened with financial risks. This is because health insurance companies, referring to these regulations and the corresponding guidelines, refund the actual costs only in part or not at all. In all other situations, physicians are obliged to provide adequate assistance whenever an illness occurs. In the case of drug addicts, however, it is up to them whether to help or not. If they consider a treatment to be reasonable, such as substitution, they are entirely free to apply it according to the principle which grants them freedom in choosing therapy. Typically, however, the costs incurred won't be refunded, due to the restrictive guideline, imposed by a panel of physicians and health insurance companies, which permit the refusal of finance for this kind of therapy. Legislation thus tolerates that the association of health insurance companies stipulates far more restrictive conditions than those required by the criminal law on narcotics. It is therefore not so much the criminal law itself, but rather a delegated body of rules, an executive law, that causes the desolate situation of programmes against drug abuse in Germany. In a democracy based on the separation of powers, this is an intolerable situation leading to a serious impediment of programmes against drug abuse even outside penal institutions.

Within the penal system in Germany it is not so much the question of costs that has rendered adequate medical care impossible, but a far too crude theory of how to prevent relapse. It is therefore necessary to analyse the prevention of recidivism as a goal of imprisonment.

In its 1994 judicial ruling on cannabis, the Bundesverfassungsgericht, the German Federal Constitutional Court, exempted the purchase of small amounts of drugs for individual consumption from strict punishability (applying to all drugs, not just cannabis) and laid down the approach of diversion.

Disregarding the dispute as to what constitutes a small amount, an unusual principle arises from this ruling: a ban without the pursuit of a conviction. Delegitimizing drug use, it relaxes the requirement of compulsory prosecution.

Those favouring legalisation or at least decriminalisation of cannabis and other harmless drugs were disappointed with this half–hearted ruling. But those who are willing and able to deal with compromises may cleverly develop this formula further. Applied to penal institutions it means that, as far as drug addicts are concerned, not prevention of relapse is the main goal of imprisonment, and that the sanctioning of drug consumption in prisons has therefore to be questioned. If outside prison walls drug consumption is not prosecuted but only delegitimized as «banned», it can not be the task of prison authorities to prevent the consumption of drugs as such at all costs.

At present prison staff follow the dogma of abstinence and the goal of strict prevention of relapse in drug use. They regularly examine urine specimens and check cells for any utensils of drug consumption (including sterile syringes). Indications of illegal drug consumption leads to direct and indirect sanctions within the institution. Privileges, for instance, as provided for by the law of prison administration, may be denied. Whether unwittingly or deliberately, this practice follows the dogma of abstinence as formulated in 1968. Since this dogma, however, turns out to be utterly unrealistic for drug addicts, it will neither avoid relapse nor guarantee basic medical care for the prisoners.

In view of the ruling of the German Federal Constitutional Court of 1994 these practices can not be accepted any longer. Considering the newly established principle that criminal prosecution authorities are obliged to abandon any prosecution of drug use (the non–presentation of charges), we can try to transfer this to an interpretation of the goal of imprisonment. It follows that drug use by itself does not warrant any sanctions (and therefore no checking either). Drug consumption has to be tolerated – within limits – provided no drug dealing is taking place at the same time. (Consumption, however, does not substantiate any justifiable suspicion of dealing.). I am fully aware that reality in prison is entirely different from my interpretation. But I think it is not unrealistic to estab-lish this principle in the future.

Modifying the goal of imprisonment in this way facilitates the next step: the assessment of relapse prevention versus programmes against drug abuse. The dilemma turns into a problem which may be handled pragmatically. It becomes possible to deal openly with the problem of drug addiction in prisons and to develop and provide relevant help schemes. The requirement for adequate medical care is given by the principles of the welfare state as well as by the specific responsibility for prisoners. Accordingly prisoners have a de jure enforceable right to basic medical care.

Not abstinence but *controlled drug use* must be the goal guiding prison administration. This means that all prisons must at least offer vari-ous substitution therapies, since otherwise it remains impossible for the addict to become used to regulated drug usage. In the long term, one might aim at allowing the prescription of heroin and other illegal hard drugs under controlled conditions, in order to offer drug addicts a realistic perspective of improving their situation. At any rate, the current situation in prisons is in conflict with the principles for prison administration law as developed here applying the constitutional court ruling mentioned above.

III Result

The dilemma can be solved. It's irreconcilable when the goal of imprisonment is stretched beyond the breaking point, i.e. when the strict prevention of relapse is made a requirement even in minor cases (as such drug use is defined by the criminal law of narcotics according to the German Federal Constitutional Court). As soon, however, as the dogma of abstinence is abandoned, because it is inconsistent with the principles of the welfare state and the fundamental right of prisoners to basic medical care in prison, one gains the necessary scope of action. Although strict adherence to norms may be required contrafactually in society (symbolic prohibition), it can not be implemented. The goal of penal institutions, defined in compliance with the constitution, is therefore not the strict prevention of relapse but a step–by–step improvement of the prisoners' prognosis. Minor criminal offences such as the mere consumption of illegal drugs have to be tolerated. The dilemma must be solved in favour of improved programmes against drug abuse, considering that medical care is a fundamental right. The state, however, maintains an interest in the ban of drug consumption as an arbitrary goal of criminal policy which can be modified by legislation at any time.

IV Institutional Consequences

Behind prison walls people are burdened with two conflicting tasks. On the one hand, they are there to help the prisoner solve his or her problems. On the other hand, they are in charge of «law», «order» and the safety within the institution and are expected to enforce goals as defined by criminal policy. This latent contradiction turns into a manifest problem if one considers – I think, realistically – drug consumption as a prerequisite to drug dealing in high amounts, which in my solution can be sanctioned. One and the same person can not prevent drug dealing and at the same time react adequately to the problems of drug addicts. Therefore there is but one reasonable institutional consequence: the tasks have to be divided amongst different groups of staff.

Let us have a look at definite improvements. For example, the approach presented in this paper is compatible with the requirement for availability of disposable syringes and easy accessibility of them. This puts the staff to a severe test. It should only be considered once the medical service has handed out sterile syringes over a trial period and only if adequate substitution therapy is available. The prison staff too must follow the maxim «Learning by Doing».

But even before the learning by doing starts, typical basic conditions will have to be modified. The staff must be instructed by the superiors not to carry out any inspections aimed solely at establishing drug consumption. According to the view discussed here, urine analysis and inspections as they are carried out at present are not consistent with the penal goal. They contravene the principles of the welfare state to minimise negative consequences of imprisonment and to guarantee fundamental rights of the prisoners, and they are inadequate or disproportionate since they impede programmes adequate drug abuse without preventing drug consumption. Drug use as such must not be declared an offence against «order» or «safety» of the prison. Since programmes against drug abuse must be the primary concern, the conventional dogma of abstinence is not an adequate organising principle.

It is, of course, implicit in the logic of imprisonment that these principles and regulations can not be implemented without circumventions and only by degrees. For this reason, programmes against drug abuse ought to be left in the hands of the medical staff or the external programmes against drug abuse. In practice, this will lead to a larger number of external welfare workers and external physicians working in prisons.

References

Holmes, S. (1993): The Anatomy of Antiliberalism, Cambridge/Mass.: Harvard University Press.

Honneth, A.(1993) (Hrsg.): Kommunitarismus, Frankfurt/New York.

AIDS Prevention Strategies: An Overview

François Wasserfallen
Dina Zeegers Paget
Pierre G. Bauer[1]

1 Introduction

After more than 10 years of AIDS prevention activities, widely varying from one country to another, it is practically impossible to give a complete overview of what has been achieved. It is, however, certainly possible to learn from several examples, to see what has been successful and what has not and to understand the difficulties encountered by AIDS prevention efforts.

In this article, three AIDS prevention programmes are examined in detail. These programmes have been selected as they are good examples of both the successes and difficulties encountered in the field of AIDS prevention. After a short presentation of the three programmes and their main results, the difficulties encountered in each of these programmes are discussed in section 5. Finally, in section 6, the lessons learned from these experiences are presented in the form of theses.

---

[1] The views expressed herein are solely those of the authors; they do not necessarily reflect any views the Swiss Federal Office of Public Health holds on the issues discussed.

2 The AIDS prevention strategy in Seattle: the media campaign[2]

The AIDS prevention strategy in Seattle is best described by its openness. The strategy includes a daring and original media campaign, which addresses subjects like sexually transmitted diseases, contraception, unwanted pregnancies, condoms and AIDS in a very open and humourous way. Examples of the messages are:

«4 out of 4 ... people prefer condoms over herpes!!!»
«condoms improved dramatically! Since your parents used them ... if they had sex, that is.»
«condoms. 250'000 cheaper! ... than the average child»

The primary target group of this campaign were the sexually active young adults aged 15-17 years. The campaign used several information channels and had three successive waves. The campaign has been very successful and 73.1% of the targeted audience reported exposure to this campaign (*see table 1*).

Table 1: Condom campaign Seattle 1995; Media Exposure Data [3]

Media channel	Exposure (%)
Radio spots	50.8
Poster	35.0
Busboard/Billboard	32.1
Exposure to any condom campaign media	73.1

[2] The information for this section was obtained with the help of Ann Downer, Programme Director, NW AIDS Education and Training Center, School of Medicine, Seattle. The authors would like to thank Ann Downer for her kind collaboration and assistance.
[3] Memorandum of the Seattle–King County Department of Public Health dated 26 January 1996, communicated to us by Ann Downer, Programme Director, NW AIDS Education and Training Center, School of Medicine, Seattle.

The open-minded nature of the AIDS prevention strategy in Seattle goes beyond the media campaign. Seattle is one of the few cities in the United States where legal needle exchange projects exist: there are six sites in Seattle and between 80'000-85'000 syringes are exchanged every month. Furthermore, the AIDS prevention strategy in Seattle includes HIV education in prison, even though it is not implemented in a consistent manner.

3 The AIDS prevention strategy in Thailand: the 100% condom programme[4]

It is well known that Thailand is a country where HIV prevalence is very high: the estimated infections in Thailand have risen tenfold since early 1990 (Merson 1994). The main way of HIV transmission in Thailand are heterosexual relationships with commercial sex workers. In order to hinder this way of transmission, the government launched an ambitious condom promotion programme, specifically aimed at commercial sex workers and their clients. The programme combines an authoritarian attitude towards brothel holders with a large information campaign. The brothel owners are forced to have all their employees use condoms in a systematic and consistent manner. This rule is controlled by an active contact tracing programme for those found with sexually transmitted diseases, which allows to identify the ,guilty' brothel. The campaign used mass media to reach potential clients of commercial sex workers and to promote a general awareness towards the AIDS epidemic.

The results of this programme are impressive:

- more than 150 million condoms were distributed by the government in the last couple of years (*see table 2*)
- the number of sexually transmitted diseases reported has decreased significantly (*see table 3*)

---

[4] This section is based mainly on Rojanapithayakorn & Hanenberg, 1996.

- the protective behaviour reported has increased significantly: 92% of all commercial sex acts occurred with a condom (*see table 4*)

Table 2: Condom distribution in Thailand

Year	Government	Commercial
1990	6'508'064	8'636'184
1991	42'086'576	33'665'416
1992	55'850'876	32'160'144
1993	46'500'192	25'056'284

Table 3: Number of male cases of sexually transmitted diseases at State clinics in Thailand

Year	Syphilis	Gonorrhea
1987	11'855	109'289
1989	11'487	84'675
1991	5'714	50'344
1994	30'279	10'211

Table 4: Commercial sex acts with condom use (%)

Month/Year	percentage of sexual acts with condoms used
before 1989	~ 14
June 1990	56
June 1991	74
June 1992	90
June 1993	94
June 1994	92

4 The AIDS prevention strategy in Switzerland: the Hindelbank experience

The Swiss AIDS prevention strategy is based on a three-level intervention method:[5]

- First, interventions for the general population. The most famous intervention at this level is the Stop AIDS campaign, which has started as early as 1987.[6] The main themes of this campaign are condom use, fidelity and solidarity. At the same time, the campaign also includes themes for specific minority groups, such as needle distribution for injecting drug users.
- Second, interventions for specific population groups, such as: commercial sex workers, injecting drug users, men having sex with men and prisoners.
- Third, interventions at an individual level. This level includes counselling, therapies, etc.

The successful pilot project of AIDS prevention including needle distribution in the prison for women of Hindelbank falls under the second level of intervention. As this project has already been discussed elsewhere, only the main results are listed here:

- no increase in drug use was observed;
- the health of prisoners improved;
- a significant decline in needle sharing could be observed;
- no new cases of HIV or hepatitis infection were seen; and
- syringes were not used as weapons.

[5] See for more detailed information: Swiss Federal Office of Public Health 1993
[6] See for more detailed information: Kocher 1993.

5 Difficulties encountered by AIDS prevention strategies

At first sight, the examples presented above seem very successful and seem to suggest that our fight against AIDS is nearly over. This, however, is too optimistic and naive. Looking at these examples again, this time in more detail, taking into account the environment, there are several difficulties and insufficiencies to be noted.

If the AIDS prevention strategy in Seattle is so successful, why was it not implemented on a national level? Why didn't it at least influence the national AIDS policy in the United States? This aspect of local effectiveness of AIDS prevention strategies in the United States can be explained by two factors:

1. there has been no national leadership in the United States concerning AIDS; and
2. there has been no openness at a national level in the United States.

There have been several efforts in the United States to set up a national strategy of AIDS prevention. However, as Francis (1994) describes: «There has been an absence of solid national leadership, and respected panels continually use phrases like 'woefully inadequate' or 'absence of leadership' to describe America's response to AIDS.»

At the same time, the national level, especially the Congress and its politicians, have shown no openness at all. This can be illustrated with two examples, which show the large influence of politicians and thereby the limits of the influence of public health experts.

The first and one of the best examples of this political influence is the question of sexual education in schools, which has been subject to a large debate on moral acceptability of such programmes. The famous federal «Helms» amendment forbids funding AIDS prevention programmes that «promote, or encourage, directly, homosexual or heterosexual activity or drug abuse» (Gostin 1989). At a State level, AIDS prevention in schools ranges from restrictive programmes, stressing abstinence, to facilitating programmes. This mainly conservative approach to sexual education in schools is all the more worrying as several projects and studies have shown that «providing explicit HIV prevention programs prior to the time that adolescents are sexually active can have greater impact than programs initiated after the initiation of sexual activity» (Choi et al 1994).

The second example concerns the question of needle exchange programmes. Bayer (1995) clearly states that: «The Congress, which easily gets caught up in crusades involving drug use, has since 1988 passed seven laws prohibiting the use of federal funds for needle exchange.»

The 100% condom programme in Thailand also seems a successful programme. However, the success of this programme is rather fragile, as the cultural and social environment which pushes girls into prostitution is not addressed. If a programme only focuses on prevention of HIV transmission, its success will be limited. In order to reach a situation where HIV transmission is prevented in the long term, programmes should also address the problematic situation of women and an improvement of social and structural aspects should be included (e.g. reach a better level of education for women in general). Without these social and structural changes, the incidence of HIV may rise again dramatically, if, for instance, the coercive measures accompanying the 100% condom programme are not rigorously implemented.

The Hindelbank pilot project in Switzerland was the third example used to describe successful AIDS prevention programmes. Even though the Hindelbank project had a positive outcome, a more detailed look provides some difficulties with AIDS prevention in prisons. Firstly, AIDS prevention in this field is hampered by its political nature as well as by the different levels of competence: the federal government is responsible for prevention of epidemics, the cantonal authorities are responsible for the prison management. This means that openness in one prison (in this case Hindelbank) does not automatically mean that a successful prevention programme is implemented in all prisons. Furthermore, as stated by Mertens et al (1994): «it is commonly found that the outcomes of health interventions are more favourable during trials than during routine practice.»

Summarizing the difficulties encountered in these three examples of successful AIDS prevention strategies, we can see the following:

- a lack of a uniform and national strategy, including unclear competences on all levels, will hamper locally achieved successes;
- a lack of openness towards new ideas, new ways of reaching and informing specific population groups will hamper AIDS prevention strategies;
- a large political influence will hamper AIDS prevention as in this case public health experts have a smaller influence on the setting up of AIDS prevention strategies;
- the continuity and valorization of pilot and local projects should be ensured in order to have a successful overall AIDS prevention strategy; and
- AIDS prevention programmes should not only focus on the individual, but should combine behavioural interventions with enabling approaches, that is create a supportive social and structural environment for the individuals (Tawil et al 1995).

6   Lessons learned for the future

The situation we face today is challenging as two new developments will influence the future of AIDS prevention strategies. The first is the fact that AIDS is slowly loosing its special status and will be integrated more and more in general public health strategies. This integration should mean that we integrate what we have learned from AIDS prevention in a public health strategy that has to be re–focused . The integration of the AIDS experience in general public health strategies should improve the latter and should also improve general enabling approaches. The second development are the decreasing funds available for AIDS prevention. This means that new priorities concerning activities and target groups have to be discussed. The choice of new priorities should be made carefully, as it is not adviseable just to favour target groups but to forget to maintain solidarity by and interest of the general population, as this could very easily lead to discrimination and isolation of seropositive people and patients with AIDS.

The challenge of today and tomorrow can only be faced if we learn from experiences made in the past. Based on the examples presented in this paper, several theses can be formulated:

1. We have seen that AIDS prevention programmes can be successful and are able to dramatically reduce unsafe behaviour. Despite of these results, resistance against AIDS prevention may continue. It is thus the task of public health experts to overcome political controversy and to convince politicians that the benefits of such programmes are greater than the assumed harms.

2. AIDS prevention does not stand by itself. Various factors, including the social and cultural environment, are playing a role in the success or failure of AIDS prevention, and should, therefore, be taken into account. Enabling approaches should be the logical complement of AIDS prevention programmes.

3. Successful pilot projects, aimed at a specific population group in a specific part of the country, are not enough to ensure AIDS prevention for the future. The valorization, the reproduction and adaptation of such projects on a wider scale are decisive for the future of AIDS prevention.

4. AIDS prevention should be a continuous effort: having one project for two years or one media campaign is not enough to sensibilize people to change their behaviour. Information and education have to be a continuous effort in order to achieve behaviour modification.

5. AIDS prevention should not focus only on one level of intervention (e.g. the general population), but should simultaneously intervene on

all levels (general, target-groups, individual) in order to ensure effectiveness.

6. There should be a certain coherence in AIDS prevention, that is, there should be one clear message, one clear strategy instead of contradictory strategies. If it is decided that needle distribution is possible in a country, this should also include the possibility of needle distribution in prison.

7. AIDS prevention should not be seen as isolated from other health-related problems, but should be integrated in general health promotion. Young adults, for instance, are more concerned by unwanted pregnancies and sexually transmitted diseases than by AIDS alone.

8. Finally, feed-back on experiences made is essential and should be given at all levels. This includes a certain openness about the successes or failures of experiences made, so that lessons can be learned. This paper can be seen as a sort of feed-back, and we hope that it will help others in their AIDS prevention efforts.

References

Bayer, R. Politics, social science and HIV prevention in the United States: looking backward, looking forward. In: Friedrich, D., Heckmann, W. (eds.). *AIDS in Europe – the behavioural aspect.* Sigma; Berlin, 1995.

Choi, K.–H., Coates, T. J. Prevention of HIV infection. *AIDS, 8*(10): 1371–1389, 1994.

Francis, D. P. Towards a comprehensive HIV prevention program for the CDC and the Nation. *JAMA, 268*(11): 1444–1447, 1994.

Gostin, L.O. Public health strategies for confronting AIDS: legislative and regulatory policy in the United States. *JAMA, 261*(11):1621–1630, 1989.

Kocher, K. Stop AIDS: the stop AIDS–story 1987–1992. Bern; Swiss AIDS Foundation/SFOPH, 1993.

Merson, M. H. Global status of the HIV/AIDS epidemic and the response. Presentation given at the Xth International Conference on AIDS in Yokohama on the 8th of August 1994.

Mertens, T., et al. Prevention indicators for evaluating the progress of national AIDS programmes. *AIDS, 8*(10): 1359–1369, 1994.

Rojanapithayakorn, W., Hanenberg, R. The 100% condom program in Thailand. *AIDS, 10*(1): 1–7, 1996.

Swiss Federal Office of Public Health/National AIDS Commission. HIV–Prevention in Switzerland: targets, strategies, interventions. Bern; SFOPH/NAC, 1993.

Tawil, O., Verster, A., O'Reilly, K. R. Enabling approaches for HIV/ AIDS prevention: can we modify the environment and minimize the risk? *AIDS, 9*(12): 1299–1306, 1995.

Drug prevention outside and inside of prison walls

Ambros Uchtenhagen

Efforts to reduce the consumption of intoxicating and habit–forming substances in the prison milieu are not well documented and even less evaluated. This is in contrast with the increased risk for drug consumption in prison inmates, due to a number of factors, such as an increased demand for psychoactive medication and the over–representation of drug use in delinquent populations.

This paper therefore tries to summarize first what can be learned from drug prevention in general, focusing then on prevention issues relevant for the prison milieu and pointing out some perspectives for future activities.

Some essentials of drug prevention

Prevention has to start by designing its objectives. Objectives may be

- to prevent first use,
- to reduce the number of users,
- to reduce the overall extent of use,
- to prevent abuse and dependance,
- to minimalize harmful use.

Prevention strategies have to be selected according to objectives.

Main strategies are

- Information through mass campaigns or targeting specific groups;
- Education (health education, social skills training);
- Counselling (e.g. for individuals at risk, for parents and peers);
- Facilitating alternative activities (sports, adventures, community activities)
- Improving quality of life at the workplace or concerning living conditions in general;
- Supply control (by interdiction, taxation, product control or privileged access).

As an example, *table 1* shows the range of strategies which can be used if the objective is to reduce the number of users.

The various strategies are based on **theoretical assumptions** about the nature and predictors of human behaviour. The range of theories includes the following:

Rationalistic theories:	People act according to their knowledge.
Utilitarian theories:	People act in order to maximize gains.
Learning theories:	People act according to previous experience.
Voluntaristic theories:	People act according to drives and needs.
Deterministic theories:	People act according to preestablished patterns of behaviour (genetically or socially determined).

Drug prevention, aiming at preventing specific types of behaviour or aiming at behaviour change, has to be explicit concerning its theoretical bases. Some of the theoretical models used in drug prevention are

- Communication/persuasion model (Mc Guire);
- Social learning model (Bandura);
- Life skills approach (Botvin);
- Healthy lifestyles approach (WHO);
- Functional equivalents to drug use (Silbereisen).

Table 1: Strategies to reduce the number of users

1. reduce the number of new users	1.1 reduce availability	1.1.1 prohibition 1.1.2 legal restrictions 1.1.3 taxation
	1.2 increase risk awareness	1.2.1 information 1.2.2 education 1.2.3 image modelling
	1.3 resistance to social pressure	1.3.1 coping abilities training 1.3.2 self-help network
	1.4 alternatives to drug use	1.4.1 job opportunities 1.4.2 leisure activities 1.4.3 social networking
2. postpone start of first use	1.1 – 1.4 2.2 keep up social control	 2.2.1 parent education 2.2.2 neighbourhood groups 2.2.3 counselling school teachers and students
3. increase the number of ex-users	3.1 drug-free treatment 3.2 substitution treatment 3.3 compulsory treatment 3.4 incarceration 3.5 opportunities for ageing-out	

Recent drug prevention activities in Europe

Two recent publications document prevention activities in a number of European countries, based on specific surveys.

The first is a catalog of 75 projects from 14 countries, published in 1993 in Spain (Zaccagnini et al 1993). *Table 2* summarizes the nature of information provided and the main topics covered in the projects.

The second publication is a report made on behalf of the council of Europe and published in 1994 (Negreiros 1994). It focuses on «the most significant prevention projects» in the participating countries (defined as being innovative, and/or evaluated, and/or successful). The questionnaire during the pilot phase asked for information about scope and objectives, target groups, planning, implementation, evaluation, and funding. In total, 47 projects from 18 countries are included (*table 3*).

Both overviews demonstrate that most activities focus on information and education for non–users, especially in schools. A minority only is directed towards behaviour change. Half of the activities are performed on the national level, practically none on the international level. Monitoring and process evaluation is more frequent than impact assessment.

Table 2: Catalogo de programmas de prevencion de la drogaddiccion, Valencia 1993 (Zaccagnini, Colom & Santacreu)

Analysis of 75 projects from 14 countries	
Information on	*Main topics*
- name of the project	- information on drugs (n=69)
- responsible agency	- education (n=62)
- date / place	- attitude change (n=25)
- scope	- sensibilisation (n=23)
- theoretical background	- behaviour change (n=3)
- hypothesis	- quality of life (n=2)
- target population	- change of milieu (n=1)
- methodology (instruments,	- school (n=38)
variables, procedure)	- general population (n=14)
- results	- prison (n=1)
- evaluation	- social mediators (n=26)
- publications	- parents (n=16)
	- teachers (n=14)

Table 3: Drug misuse prevention projects in Europe

Objectives «specific»	– information about drugs (20.6 %) – change of attitudes and behaviours towards drugs (22.3 %)	
«non–specific»	– increase the acquisition of life skills (19.4 %)	
Combination of «specific» and «non–specific» objectives in 74 %		
Scope	– drug–specific projects:	n = 33
	– non drug–specific projects:	n = 27
	large overlap!	
Drug–specific projects focus mostly on legal and illegal substances (70 %). Focus on legal drugs only: 6 %		
Target population direct targets	– problem drug users – addicts – groups at risk – non–users (n=32) – general population, youth – school children	
indirect targets	– parents – teachers – local community – specific social groups – sports associations	

Table 3 (continued)

Implementation	– local level (33 %)
	– regional level (18 %)
	– national level (49 %)
	– international level (–)
Conceptualisation by	– practitioners (43 %)
	– practitioners and scientists (38 %)
	– scientists (6 %)
Implementation agency	– specialized prevention service (55 %)
	– teachers (25 %)
	– peers (15 %)
	– parents (8.5 %)
	– health care system (2.2 %)
Evaluation	– monitoring or process evaluation n = 32
	– impact assessment n = 19
	– process and outcome evaluation n = 14
	– no evaluation n = 3

Evaluation of prevention activities

Controlled studies from the USA have demonstrated a number of essential findings concerning drug education and health education. Controlled studies on primary prevention in schools in European countries have been collected recently by a working group of a COST–project (Cost A-6 «Evaluation of action against drug abuse in Europe»), confirming some of the main findings.

Table 4: Primary prevention in schools

Successful programs focus on	– life skills – social competence – resistance to peer influence – assertiveness and self–esteem
caveats	– effects on attitudes and knowledge do not correlate with changes in consumption behaviour – short programs (less than 10 sessions) are ineffective – positive effects last max 2 years (booster sessions are needed) – programs reach mostly persons at low risk
Netherlands	– «mild horror approach» and factual approach are followed by increased use – «Personal approach» has the least negative effects – shift from «increasing knowledge» to «changing attitudes and behaviour»
Ireland	– attitudes and beliefs improved – no effects on consumption of alcohol, cigarettes, illegal drugs
Greece	– decreased intentions to use drugs – increased consumption of alcohol, cigarettes, illegal drugs
Finland	– positive change in attitudes and fantasies about drugs – no effect on (low) consumption

From the USA, we also have evaluation studies on secondary prevention for high–risk–groups in community settings. The findings may be summarised as follows:

- short term effects: decreased use, less dangerous drugs and use patterns
- mid/long–term effects unknown
- involvement of parents: better results

pport and training in social relationships are better than
on

- inadequate strategies to reach those who are most in need
- negative stigmatising effects for those labelled «high–risk»

The main messages are that knowledge and attitudes can be improved, but with unreliable impact on consumption behaviour, that short programs are not effective and that most programs cannot adequately reach those who are most in need of them.

Such findings confirmed the necessity to implement drug prevention programs in prisons with their high–risk–populations.

Drug prevention issues and strategies in prisons

There are at least five categories of populations at risk:

- inmates who never used drugs: exposure to first use while in prison,
- inmates who are non–dependent users: risk for developing dependence during stay in prison,
- inmates dependent on drugs: risk for secondary infections, increased management problems,
- inmates who are ex–users: relapse risk while in prison,
- inmates with specific delinquency risks: relapse after discharge (e.g. driving while intoxicated).

Drug prevention therefore has manyfold issues to cope with, such as the following:

- to prevent non–users to start drug use while in prison,
- to prevent development of abuse and dependence in persons with controlled use,
- to prevent relapse during stay in prison,
- to prevent relapse in specific delinquency after release from prison.

A range of strategies therefore has to be considered, some of which are applicable for all groups at risk, whereas others are more specific. Selected drug prevention strategies in prison are:

- Supply control (checks);
- User control (urinanalysis, separating heavy users from non–users);
- Medical and psychosocial assessment and counselling/care for users and non–users;
- User treatment and management (drug–free, substitution, psychopharmacological, medical and psychosocial care, family/spouse counselling);
- Hygienic measures to avoid harmful use (bleach, syringe exchange);
- Nutrition (alternative source of satisfaction and wellbeing);
- Options for leisure activities and initiatives;
- Information/education (drug specific and/or general health education);
- Pharmacological relapse prevention (Antabus, Naltrexone);
- Psychosocial relapse prevention (release preparation, after–care).

A starting point for identifying risk groups and appropriate strategies in a given prison are detailed knowledge on user categories, psychiatric and health status of inmates, length of stay in prison and milieus where inmates are returning to. A good example is the implementation of specialised teams in French prisons (antenne–toxicomanie) which have to screen all inmates at entry for drug use and social problems, which provide anonymised data, centrally evaluated at INSERM, and which offer individual care, sports, and cultural activities, prepare release and establish contacts with agencies outside prisons for follow up. Some of the data are especially relevant for prevention purposes: such as the high rates of drug using partners (25%), drug using siblings (22%) and children at risk (27%) (Facy 1989-1990).

Evaluation of drug prevention in prisons

Evaluation studies are extremely rare. The above mentioned overviews include only 1 project from Sweden, and a comprehensive literature search resulted in two recent US–studies.

The national Swedish Board of Health and Welfare implemented in 1987 a one–month information course on drug related issues for staff working in correctional centres. This course used an information package developed for staff working with drunken drivers. Evaluation is planned, results are not available yet.

A study by Peyrot et al (1994), using a cognitive–behavioural approach, evidenced an improvement of knowledge and attitudes, but no behaviour change. Barbor (1993) evaluated a program aiming at interactive coping skills for high–risk situations (relapse prevention) and found on short–term improved self–efficacy, but on mid–term no difference to a control group regarding consumption and self–efficacy.

There are a number of reasons which account for the scarcity of systematic drug prevention programs in prisons and especially for an evaluation of those. Nevertheless, with increasing numbers of drug users in prisons, with increased health and management problems and with high relapse rates documented, additional efforts are asked for.

Perspectives for the future

Not knowing what strategies and programs are feasible and effective, well–designed pilot projects are recommended, including independent evaluation. In the preparation of projects, the results from drug education programs outside prison milieus and from other approaches have to be taken into account.

As a basis for more systematic implementation of drug prevention in prisons, a systematic collection of relevant information on inmates is essential. Available data are in favour of

- combined care and prevention projects for those who are already involved in drug use,
- a special focus on relapse prevention,
- adequate networking with after–care and agencies outside of prison,
- active participation by inmates, in order to improve projects and to improve compliance.

Literature

Barber, J.G.: An application of microcomputer technology to the drug education of prisoners. Journal of Alcohol & Drug Education 1993, 38(2) 14–22.

Facy, F.: Toxicomanes incarcérés vus dans les antennes–toxicomanie, enquète épidémiologique 1989–1990. Convention entre le ministère des affaires sociales, le ministère de la justice et l'institut national de la santé et de la recherche médicale.

Negreiros, J.: Drug misuse prevention projects in Europe. University of Porto (Portugal), P–PG (94) 25, Cooperation group to combat drug abuse and illicit trafficking in drugs (Pompidou Group), Council of Europe.

Peyrot, M. et al.: Shortterm substance abuse prevention in jail: A cognitive behavioral approach. Journal of Drug Education 1994, 24(1) 33–47.

World Health Organization: Programme on substance abuse. Guidelines for assessing alcohol and drug prevention programmes, WHO/PSA/91.4.

Zaccagnini, J.L. et al.: Catalogo de programas de prevencion de la drogadiccion. Promolibro Valencia 1993.

AIDS, drugs and risk behaviour in prison: State of the art

Kate Dolan

Introduction

Prisons are probably one of the most difficult settings for the study of HIV risk behaviour and transmission. This chapter will mainly cover prisons in developed countries as most of the literature comes from these countries. However, there has been an indication from at least one developing country, Thailand, that prisons can play a crucial role in the transmission of HIV (Wright et al 1994). After considering the characteristics of prisoners and ethics of prison research, this chapter reviews the literature on the prevalence of HIV infection among prisoners, the proportion of prisoners who are drug injectors and the risk behaviours in which prisoners engage such as drug injecting, tattooing and sexual activity. In order to improve our understanding of the likelihood of HIV infection in prison, the evidence of HIV transmission in prison is also reviewed and the notion of mixing, or the extent of intermingling of inmates that is integral to prison systems is considered.

Attributes of prisoners and prisons

Prisoners are failed risk takers. They are predominately males aged between 20 and 40 years and a group usually considered to be sexually very active. Most come from disadvantaged backgrounds and have low levels of education. Minority groups, such as blacks in the US and Aboriginals in Australia, are vastly overrepresented in prison populations. Alcohol (Wright, 1993) and drug (Dolan et al, 1995) problems are very common among prisoners worldwide. The prevalence of infections linked to drug injecting such as hepatitis B and C (Crofts et al, 1995) and sexually transmissible diseases (Cohen et al, 1992) are several times higher among prison entrants than among the general population. Female prisoners are generally more likely than male prisoners to report a history of drug injecting (35% vs 18%; Patel et al, 1990) and therefore to be infected with HIV (Vlahov et al, 1991).

Correctional facilities can be stressful, crowded and violent places where drug withdrawal is common (Turnbull & Stimson, 1994). Although imprisonment has been shown in some studies to reduce drug use (Shewan et al, 1994), inmates have reported injecting drugs (Taylor et al, 1995) and engaging in homosexual activities (Dolan, 1994) for the first time while incarcerated. These have been attributed to boredom and the single sex nature of correctional establishments.

The ethics of prison research

Research into special populations usually raises a number of ethical issues. Prisoners, having lost many basic civil rights, are a particularly vulnerable group. The World Health Organisation emphasised the importance of ethics committees in their guidelines for HIV research in prison: *independent examination by an ethical review committee should be carried out for all research procedures in prisons and ethical principles must be strictly observed. The results of such studies should be used to benefit prisoners* (WHO, 1993; p 2).

One major role of ethics committees is to ensure that potential respondents or subjects are not harmed by research. But ethics committees also have the potential to produce long term detrimental effects on the very populations they are trying to protect. The lack of prison data has made it difficult to argue a case for implementing HIV prevention in correctional facilities. It was reported in a study of HIV transmission in a US prison that, *prior ethic committee review precluded individual interviews for high risk histories* (Brewer et al, 1988; p 366). Consequently, the study was unable to determine whether HIV transmission occurred in prison or prior to prison and also it was impossible to obtain an appropriate denominator for the measurement of incidence, ie confining the population studied to those who reported engaging in risk behaviour in prison rather than the entire study sample. Inmates' knowledge, attitudes and behaviour were studied in Toronto in order to produce AIDS educational material. But the effectiveness of such material produced is likely to have been impaired as *permission to conduct (the) study was granted providing the behaviour questions did not inquire about sex and drug use in prison* (Toepell, 1992, p 39).

The WHO guidelines on HIV in prison recommend studies of risk behaviour to inform planning policies and intervention, but they stipulate that *prison administrations should not seek to influence the scientific aspects of such research procedures, their interpretation or their publication* (1993, p2). Collecting data on risk behaviours in prison is important because the absence of such data can be used to justify inaction. In the UK, for example, *Home Office Ministers have not been convinced that making condoms available for use in prison would be appropriate or helpful* (Groves, 1991). This suggests that the Ministers leave open the possibility that in the future they may be convinced of the appropriateness of providing condoms in prison. They have however, ruled out the possibility of syringe exchange *even though the [prison medical] service recognises that some inmates will gain access to injectable drugs and will share injecting equipment, needle exchange schemes in prison cannot be contemplated* (Groves, 1991).

Most prison authorities have had policies to test prison entrants for HIV infection (Harding & Schaller, 1992). Sometimes this has been on a mandatory basis even though voluntary testing can be just as accurate in determining HIV prevalence (Hoxie et al, 1990). However in a voluntary pilot HIV testing program among inmates in London, only 0.3% of the

54 percent who agreed to participate tested positive. This was probably an under estimate as another study found five percent of recently released prisoners were infected in 1990 (Turnbull et al, 1992). This low level of compliance may partly be a result of the restrictions imposed on infected inmates or inmates thought to be infected (Turnbull et al, 1993). Infected inmates are often segregated which precludes confidentiality of their HIV status (Harding & Schaller, 1992).

Duty of Care

The American AIDS Litigation Project examined the legal aspects of AIDS (Gostin, 1990). According to the Eighth Amendment in the US constitution, US prisoners are to be protected from cruel and unusual punishment. This is considered to include contracting communicable disease. Claims that compulsory screening and segregation are necessary to prevent HIV transmission in prison have been rejected by US courts on the grounds of insufficient evidence. But the necessity of providing AIDS education in prison has been recognised by US courts as failure to provide it can create distress (which is considered tantamount to cruel and unusual punishment).

Prevalence of HIV and AIDS

By 1995, over one million cases of AIDS had been reported to the World Health Organization (WHO, 1994). A comparison of estimated cumulative incidence and rates of HIV and AIDS per million of population in eight European countries, Australia and the USA appear in *table 1*. The USA, Spain, France and Italy have some of the highest rates of HIV infection – between 2,000 and 4,000 cases per million population.

HIV infection among inmates

HIV infection is more prevalent in prison populations than in the corresponding community because of the increased prevalence of HIV infection in injecting drug users (IDUs) and the high proportion of IDUs in prison populations (Harding, 1987). As early as 1988, about half of the inmates in Madrid prisons (Estebanez et al, 1988) and twenty percent of prisoners in New York City tested HIV positive (Truman et al, 1988). Within prison populations certain groups have higher levels. In 10 US correctional systems, infection levels were higher among women (15%) than men (8%), among younger women (5%) than younger men (2%) and among non caucasians (5%) than caucasians (3%) (Vlahov et al, 1991). It was estimated that in New York State prisons in 1988 there were 2,200 male and 200 female HIV positive entrants, making HIV the leading medical problem among inmates (Smith et al, 1991).

HIV surveillance has been the most common form of HIV research in prison (see *table 2*). HIV prevalence among prisoners has ranged from zero percent in Iowa, USA in 1986 (Glass et al, 1988) to 34 percent in Catalonia, Spain in 1989 (Martin et al, 1990). The high prevalence reported among Spanish prisoners reflects the high prevalence of HIV among IDUs and their considerable over–representation in the prison population.

Evidence of HIV transmission in prison

Demonstration of HIV transmission in prison has proven to be remarkably difficult. Of the seven published studies investigating HIV transmission in prison, six failed to prove conclusively that transmission had occurred in prison and all six concluded that such transmission was rare. However, these six studies sampled only long term prisoners. Paradoxically, this group is probably at lower risk of infection than short term prisoners because they reside in maximum security institutions where opportunities to associate, engage in risk activity and become infected are more restricted in comparison with inmates in lower security institutions.

The only study to conclusively demonstrate significant HIV transmission in prison setting (Taylor et al, 1995) was fortuitously prompted by several acute cases of hepatitis B infections. These infections, along

Table 1: Cumulative cases and rates of HIV and AIDS per million

Country	Cumulative HIV rate	HIV rate per million	Cumulative AIDS rate	AIDS rate per million
Sweden	3,246	373	976	112
Germany	31,979	394	11,250	139
Netherlands	8,874	584	3,025	199
UK	40,294	695	9,021	156
Australia	15,200	854	4,896	275
Switzerland	9,055	1,294	3,845	549
Italy	112,165	1,941	21,464	371
France	126,656	2,195	30,089	522
Spain	168,889	4,319	24,205	619
USA	1,050,000	4,065	400,418	1,550

Source: Feachem 1995

Table 2: HIV prevalence among inmates

Year	City	n	%	Reference
1986	Iowa	859	0	Glass 88
1988	Michigan	802	1	Patel 90
1987	Oregan	977	1.2	Andrus 89
1988	Wisconsin	1621	0.6	Hoxie 90
1987	Maryland	1488	7	Vlahov 89
1988	California	6179	3	Singleton 90
1985/89	Rhode Island	1239	12	Dixon 93
1991	Orange City	801	1.7	Gellert 93
1991	Edinburgh	375	4.5	Bird 92
1994	Glasgow	293	2.4	Gore 95
1993	London	584	0.3	PHLS 95
1987/88	Catalonia	631	34	Martin 90
1989	Alicante	682	30	Acedo 89

with two possible primary HIV infections, suggested surprisingly high levels of risk behaviours. (This study is described below as *Study 7*).

The most common methodology used to study HIV incidence in prison has been repeated mass screening of inmates, usually on entry and annual follow up. This method underestimates HIV incidence for several reasons. Prisons are dynamic institutions where the number of annual prison entrants and internal transfers is usually double and treble the daily census. With so many movements into, out of and around the prison system, annual cohort studies will overrepresent inmates with longer sentences who are less likely to become infected with HIV. Conversely, drug using offenders who are at most risk of infection in prison will be underrepresented in cohort studies as they tend to be held on remand (awaiting trial) or serve short sentences.

The next most common methodology is studies of inmates incarcerated for very lengthy periods. The extensive duration of imprisonment suggests that it was highly unlikely that the inmates could have acquired HIV infection prior to imprisonment and still be alive. However, the main shortcoming with these studies is that the denominator for the number infected is unknown and so rates of transmission cannot be estimated.

In the following section, evidence of HIV transmission in prison from reports and studies was considered in three ways. Evidence was considered first on the strength of methodology to demonstrate transmission; second, on the extent of transmission that may have occurred and third, on aspects of the study design which may have influenced the results.

Report 1
HIV infection among IDUs presenting for drug treatment in Bangkok rose from two percent in early February to 27 percent by early March in 1987 (Wright et al, 1994) and up to 43 percent in September 1988 (Choopanya, 1989). The dramatic increase closely followed an amnesty on the King's birthday when numerous prisoners were released. Substan-

tial HIV transmission in prison is believed to have been responsible for rapid dissemination of HIV (Wright et al, 1994).

This study was only suggestive of transmission having occurred in prison, but indicated that the extent can potentially be considerable.

Report 2

In New York, six HIV infected inmates were identified who had been incarcerated without interruption prior to infection becoming prevalent in their communities (Gaunay & Gido, 1986).

This evidence is only suggestive of HIV infection in prison and there was no indication of the extent of transmission as no denominator was provided.

Report 3

In Australia, one inmate was reported to have tested negative after six years in prison and then tested positive while incarcerated without interruption. Medical files confirmed his reports of severe symptoms consistent with primary HIV infection (Dolan et al, 1994).

This can be regarded as a definite case of HIV infection occurring in prison, but no indication of the extent of transmission can be made.

Study 1

HIV testing was offered to inmates who had been imprisoned in Maryland for at least 7 years in 1985. Of 137 (38%) inmates who accepted testing, two (1%) infected inmates were detected both of whom had been incarcerated for nine years. The unknown effect of selection bias was acknowledged by the authors (Centers for Disease Control, 1986).

The possibility that the inmates were infected prior to entering prison can not be excluded. The extent of reported transmission was very low, but the study sampled only long term prisoners and the extent of transmission may have been underestimated.

Study 2

In Florida, 87 of 556 prisoners (16%) who had been continuously incarcerated since 1977 had an HIV test result recorded in their prison medical files by 1991. A positive test result was recorded for 18 (21%) of these inmates. Eight of these (44%) were still without symptoms at the end of 1991, which suggests that HIV infection occurred in prison. The authors acknowledged that the evidence of prison transmission was presumptive, though strong. The authors suggested that a great deal of sexual activity was occurring in prison and recommended condom provision (Mutter et al, 1994).

The evidence of infection occurring in prison was strong but not beyond doubt. Again, the sample studied was long term prisoners who are probably at lower risk.

Study 3

One percent of 913 inmates in an American maximum security military prison tested HIV positive in 1983 (Kelley et al, 1986). Repeated testing of the 542 inmates who were still incarcerated at follow–up in 1985 found no cases of seroconversion (95% confidence interval 0% to 0.5%). These data represented 685 person years of incarceration. Data representing an additional 641 person years of follow–up were obtained by pairing 199 specimens collected in July 1985 with samples collected in May 1982, but again no new HTLV–III (HIV) infections were detected. This gave a combined annual seroconversion rate of 0.0% (95% CI 0.0 to 0.2%). Some segregation of HIV positive inmates occurred. However, 25 hepatitis B seroconverters were identified by pairing sera collected during the same period, giving an annual incidence of two percent for HBV.

No evidence of HIV transmission was detected in the above study. However, the only data presented on the sample suggested that this military sample was atypical of civilian prison populations. In the sample, 15 percent and 38 percent of inmates had drug and sex offences respectively. As these proportions in general prison population are normally reversed, it would be unwise to generalise to other prison systems. As previously indicated, inmates in maximum security institutions generally have very limited opportunities to associate with other inmates, engage in risk behaviour and to become infected with HIV. The policy of segregating HIV infected inmates may also have reduced the risk of HIV transmission. No information was provided on how the 913 inmates who were tested had been selected. The follow–up rate was low (59%) although the duration of follow–up was long (mean = 15 months; 542 inmates represented 685 person years of prison).

The two percent incidence for hepatitis B was high, but it was not possible to determine whether these transmissions occurred in prison. Also, no information was provided on the baseline prevalence of hepatitis B, risk behaviours or whether these inmates were segregated. Although no evidence of HIV transmission emerged, the extent to which generalisations can be made from a maximum security military prison to prisons with different security levels or with a civilian population is unclear.

Study 4
Seven percent of 422 prison entrants in Maryland were positive for HIV in 1985. Infected inmates were more likely to be non–violent offenders, committed in Baltimore City and be black. Repeated testing of 393 prisoners (representing 482 prison years) in 1987 detected two prisoners who had seroconverted in prison. They had been incarcerated for 69 and 146 days at baseline testing. HIV incidence was 0.41 percent per prison–year (Brewer et al, 1988).

Inmates who refused to participate or were missed in the follow up were significantly more likely to have been committed for a drug offence, be black, or have a sentence of less than 5 years. Furthermore, inmates who had been released prior to generating eligibility lists differed on most characteristics from those enrolled in the study. These characteristics were thought to be associated with shorter sentence lengths. The authors noted that *prior ethic committee review precluded individual interviews for high risk histories* (p 366, 1988).

Although the study demonstrated HIV transmission had occurred, it was unclear whether inmates had become infected before or during imprisonment. The study concluded that the extent of transmission was limited to two inmates. However, 83% of all prison entrants were excluded from the study and excluded inmates were similar to inmates who were infected at entry. The study sample underrepresented drug injectors who would be at far greater risk of HIV infection than other prisoners. This suggests that the study design may have resulted in transmission being underestimated. Nevertheless application of this incidence figure to the Maryland prison population indicates that 60 HIV infections occur annually (Hammett, 1993).

Study 5
All prison entrants and all current inmates in Nevada were tested for HIV in 1985. Two percent in each group were found to be positive. Repeated testing of 1,069 inmates nearing release detected three inmates who had seroconverted in prison. Those inmates had spent 130, 20 and 7 days in prison when they tested negative. The sample represented 1,207 person years of imprisonment and provided a seroconversion rate of one person per 604 prison years (0.2%). The authors concluded that the reported rates were maximum estimates of transmission and that HIV transmission among inmates in Nevada was rare (Horsburgh et al, 1990).

It was unclear whether the infections occurred in prison as inmates had only been incarcerated for a relatively short period before they tested negative. The extent of transmission was limited to three inmates becoming infected. However, inmates on short sentences were underrepresented and consequently incidence may also have been underrepresented.

Study 6
HIV prevalence among all prison entrants in Illinois was 3.3% in 1988 and 3.9% in 1989. Among inmates who had already served one year, 3.2% were positive in 1989. After one year, eight inmates who had tested negative at baseline had later tested positive. HIV incidence was 0.33%

(95% CI 0.14–0.64) among the 2390 susceptible inmates (Castro et al, 1991).

The evidence of transmission in prison was strong but infection could have still occurred prior to incarceration. The extent of transmission was higher than all other studies but was still low. The study relied on mass screening over a one year period which meant short term prisoners were missed.

Study 7

An investigation was prompted by several acute cases of hepatitis B infection and two primary HIV infections in a prison in Glasgow. Of 636 inmates at Glenochil Prison between 1 January and 30 June 1993, 378 inmates (59%) were still incarcerated when the investigation was launched. Among the 258 inmates who were not present, most (74%) had been transferred to another prison and the rest (26%) had been released. Of the 378 inmates still incarcerated, 60 percent accepted counselling. Uptake of counselling ranged from 43 percent to 84 percent in the 11 subunits in Glenochil prison. Many of those who declined counselling were believed to be injectors from a subunit of the prison where injecting was particularly prevalent. Of the 227 inmates counselled, one third (33%) had a history of injecting. Almost half (43%) of IDU prisoners admitted injecting in Glenochil prison. Of these 33 injectors, 29 were tested for HIV and 14 were positive (48%).

Although only 38 percent of drug injecting inmates were tested, there was a strong association between becoming infected and injecting in prison in early 1993 (p<0.01). Fifteen inmates who had injected in Glenochil tested negative but were still in the window period for HIV seroconversion at the time of the study.

Definitive evidence that HIV infection had occurred in prison was based on: early banding patterns on Western Blot tests, antigen results, HIV negative and positive test results, primary symptomatic HIV infection and dates of incarceration. Of the 14 infected inmates, definite evidence of HIV transmission in prison existed for eight of whom six had become infected in Glenochil prison while the possibility of infection in another prison could not be excluded for two others. Another six infections also possibly occurred in prison but infection occurring outside prison could not be excluded. All inmates infected in prison reported extended periods of sharing.

This study differed from previous studies in three ways: firstly, it comprised a methodical approach to an apparent outbreak; secondly, it used precise biological measures to provide irrefutable confirmation of behavioural data and thirdly, risk behaviour data were collected. It was unfortunate that the inmates who had been transferred to other prisons or released were not followed up. However, the official report speculated on the possible extent of the outbreak in Glenochil (Scottish Affairs Committee 1994) after discussions with prison medical officers and estimated that assuming untested inmates were as likely to be IDUs (and therefore become infected) as those who had been tested, then the total number of infected inmates would be between 22 and 43 inmates (compared with the eight detected cases). They also acknowledged that 258 inmates were missed because they were either transferred (74%) or released (26%) within the six month study period and that some of these may have been infected.

Other evidence

Two studies which employed mathematical modelling techniques estimated the potential for HIV to spread among prisoners. They concluded that approximately 62 prisoners become infected in England (Medley et al, 1992) and 38 in New South Wales (Dolan et al, 1994) each year.

Risk Behaviour

Injecting drug use and homosexuality are not commonly reported in general populations. Less than one percent of respondents reported a history of injecting drug use while six percent of males reported a homo-

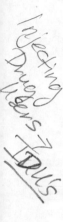

erience (Johnson et al, 1992) in a large scale English study). The rate of injecting in 17 European countries has range o 230 per 100,000 of population (European Centre, 1994, pp 88).

The proportion of IDUs in prison populations can be measured in two ways. First, by the proportion of prisoners reporting a history of injecting drug use (see *table 3*) and second by the proportion of IDUs reporting a history of imprisonment (see *table 4*). In a multi site study of IDUs in Europe, between 20 and 57 percent of IDUs reported a previous incarceration and on a mean of two occasions. With few incentives to report either an history of injecting or imprisonment, these figures would probably be underestimates. In this study, only 27 percent of IDUs in London reported a history of imprisonment, whereas three others studies of IDUs in London found previous imprisonment rates of over 50 percent (Dolan et al, 1993).

Being in prison does not necessarily mean that IDUs will engage in risk behaviour. Indeed, IDUs are more likely to stop injecting than continue while in prison (Shewan et al, 1994). Approximately one in four injectors reported continuing to inject drugs while in prison in the UK (see *table 5*). Likewise injecting in prison is not a risk for HIV unless syringes are shared. Therefore ascertaining the likelihood of sharing is crucial to understanding the potential for HIV spread in prison. Injecting equipment is scarce in prisons and is therefore often shared (as shown in *table 5*). Even though fewer IDUs inject in prison, a higher proportion of IDUs overall share in prison than in the community (Dolan et al, 1996). While only one quarter of IDUs imprisoned in the UK were injecting, approximately two thirds of these shared syringes while incarcerated.

Based on current UK data, we can estimate that for every 100 IDUs in a one year period, twenty will go to prison, five will inject in prison and three of these will share syringes. With the number of IDUs in England (conservatively) estimated to be 75,000 (ACMD, 1988), then each year approximately 15,000 IDUs are likely to be imprisoned of whom 3,750

IDUs will inject and 2,475 IDUs will share injecting equipment while in prison.

Table 3: Risk behaviour before prison entry

Location		n	%IDU	Reference
USA	New Mexico	455	41	Hull 85
	Iowa	363	25	Glass 88
	NYS	480	29	Smith 91
	Oregon	977	53	Andrus 89
GB	Edinburgh	421	17	Bird 93
	Glasgow	284	27	Gore 95
	England	755	11	Maden 92
	London	582	28	Power 92
	Scotland	559	15	PHLS 95
Spain	Catalonia	624	57	Martin 90

Table 4: IDUs reporting a history of imprisonment

City	% in prison	n
Antwerp	48	94
Copenhagen	34	67
Paris	53	105
Berlin	49	95
London	27	51
Athens	40	80
Dublin	45	68
Rome	36	71
Amsterdam	21	41
Coimbra	65	123
Madrid	57	108
Stockholm	47	99

Source: European Centre for the Epidemiological Monitoring of AIDS.

Table 5: Injecting and sharing by IDUs when last in custody

Yr	Location	n	inject %	share %	Reference
1988	England	80	25	75	Stimson 88
1989	England	286	30	67	Donoghoe 91
1989	London Bristol	113	27	61	Dolan 92
1990	England	474	25	62	Donoghoe 91
1990	England	168	27	73	Turnbull 91
1990	Edinburgh	43	67	76	Dye 91
199?	Glasgow	56	25	43	Kennedy 91
1990	Scotland	154	28	74	Power 92
1993	Edinburgh	60	13	75	Shewan 94

Prison injecting equipment

Few qualitative data exist on HIV risk behaviour in prison. In one study, drug injecting was observed by an inmate in an English women's prison in the early 1990s. A total of 92 injections were observed. Of the eleven sets of injecting equipment that were known to exist, six sets were brought in by visitors, two sets by inmates after court appearances and three sets came from the hospital wing. Nine sets were known to have been shared by at least 41 individuals (mean 4.5 IDUs per set, range 2–8 IDUs per set). During five days, one set of injecting equipment was used by seven individuals in four areas of the prison (Pickering & Stimson, 1993).

During an amnesty at Oxford Prison in England, inmates were asked to surrender their syringes. HIV antibodies were detected in two of the three syringes surrendered (Farmer et al, 1989). In South Australia, examination of 58 syringes confiscated from prison revealed the following: most were 1 ml in size (95%), one quarter had visible blood, over one half showed signs of multiple use and two thirds were refashioned, most commonly cut in half (Seamark & Gaughwin, 1994). The condition of syringes in prison has not been taken into account when guidelines for cleaning injecting equipment have been devised.

Tattooing in prison

Few studies have investigated tattooing in prison (see *table 6*). In Norway, tattooing was found to be associated with hepatitis C infection among prisoners (Holsen et al, 1993). High prevalences of tattooing were found especially among IDUs prisoners. Tattooing may provide a link between non injecting and injecting inmates thus enabling blood borne infections to be disseminated. Only six percent of ex–prisoners in England reported being tattooed during their last imprisonment, but half of those reported sharing the tattoo implements (Turnbull et al, 1991). However, the number of IDUs recruited in this study was limited which probably accounts for the low prevalence of tattooing reported.

Table 6: Tattooing among inmates

Location	n	% tattooed	Reference
New Mexico	455	82	Hull 85
Catalonia	631	75	Martin 90
Catalonia	idu 360	91	Martin 90
Catalonia	non idu 271	53	Martin 90
US	female 480	24	Smith 91
England	452	6	Turnbull 91
New South Wales	176	16	Dolan 94

Sexual behaviour

The third risk behaviour of importance in the prison environment is male to male sexual activity. Correctional facilities can help control sexually transmitted diseases at the population level by treating large numbers of infected inmates, many of whom serve short sentences (Cohen et al, 1992). Ten percent of inmates in a New York City Jail had acquired gonorrhoea during a three month period in 1986 (van Hoeven et al, 1990) which apparently persuaded prison administrators that condom distribution was justified.

Few male prisoners report being sexually active in prison (see *table 7*). Although slightly more male IDU prisoners report male to male sexual activity (see *table 8*). Some prisoners are particularly vulnerable to sexual assault, such as young prisoners (Heilpern, 1995) and transgender prisoners (Dolan et al, 1996).

Table 7: Percent of inmates who were sexually active in prison

Location	n	% homo-sexually active	Reference
New Mexico	455	3.6	Hull 85
Iowa	341	3	Glass 88
New South Wales	102	2	Dolan 96
Scotland	480	0.2	Power 92
Edinburgh	421	0.7	Bird 93

Table 8: Percent of IDUs who were sexually active in prison

Year	Location	n	%	Reference
1988	UK	139	6	Dolan 90
1989	London	50	10	Carvell 90
1989/90	England	474	3	Donoghoe 91
1989/90	London Bristol	207	6	Dolan 91

HIV positive inmates

The risk behaviours of HIV infected inmates, which determine the extent of HIV spread in prison, have been studied in New South Wales, South Australia, England and Scotland. HIV positive IDUs were significantly more likely to inject in prison than IDUs who were HIV negative or unaware of their HIV status in England (Dolan et al, 1990) and in Scotland (Dye & Isaacs, 1991). Virtually all HIV infected inmates who had injected also reported sharing injecting equipment. In New South Wales, HIV infected inmates were significantly more likely to have sex in prison than uninfected ones (Dolan et al, 1996).

Associations with imprisonment

HIV infection has been associated with imprisonment in France (Richardson et al, 1993) and Spain (Granados et al, 1991). Almost half (48%) of those imprisoned on four or more occasions in Spain were infected, compared with one fifth (21%) of those imprisoned less often. Injecting drug use prior to imprisonment was the most common exposure category for HIV positive inmates in New York (Vlahov et al, 1991).

Factors identified with syringe sharing among Scottish prisoners were: injecting a wide range of drugs in prison, using temgesic and discontinuing methadone treatment on prison entry (Shewan et al, 1994).

Mixing

From an epidemiological perspective, prisons play a pivotal role in the random mixing of disparate individuals. For example, the daily prison census in New South Wales in 1993 was approximately 6,000. Yet 14,000 individuals entered and were released from the prison system while a staggering 20,000 internal transfers of inmates occurred (NSW Department of Corrective Services, 1994). Although nearly all prisoners are eventually released, about half will be reimprisoned at some stage. The random mixing promoted by inmate movement is common to many prison systems but is not generally appreciated. Those unfamiliar with prison systems often perceive offenders as being isolated from society for extended periods. Nothing could be further from reality.

Conclusions and recommendations

The approach of most prison authorities to HIV infection conflicts with that of authorities in community settings. Prison authorities in many jurisdictions have vigorously pursued HIV testing programs in preference to implementing prevention strategies. Therefore HIV prevalence among prison entrants has been well documented in most countries (although England and Wales are exceptions). Also ample data exist on inmates' risk behaviours in a number of countries. One of the major challenges lies in collecting definite evidence of HIV transmission occurring in prison. Transmission data may best be obtained by a case study approach involving short term prisoners.

While prisons have the potential for transmitting infections, such as HIV and tuberculosis, they also present opportunities to provide prevention and treatment to a vast number of individuals. But correctional authorities are often (understandably) conservative in their management of prisons while prison medical services are almost always underfunded. These two factors have resulted in poor health care for prisoners, a very disadvantaged population compared with community members. The medical case load would be proportionally greater among prison populations and therefore prison medical services require proportionately more funding.

Prisoners are a very vulnerable population in many ways and often treated in a manner that has no parallel in the community. It has been recommended that *for practical and ethical reasons, measures for the control of AIDS in the prison environment should follow closely the strategy for the community in general. This policy implies an approach based on individual responsibility, in which each prisoner is treated as being autonomous and personally responsible for his own health and for the consequences of his behaviour. Prisoners should be informed about AIDS risk and given the opportunity to take prophylactic measures* (Harding, 1987, p1262).

The notion of mixing, as mentioned earlier, has potentially dire consequences for public health, as experienced in Bangkok. The general population needs to be informed about the vast level of intermingling that prison systems promote. Perhaps then the priority of infection prevention among prisoners may receive the attention it deserves. Prison authorities need to be reminded of their duty to care for those in their custody. Some successive attempts to improve a number of HIV issues in prison have been the result of lengthy court battles.

References

Acedo, A., Campos, A., Bauza, J., Ayala, C., Jover, M., Herrero, L., Canigral, G. & Tascon, A. (1989). HIV infection, hepatitis and syphilis in Spanish prisons. The Lancet, July 22, 226.

Advisory Committee on the Misuse of Drugs (1988). AIDS and drug misuse. London HMSO.

Andrus, J.K., Fleming, D.W., Knox, C., McAlister, R.O., Skeels, M.R., Conrad, R.E., Horan, J.M. & Foster, L.R. (1989). HIV testing in prisoners: Is mandatory testing mandatory? AJPH, 79(7), 840–842.

Bird, A.G., Gore, S.M., Jolliffe, D.W. & Burns, S.M. (1993). Second anonymous HIV surveillance in Saughton prison. Edinburgh prisoners give a lead to other heterosexuals on being HIV tested. AIDS 7: 277–9

Bird, A.G., Gore, S.M., Jolliffe, D.W. & Burns, S.M. (1992). Anonymous HIV surveillance in Saughton prison Edinburgh. AIDS, 6: 725–733.

Brewer, T.F., Vlahov, D., Taylor, E., Hall, D., Munoz, A. & Polk, F. (1988). Transmission of HIV–1 within a statewide prison system. AIDS, 2, 363–367.

Carvell, A.L.M. & Hart, G.J. (1990). Risk behaviours for HIV infection among injecting drug users. British Medical Journal, 300, 1383–1384.

Castro, K., Shansky, R., Scardino, V., Narkunas, J., Coe, J. & Hammett, T. (1991). HIV transmission in correctional facilities. Paper presented at the VIIth International Conference on AIDS, Florence, 16–21 June, Abstract no: M.C.3067 p.314.

Centers for Disease Control (1986). Acquired immunodeficiency syndrome in correctional facilities: a report of the National Institute of Justice and the American Correctional Association. MMWR, 35(12), 195–199.

Cohen, D., Scribner, R., Clarke, J. & Cory, D. (1992). The potential role of custody facilities in controlling sexually transmitted diseases. AJPH, 82(4), 552–556.

Choopanya, K. (1989). AIDS and drug addicts in Thailand, Bangkok. Bangkok Metropolitan Authority Department of Health. Bangkok.

Crofts, N., Stewart, T., Hearne, P., Ping, X.Y., Breschkin, A.M. & Locarnini, S.A. (1995). Spread of blood–borne viruses among Australian prison entrants. British Medical Journal, 310, 285–88.

Dixon, P.S., Flanigan, T.P., De Buono, B.A., Laurie, J.L., De Ciantis, M.L., Hoy, J., Stein, M., Scott, H.D. & Carpenter, C.C.J. (1993). Infection with the human immunodeficiency virus in prisoners: Meeting the health care challenge. The American Journal of Medicine, 95, 629–635.

Dolan, K., Wodak, A., Hall, W., Gaughwin, M. and Rae, F. (1996). HIV risk behaviour before, during and after imprisonment in New South Wales. Addiction Research 4(2), 151-160.

Dolan K, Shearer J, Hall W and Wodak A. (1996) Bleach is easier to obtain but inmates are still risking infection in New South Wales prisons. Technical Report. Sydney National Drug and Alcohol Research Centre.

Dolan, K., Wodak A and Penny R (1995). AIDS behind bars: preventing HIV spread among incarcerated drug injectors. AIDS, 9:825–32.

Dolan, K., Kaplan, E., Wodak, A., Hall, W. & Gaughwin, M. (1994). Modelling HIV transmission in NSW prisons, Australia. Tenth International Conference on AIDS, Yokohama abstract no. PD 0524. pp 336.

Dolan, K., Hall, W., Wodak, A., and Gaughwin, M. (1994) Evidence of HIV transmission in an Australian prison. Letter MJA, 160, 734.

Dolan, K., Hall, W., Wodak, A. (1994) Bleach availability and risk behaviour in prison in New South Wales. Technical Report No 22, Sydney: National Drug and Alcohol Research Centre.

Dolan, K. (1994). Sex in the slammer. National AIDS Bulletin 8:6, 12–13. Australian Federation of AIDS Organisations, Sydney.

Dolan, K.A. (1993). Drug injectors in prison and the community in England. International Journal of Drug Policy, 4(4), 179–183.

Dolan, K.A., Donoghoe, M.C., Jones, S. & Stimson, G.V. (1992). A cohort study of syringe exchange clients and other drug injectors in England, 1989 to 1990. Report to the Department of Health. London: Monitoring Research Group, The Centre for Drugs and Health Behaviour, Charing Cross and Westminster Medical School, London.

Dolan, K.A., Donoghoe, M. & Stimson, G. (1990). Drug injecting and syringe sharing in custody and in the community: an exploratory survey of HIV risk behaviour. The Howard Journal, 29(3), 177–186.

Donoghoe, M.C., Dolan, K.A. & Stimson, G.V. (1991). The 1989–1990 National Monitoring Study. Monitoring Research Group. The Centre for Research on Drugs and Health Behaviour. Charing Cross and Westminster Medical School, London.

Dye, S. & Isaacs, C. (1991). Intravenous drug misuse among prison inmates: implications for spread of HIV. British Medical Journal, 302, 1506.

Estebanez, P., Coloma, C., Zunzunegui, M.V. & Rua, M. (1988). Prevalence and risk factors for HIV infection among inmates. IV International Conference on AIDS Stockholm, Abstract no. 4202.

European Centre for the Epidemiological Monitoring of AIDS (1994). Surveillance of AIDS/HIV in Europe, 1984–1994. Saint Maurice, France.

Farmer, R., Preston, D., Emami, J & Barker, M. (1989). The transmission of HIV within prisons and its likely effect on the growth of the epidemic in the general population. University of London.

Feachem, R.G. (1995). Valuing the past...investing in the future. Evaluation of the National HIV/AIDS strategy 1993–94 to 1995–96. Australian Government Publishing Service, Canberra.

Gaunay, W. & Gido, R. (1986) AIDS, a demographic profile of New York State inmates mortalities 1981–1985. New York: New York State Commission of Correction.

Gellert, G.A., Maxwell, R.M., Higgins, K.V., et al (1993). HIV infection in the women's jail, Orange County, California, 1985 through 1991. American Journal of Public Health, 83 (10), 1454–56.

Glass, G.E., Hausler, W.J., Loeffelholz, P.L. & Yesalis, C.E. (1988). Seroprevalence of HIV antibody among individuals entering the Iowa prison system. AJPH, 78(4), 447–449.

Gore, S.M., Bird, A.G., Burns, S.M., Goldberg, D.J., Ross, A.J. & Macgregor, J. (1995). Drug injection and HIV prevalence in inmates of Glenochil prison. BMJ, 310, 293–296.

Gostin, L.O. (1990). The AIDS Litigation Project – A National review of courts & human rights commission decisions, Part 1: The social impact of AIDS. Law & Medicine, 263 (14), 1961–1970.

Granados A. Miranda M.J. & Martin L. (1990). HIV seropositivity in Spanish prisons. Presented at the VIth International AIDS Conference, San Francisco Abstract no Th.D.116.

Groves, T. (1991). Prison policies on HIV under review. BMJ, 303.

Hammett, T.M., Harrold, L., Gross, M. & Epstein, J. (1993). 1992 Update: AIDS in correctional facilities, issues & options. Abt Associates Inc.

Harding, T. (1987). AIDS in prison. The Lancet, Nov 28 1260–63.

Harding, T. & Schaller, G. (unpub). HIV/AIDS and prisons: update and policy review, June 1992, University Institute of Legal Medicine, Geneva.

Heilpern, D. (1995). Sexual assault of New South Wales prisoners. Current Issues in Criminal Justice 6:327–334.

Horsburgh, C.R., Jarvis, J.Q., McArthur, T., Ignacio, T. & Stock, P. (1990). Seroconversion to human immunodeficiency virus in prison inmates. American Journal of Public Health, 80(2), 209–10.

Holsen, D.S., Harthug, H. & Myrmel, H. (1993). Prevalence of antibodies to hepatitis C virus and association with intravenous drug abuse and tattooing in a national prison in Norway. Eur J Clin Microbiol Infect Dis, 12(9) 673–676.

Hoxie, N.J., Vergeront, J.M., Frisby, H.R., Pfister, J.R., Golubjatnikov, R. & Davis, J.P. (1990). HIV seroprevalence and the acceptance of voluntary HIV testing among newly incarcerated male prison inmates in Wisconsin. American Journal of Public Health, 80(9), 1129–1131.

Hull, H.F., Lyons, L.H., Mann, J.M., Hadler, S.C., Steece, R. & Skeels, M.R. (1985). Incidence of hepatitis B in the penitentiary of New Mexico. American Journal of Public Health, 75(10), 1213–1214.

Johnson, A.M., Wadsworth, J., Wellings, K., Bradshaw, S. & Field, J. (1992). Sexual lifestyles and HIV risk. Nature, 360, 3 December.

Kelley, P.W., Redfield, R.R., Ward, D.L., Burke, D.S. & Miller, R.N. (1986). Prevalence and incidence of HTLV–111 infection in a prison. JAMA, 256(16), 2198–99.

Kennedy, D.H., Nair, G., Elliott, L. & Ditton, J. (1991). Drug misuse and sharing of needles in Scottish prisons. BMJ, 302, 1507.

Maden, A., Swinton, M. & Gunn, J. (1992). A survey of pre–arrest drug use in sentenced prisoners. British Journal of Addiction, 87, 27–33.

Martin, V., Bayas, J.M., Laliga, A., Pumarola, T., Vidal, J., Jimenez de Anta, M.T. & Salleras, L. (1990). Seroepidemiology of HIV –1 infection in a Catalonian penitentiary. AIDS, 4, 1023–26.

Medley, G., Dolan, K.A. & Stimson, G. (1992). A model of HIV transmission by syringe sharing in English prisons using surveys of injecting drug users. Presented at the VIIIth International Conference on AIDS, Amsterdam, Abstract number MoD 0038, pp 75.

Mutter, R.C., Grimes, R.M. & Labarthe, D. (1994). Evidence of intraprison spread of HIV infection. Archives of Internal Medicine, 154, 793–795.

NSW Department of Corrective Services (1994). Annual Report 1993–1994. Sydney.

Patel, K.K., Hutchinson, C. & Sienko, D.G. (1990). Sentinel surveillance of HIV infection among new inmates and implications for policies of corrections facilities. Public Health Reports, 105(5), 510–14.

Pickering, H. & Stimson, G.V. (1993). Syringe sharing in prison. The Lancet, 342, 621–622.

Power, K.G., Markaova, I., Rowlands, A., McKee, K.J., Anslow, P.J. & Kilfedder, C. (1992). Comparison of sexual behaviour and risk of transmission of Scottish inmates, with or without a history of intravenous drug use. AIDS Care, 4(1), 53–67.

Public Health Laboratory Service (1995). Unlinked anonymous HIV seroprevalence monitoring programme in England and Wales. Department of Health, London.

Seamark, R. & Gaughwin, M. (1994). Jabs in the dark: Injecting equipment found in prisons, and the risks of viral transmission. AUST JPH, 18(1), 113–116.

Scottish Affairs Committee (1994). Drug abuse in Scotland, Report. London HMSO.

Shewan, D., Gemmell A. & Davis, J.B. (1994). Behavioural change amongst drug injectors in Scottish prisons. Soc Sci Med. 39(11), 1585–86.

Singleton, J.A., Perkins, C.I., Trachtenberg, A.I., Hughes, M.J., Kizer, K.W. & Ascher, M. (1990). HIV antibody seroprevalence among prisoners entering the California correctional system. West J Med, 153, 394–399.

Smith, P.F., Mikl, J., Truman, B.I., Lessner, L., Lehman, J.S., Stevens, R.W., Lord, E.A., Broaddus, R.K. & Morse, D.L. (1991). HIV infection among women entering the New Yorrk state correctional system. American Journal of Public Health, 81, 35–40.

Stimson, G.V., Alldritt, L., Dolan, K.A., & Donoghoe, M. (1988). Injecting equipment exchange schemes: A final report on research. Goldsmiths' College 1988.

Toepell, A. (1992). Prisoners and AIDS. Knowledge, attitude and behaviour. National Clearing House on AIDS. Ontario, Canada.

Taylor, A., Goldberg, D., Emslie, J., Wrench, J., Gruer, L., Cameron, S., Black, J., Davis, B., McGregor, J., Follett, E., Harvey, J., Basson, J. & McGavigan, J. (1995). Outbreak of HIV infection in a Scottish prison. BMJ, 310, 289–292.

Turnbull, P. & Stimson, G. (1994). Drug Use in Prison. Letter. BMJ, 308, 1716.

Turnbull, P.J., Dolan, K.A. & Stimson, G.V. (1991). Prisons, HIV and AIDS: Risks and experiences in custodial care. Avert, Horsham, England.

Truman, B.I., Morse, D., Mikl, J., Lehman, S., Forte, A., Broaddus, R. & Stevens, R. (1988). HIV seroprevalence and risk factors among prison inmates entering New York State Prisons. Presented at the IVth International Conference on AIDS, abstract no.4207.

van Hoeven, K.H., Rooney, W.C., & Joseph, S.C. (1990). Evidence of gonococcal transmission within a correctional system. American Journal of Public Health, 80(12), 1505–1506.

Vlahov, D., Brewer, T.F., Castro, K.G., Narkunas, J.P., Salive, M.E., Ullrich, J. & Munoz, A. (1991). Prevalence of antibody to HIV–1 among entrants to US Correctional Facilities. JAMA, 265(9), 1129–1132.

Vlahov, D., Brewer, F., Munoz, A., Hall, D., Taylor, E. & Polk, B.F. (1989). Temporal trends of Human Immunodeficiency Virus Type 1 (HIV–1) infection among inmates entering a statewide prison system, 1985–1987. JAIDS, 2(3), 283–290.

World Health Organization (1993). WHO Guidelines on HIV infection and AIDS in prisons. Geneva WHO.

Wright, K.N. (1993). Alcohol use by prisoners. Alcohol Health & Research World, 17(2), 157–161.

Wright, N.H., Vanichseni, S., Akarasewi, P., Wasi, C., & Choopanya K. (1994). Was the 1988 HIV epidemic among Bangkok's injecting drug users a common source outbreak? AIDS 8: 529–532.

Provision of syringes[1] and prescription of heroin[2] in prison: The swiss experience in the prisons of Hindelbank and Oberschöngrün

[1]Joachim Nelles, [2]Anja Dobler–Mikola and Beat Kaufmann

I Provision of Syringes in Prison

Introduction

Problem

Consumption of illicit drugs and risk behaviour, such as exchange of used syringes among intravenous drug dependent inmates and unprotected sexual contacts, do exist in prisons all over the world (Hardding 1987, Brewer 1992, Thomas & Moerings 1994, Dolan 1995). However, the assessment of problems concerning these conditions by prison administrators and politicians vary from complete denial to serious concern.

Although there are plenty of publications available concerning the special situation in prison, there is still a lack of knowledge, since data gathered in different countries are difficult to compare. This is due to the variety of research designs and national prison systems. Nevertheless, a coarse overview giving an idea about the extent of drug use and prevalence of HIV and hepatitis infection in prison is presented in *table 1*. These data, published between 1988 and 1995, show a broad spectrum of results, especially regarding HIV infection. The severity of the problem becomes more apparent when the data are compared with the situation in the communitiy. HIV prevalence for instance is 0.2% in the Swiss general public (BAG 1993), while the corresponding figure in prison is approximately 20 to 60 times higher. The prevalence of hepatitis C in prison is strikingly high. Hepatitis C must be considered as *the* infection in prison, nevertheless, it remains widely forgotten (Gaube 1993, Keppler 1994).

Strategies

Drug and harm reduction policy in prison differs from country to country, and even from prison to prison. Segregation of HIV positive individuals, mandatory and voluntary HIV testing, general and personal information, counselling and therapy, distribution of condoms, methadone substitution and providing inmates with disinfectants are

Table 1: Drug use and prevalence of HIV and hepatitis infection in prison

	i.v. drug consumption %	HIV prevalence %	Hepatitis C prevalence %
Australia	36-46	0.5-3	37-67
Canada	30-50	1.1-7.2	
France		0.5-1.5	
Germany		1.2-8	21.9
Italy	19-32	13.4-13.6	
Netherlands	33	6.3-8	
Norway	44	13	41.8
Scotland	18-27.5	2.4-8.6	
Spain	44	20.6-28.4	
Switzerland	25-70	3.5-12.5	
United States	40-80	<1-20	38.1

Source: see Nelles et al 1995

applied strategies. In Switzerland, established prevention strategies and harm reduction efforts in the community also consist in unrestricted distribution of syringes and condoms, in widespread substitution of methadone and in establishing shooting galleries in most of the greater towns. Furthermore, first experiences on the prescription of illicit drugs are available now (Rihs 1995). These progressive strategies however have not passed prison walls until now and remain highly disputed. This might be due to the fact that particularly in prison narcotic laws prohibiting drugs on the one hand and health care claiming for harm reduction on the other hand are more likely interpreted as to contradict each other, thus blocking further development. Consequently, political opposition arises as soon as such harm reduction measures shall be introduced in prisons. It therefore does not surprise that international recommendations by both the World Health Organisation and the Council of Europe regarding adequate prevention measures in prison (WHO 1993, Council of Europe 1993) have largely been ignored by politicians and prison administrations.

New approaches in Switzerland

Distribution of sterile injection material inside prison initiated in 1993 as an act of medical disobedience, when the physician of Oberschöngrün Prison in the Swiss Canton of Solothurn decided to provide inmates with sterile syringes without being authorised (Nelles & Harding 1995).

In 1994, a pilot project of HIV prevention, including distribution of sterile syringes, was installed in the Swiss prison of Hindelbank as a result of a long lasting decision making process on the political level. This process had started in 1991, when the medical service of Hindelbank Prison presented alarming figures about drug abuse, HIV prevalence and syringe exchange among drug dependent inmates. The process to launch a pilot study was carried on by the Swiss Federal Office of Public Health, which made it possible to overcome the doubts and reservations of political authorities in the Canton of Berne. The results of this project will be presented in this chapter.

Recently even prescription of injectable heroin to a limited number of severely drug addicted male inmates has become available in the framework of a scientific study that started in July 1995 in Oberschöngrün Prison. This project will be presented in chapter II.

Drug and AIDS Prevention in Hindelbank Prison

Study design and evaluation programme

The pilot project was carried out over a period of twelve months (June 1994–May 1995). Prevention efforts and evaluation were accomplished by two independent external groups.

The prevention programme consisted of plenary sessions and sessions in small groups, socio–medical personal counselling, provision of information leaflets and condoms and distribution of sterile syringes by means of one–to–one automatic dispensers. Group sessions and personal counselling took place in rooms reserved for the project. Syringe dispensers had been installed in each of the six divisions of the prison. The prevention programme was aimed at all prisoners and as far as convenient at the relevant prison personnel as well. The information meetings focused upon topics such as hepatitis and HIV infection, corresponding protection measures and assistance in drug related emergencies. The group encounters included meetings, discussions and role playing. The whole programme was held in French, German, English and Spanish (Baechtold 1995).

The objective of the subsequent evaluation was to analyse the efficacy of the prevention programme, to detect any undesirable developments and to elaborate, on the basis of the obtained results, general recommendations on how to proceed after termination of the pilot project as well as on the introduction of syringe distribution in other prisons. The evaluation was based mainly on standardised interviews.

They were carried out before launching the prevention programme as well as three, six and twelve months thereafter. The interviews included questions on the socio–cultural context of the individual, the consumption of drugs (past and present), risk behaviour regarding sexuality and consumption of drugs, the level of knowledge concerning AIDS and hepatitis as well as the acceptance and use of the offer of preventive measures. Additionally, data such as the number of syringes used, the number and nature of sanctions, particular incidents, and data from the prisoners' medical examinations were gathered.

Participation:

Participation in the interviews by the inmates was high. From a total of 189 women, 155 had been invited for the interviews, and 137 took part. Comparisons of socio–demographic data with the whole inmate population revealed this sample to be representative. Acceptance of the detailed interview by the staff on the other hand was low. Only 48 out of 111 persons participated in the first interview. Consequently modified questionnaires (handed out to all staff members) did not change the situation markedly. Nevertheless, finally 86 members of the personnel took part at least in one interview or returned a questionnaire.

Socio–demographic aspects

The inmate population of Hindelbank Prison, which serves the whole of the Swiss Confederation, was very international. Only 40% of the inmates were of Swiss origin (*figure 1*). The data on age, education level, and further socio–demographic aspects were comparable with other prisons for women. 60% of the inmates have been sentenced because of offences against the Swiss law on narcotics.

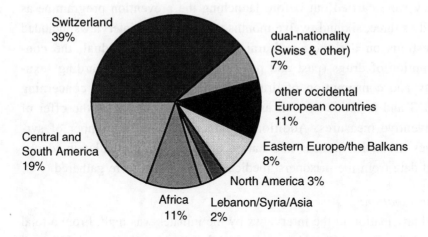

Switzerland 39%

dual-nationality (Swiss & other) 7%

other occidental European countries 11%

Central and South America 19%

Eastern Europe/the Balkans 8%

North America 3%

Africa 11%

Lebanon/Syria/Asia 2%

Hindelbank Prison is very international. More than half of the inmates are foreigners. All prevention measures and evaluation instruments had to be offered in four languages (German, English, French and Spanish).

Figure 1: Origin of interviewed prisoners

Drug consumption before and during imprisonment

The spectrum of drug consumption before and while being in prison is presented in detail in *figure 2*. As expected, intake of nicotine and heroin remained almost unchanged, whereas the intake of alcohol and cocaine decreased markedly. Consumption of cannabis increased. A comparable elevation was observed in the intake of sleeping, tranquillising and anti–depressant drugs as well. The results correspond with the well-known fact that alcohol and cocaine are much rarer in prison than heroin and cannabis. Cigarettes are sold at the prison's kiosk, prescription of medicaments depends on medical treatment. The data are comparable with investigations performed in other prisons. In the interviews three, six and twelve months after beginning of the project almost the same pattern of answers was given by the inmates, indicating that the spectrum of drug intake remained stable during the pilot phase.

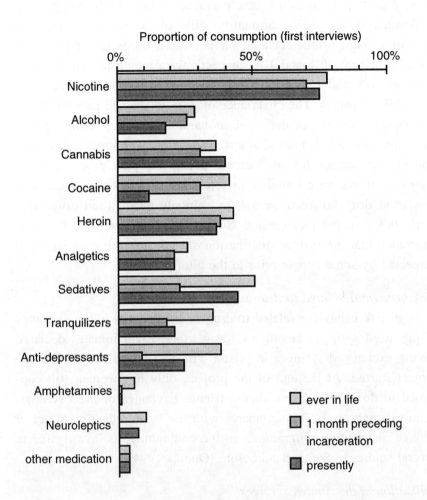

Proportion of consumption (first interviews)

Figure 2: Drug spectrum (interviews at the beginning of the prevention programme)

Inmates were asked about their drug consumption ever in life, during the month preceding incarceration and presently. In the three following interviews, the pattern of their answers remained almost the same indicating that there was no elevation of drug consumption during the pilot project.

Figure 2: Drug spectrum (interviews at the beginning of the prevention programme)

It is important to mention that prisoners taking illicit drugs were predominantly of Swiss nationality: 80% of the Swiss inmates and 20% of foreign origin declared having taken drugs regularly before being in prison; 70% and 10% respectively a month preceding incarceration. 50% and 15% respectively declared to take illicit drugs actually while in prison. The covariance of drug intake and nationality unfortunately restricts calculation of co–variables for drug intake such as age, education level, marital status, and so on. The observed proportion of drug intake did not increase during the pilot phase. No new drug consumers were found in prison either. Those few inmates who re–started drug intake in prison had already taken illicit drugs regularly before being incarcerated. Summarising these results, it can be concluded that the syringe distribution did not increase drug intake as suspected by some people prior to the pilot project.

Risk behaviour related to drug intake

High risk behaviour related to drug intake consists in the exchange of pre–used syringes among i.v. drug users. Eight inmates declared having exchanged syringes in prison with various persons before the project started. At the end of the project, only one woman still continued to do so with her addicted friend. Exchange of used syringes almost disappeared. This compares with the harm reduction effect of syringe distribution programmes in the community, as investigated in several studies in Switzerland before (Dubois 1994).

Utilisation of distributed syringes

The number of syringes distributed and the course of sanctions are presented in *figure 3*. The curve of syringe distribution starts on a high level and reaches another peak in October and November 1994. It decreases during the following months and remains finally on a quite low level when compared with the beginning. The course of sanctions related to drug intake clearly correlates with the number of syringes distributed, whereas the course of sanctions related to other

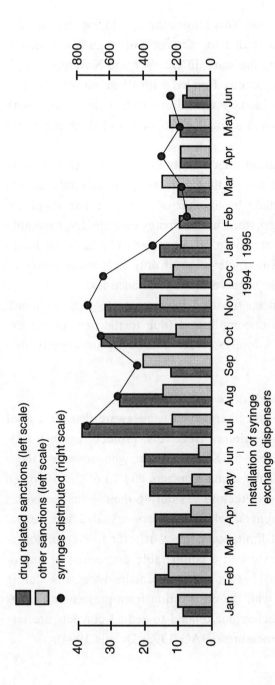

Distribution of syringes by one-to-one exchange dispensers was measured and compared with the number of sanctions related to drug consumption and to other disciplinary offences. The distribution curve and the curve of drug related sanctions run clearly parallel, whereas sanctions caused by other offences do not. The high distribution rate at the beginning might be due to an effect of the start of the project. The second peak in October and November 1994 is due to a temporary increase of the availability of illegal drugs. From February to June 1995 the total number of drug addicted women was lower and in addition there were less illegal drugs available in the prison. The results may be interpreted as follows: Syringes are used for drug consumption. Elevated drug consumption is followed by consequent sanctioning by the staff.

Figure 3: Distribution of syringes and course of sanctions (per month)

disciplinary offences does not. This allows the conclusion that the elevated syringe distribution is due to increased drug intake, which is
consequently sanctioned by the staff. In October and November 1994,
Hindelbank Prison was apparently flooded with illegal drugs. The low
syringe distribution from January until June 1995 is associated with
low drug use at that time and a smaller proportion of drug dependent
women in prison.

These observations indicate that distribution of syringes is closely
related to availability and use of illegal drugs, predominantly heroin.
This conclusion is confirmed by another observation: The supply of
syringes was elevated in the week after inmates received their monthly
wages (*figure 4*); Having money in prison seems to be associated with
an increase in drug acquisition, elevation of drug intake and supply of
syringes, followed by a rise in surveillance and sanctions.

Syringes have never been misused by inmates (e.g. as weapon).
Disposal of syringes was uncomplicated (due to the one–to–one exchange machines) and no injuries were caused by unproperly dis-
posed syringes.

Risk behaviour related to sexual contacts

The majority of the prisoners interviewed were aware that the use of
condoms during sexual relations effectively protects against HIV
infection. Nevertheless, from 58 Swiss women who answered these
questions, 35 declared to have sexual contacts and 25 of those women
(70%) did usually not protect themselves during their sexual activities
by using condoms. Foreigners, whose answers revealed less sexual
contacts (due to a general limitation of day–offs for foreign prisoners
and less social contacts), showed a comparable proportion of unprotected sexual practices (76%). This situation remained the same during
the project and compares with the observation from prevention studies
outside prisons that risk behaviour related to sexual contacts are less
influenced by preventive measures (BAG 1993, Dubois 1994).

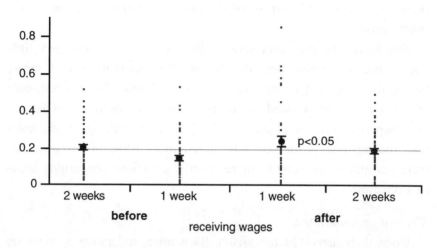

One week after inmates receive their monthly wages the distribution of syringes is significantly elevated, thus indicating that having money is associated with drug acquisition and drug consumption and followed by an elevated demand for syringes. This is an additional indicator that syringes supplied are directly related to drug consumption – an effect that has been desired as a basic aim of harm reduction with the implementation of the project.

Figure 4: Distribution of syringes related to receiving wages

Knowledge on HIV/AIDS and hepatitis infection

Knowledge on HIV infection and AIDS remained unchanged, but on a sufficiently high level. The inmates were already well informed at the beginning of the project; and during the time, only slight differentiation of the pre–existing knowledge occurred. Variation analysis indicates that this slight improvement is rather due to repeated interviewing than to information lectures. Despite the solid elementary knowledge that was displayed, 35% of the prisoners committed «fatal» judgement errors: behaviours that undeniably include the risk of infection, e.g. sexual relations between women, were falsely estimated to be out of risk. Surprisingly, drug addicted prisoners most often committed such errors, even though they showed themselves to be better informed in almost all of the other awareness areas than their fellow prisoners.

Strikingly, the prisoners showed themselves to possess very little knowledge concerning hepatitis, despite the fact that, as it is shown below, this infection is wide–spread at Hindelbank. For instance, 60% of the inmates interviewed could not answer the question: «What is a viral hepatitis (infectious jaundice)?». Only half of the prisoners knew how the hepatitis virus could be transmitted. Most of the prisoners were not able to respond to more specific questions concerning hepatitis infection.

Medical examinations

Upon their arrival at the prison, 94 women underwent a voluntary blood analysis. The results revealed, in addition to HIV infections, a significant number of hepatitis infections. Of the women examined, one out of two was hepatitis B positive and more than one in three was shown to be hepatitis C positive (*figure 5*). In re–tests on release (51 cases; investigation within an average of 5 months) no new infection (sero–conversion), neither wit HIV nor with hepatitis B or C was diagnosed.

During the project time no abscesses related to injection in prison occurred.

Incidents

During the pilot project, no incident concerning distribution and use of syringes was observed. As expected, the number of overdoses (1 in 12 months) and the level of drug related deaths (1 in 12 months) did not increase either.

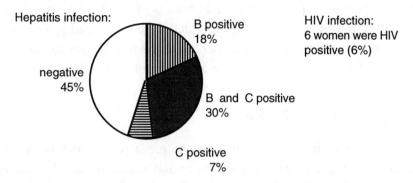

Prevalence of hepatitis B and C, measured with common immuno antibody tests, is strikingly high. Almost 50% of the tested inmates were infected with the hepatitis B virus and about 40% with the hepatitis C virus. 5% of the hepatitis B were still infectious, whereas this proportion could not be determined in hepatitis C infections because of a lack of sufficient follow up measurements of liver transaminases. However, in 51 serological retests no sero-conversion related to hepatitis and HIV infections was observed (retests within a mean time of 6 months). The prevalence of HIV infection is comparable with international results, the infection rate with hepatitis B and C is clearly higher, a fact that cannot be interpreted so far.

Figure 5: Results of voluntary blood analysis

Distribution of Syringes in the Prison of Oberschöngrün

Since 1993, the physician of the prison in Oberschöngrün, a prison for about 75 male inmates with a permanent number of some 15 drug addicts, hands out himself about 700 syringes a year. The syringes are given directly to the prisoners on their demand. The effect of the syringe distribution has not been evaluated scientifically, but the observations made in Oberschöngrün (given in detail in a personal communication) compare with the results of the pilot project in Hindelbank. In Oberschöngrün, neither incidents concerning distribution and use of syringes, nor an elevation of the number of overdoses or drug related deaths occurred. Furthermore, no abscesses related to

drug injection in prison and no elevation of drug intake were observed. Removal of used syringes (which were exchanged against new
ones) did not cause any injuries, neither to the inmates nor to the staff.
Syringes have not been misused in any harmful way either.

Interpretation of the Findings

The proportion of drug consumption, the prevalence of risk behaviour
related to drug consumption and to sexual practices and the rate of
HIV and of hepatitis infection in the prison of Hindelbank reflect the
situation on an international level.

The results of the pilot project carried out at Hindelbank Prison do
not furnish any arguments against the continuation of the distribution
of sterile syringes. The initial fears that were expressed – that the consumption of drugs would increase, syringes would be used negligently
or as weapons or would cause injuries – were not confirmed. In contrast, no abscesses related to drug injection in prison were found during the pilot project, the exchange of syringes among prisoners almost
ceased and no new cases of HIV or hepatitis infection surfaced. Abol-
ishing the distribution of sterile syringes would undermine the success
achieved thus far in this project.

The results compare with the experience of syringe distribution in
Oberschöngrün Prison, indicating that distribution of syringes is
feasible in prisons for men as well. However, there is one considerable
limitation regarding the conclusions: both Swiss prisons are of
relatively small size.

The level of knowledge about HIV infection and AIDS was fairly
high already before launching the project, whereas awareness of the
comparable dangerous hepatitis infections was very low in both
groups, the inmates and the personnel. There is an urgent need in
sensitisation of the prisons to these harming infections.

Both, the positive effects of syringe distribution programmes on
harm reduction in Hindelbank and in Oberschöngrün, and the fact

that the consumption of drugs, behaviour detrimental to good health as well as a high prevalence of HIV and hepatitis infections are undeniable realities of prison life lead to the conclusion that syringe distribution should be considered in addition to routine prevention activities in other prisons as well.

As a consequence of the project results, providing the inmates of Hindelbank Prison with sterile syringes has been prolonged by the cantonal police director for at least one year, but with a lower level of accompanying preventive measures. A follow–up evaluation is planned twelve months after ceasing of the pilot project.

II Controlled Opiate Maintenance Treatment in the Penal Institution of Oberschöngrün

Introduction

In the following chapter some first impressions on the study on heroin maintenance treatment in the penal institution Oberschöngrün will be presented. This programme is part of the Swiss multicenter opiate trial. In the beginning of the nineties, the Swiss Federal government started a longitudinal study in order to analyse the long–term effects of diversified medical prescription of different narcotics on long–term drug addicts with signs of social marginality. According to the research plan, the type of narcotic prescription was diversified, including the prescription of i.v. heroin, i.v. morphine and i.v methadone. Some experiments mainly used the double–blind approach (in which neither the participant nor the therapist knows which substance the participant receives) to investigate objectively the differences in the effectiveness of narcotics, while others concentrated either on random prescription to enable a comparison of therapeutic characteristics or on prescription by individual indication to investigate the effect and suitability of the narcotics in view of the subjective experiences and expectations. This study design was once adjusted and once modified: The number of planned morphine treatments was reduced because of certain unfavourable experiences with prescribing intravenous morphine (Uch-tenhagen 1995). A similar reduction with intravenous methadone was carried out. In May 1995 the Swiss Council of Ministers resolved to expand the programme with additional questions and pilot studies, including the research question concerning the feasibility of heroin maintenance treatment within the penal system.

This study started in August 1995. Accordingly the following proceedings are based on the preliminary data from the starting phase. Nevertheless, we wish to be able to give some first impressions on the evaluation setting and approach. For that we will present the baselines of the research design and describe the implementation of the project. Finally we will discuss some initial results that are based on the first qualitative analysis of the verbal interviews with inmates and with the staff members.

Research questions

As mentioned above, the heroin maintenance trial in the prison is a special project within the Swiss national project on medical prescrip-tion of narcotics. Accordingly it follows the same basic objectives as the trials outside prison walls, especially to reach addicts unable to profit from other forms of treatment, to improve health and social status and to reduce risk behaviour.

However, in the special environment of the penal system there are also specific questions concerning the participants: Is there an im-provement in the general adjustment of the participants because of the heroin substitution in the penal institution? And concerning the organisation and realisation: Which are the negative and positive effects of the heroin substitution in penal institutions?

Study design

In general the participants in the prison have to fulfil the same entry criteria as in the trials outside prison walls. They have to prove that they have been heroin dependent for at least two years and that earlier therapeutic efforts have failed. They should not be younger than twenty years and deficiencies concerning the social integration and/or psychological well–being and/or health should be presented. Additionally, the target population in the prison includes only heroin addicted inmates with at least 9 months of sentence remaining (Schaefer 1995). This because it makes little sense to provide heroin only for a few months without security of continuity of the programme after discharge. The trial is also open for inmates from other penal institutions, but their sentences have to be compatible with the semi–confined imprisonment of Oberschöngrün.

Within the penal institution of Oberschöngrün the trial is separated from the main part of the prison, located in a special building about three kilometres outside the main buildings. The participants live and work in a small group setting. The heroin is provided three times a day by trained female staff (nurses) and the provision is supervised by a prison warder. Additionally the participants receive psycho–social counselling and care based on the general guidelines for the Swiss heroin trials.

The first participants entered the trial in September 1995. In an initial pilot phase, four inmates were admitted. After three months the trial was opened for eight persons. All these places are occupied today. After some initial difficulties the daily routine normalised rapidly. The difficulties resulted from the strange new elements in the penal setting: The inmates as well as the warders needed some time to get used to a very unusual situation of allowed injection of heroin by inmates under the eyes of prison warders.

Research design

As mentioned above, the trial in the prison has to answer special research questions on two levels: Concerning the participants and concerning the implementation in the penal system. Such questions refer to negative and positive effects of the legal heroin in the penal institution. This issue is sure to be controversial because of the illegality of heroin in general. It is however possible that the availability of heroin maintenance treatment diminishes the other drug problems in the prison.

Due to the intricate circumstances a multilevel methodology is needed. The research design is therefore based on a single case study design (Lamnek 1993, US G.A.O. 1990) aimed at multilevel understanding of the ongoing process after the implementation of heroin maintenance. Important features are prospectivity, qualitative research paradigm and multi–methodological data collection (Mayring 1990). The following levels are included in the data collection: Focused semi–structured interviews, internal documents, standardised records (daily, weekly and monthly), standardised records of group meetings and standardised staff questionnaires. This kind of data collection is based on several instruments on different levels. In the beginning data about the selection and admission are collected by standardised instruments that allow to analyse the population as well as to make an eventual selection of it. The questions concerning somatic and psychic health are documented during the medical care. Data should be collected at entry and during the heroin substitution. The instruments applied are the same as the ones from the other Swiss narcotic prescription programmes, because the state of health in a penal institution is expected to show the same characteristics as in an ambulant care. These instruments are registration of the doctor's conversation, registration of somatic and psychic status and registration of laboratory parameters. The features of substitution are of special interest. The corresponding questions concern dosage, incidents and organisational problems. They can be analysed through the systematic documentation of the substitution programme. The living–environment of inmates in the trial is documented by daily protocols. This documentation is concentrated on questions about work performance, leisure time and questions about control and discipline. Additionally there are also external inquiries. They are an important instrument of the general evaluation. In the penal institution external inquiries propose an additional non controllable factor. At the planning level the pros and contras of external inquiries should be checked carefully. Since they offer a very wide range of information, they should be taken into consideration. Analogue to the questionnaires of the general evaluation specific forms are evaluated. The forms should consider the specific goals in penal institutions. Since the total number of participants is only eight, half–standardised questionnaires can be used.

Preliminary results

Until now the quantitative and qualitative data from the starting period on the four first participants has been collected and coded. In order to give some first impressions of ongoing processes the following topics, which we identified during the first analysis of the qualitative data will be discussed: Treatment specific interactions, dependency relationships and contradictions of heroin maintenance within the penal system. Regarding the treatment specific interactions we can see that the heroin maintenance initiates a new quality in the interactions within the penal system, which is perceived by the inmates and by the staff: Intensified care and heightened empathy can be observed. The participants' experience increased empathy positively (Dahle & Steller 1990). The contact with female staff members in the context of heroin distribution has been experienced as an enrichment. There is an increasing frequency of contacts between medical staff and inmates, which produces new qualities in the relationship. The biweekly group sessions have effects in the same direction. Increased involvement by the social services of the penal institution is also a new feature within this penal system. The inmates get additional attention by the regular interviews with external personnel. To sum up, all these elements include an increase of positive attention. It will be interesting to analyse in the follow–up the consequences of this kind of attention for the inmate's identity and for the informal structures inside prison walls.

The inmates also perceive an increase of control: The participants are required to comply with a schedule of distribution within a defined distribution context. Adjustment of dosage is based on a specified dosage regime. The superintendent of the institution is authorised to exclude inmates for several days from the heroin maintenance programme in case of disciplinary transgressions. On leave of absence, participants are required to seek methadone from a methadone distribution centre. Summarising these facts, we see that the inmates aren't anymore independent in their heroin use. Another consequence of the heroin maintenance treatment is a rise of new interdependencies. Dependency of the participants on controlled opiate availability includes the following aspects: Anxieties regarding the cessation of the project KOST (controlled opiate prescription therapy), anxieties regarding increased opiate dependency, anxieties regarding the dependency on the substance distributing agent. The project KOST and the penal institution are also dependent on the participant: The participating inmates can not be transferred to other institutions in case of disciplinary conflicts. As a consequence to these observed interdependencies some inmates refuse to participate in the study. They base their refusal on fears of entering into a dependent relationship. The contradictions implied with heroin maintenance treatment within the penal system can also be identified in the beginning of the study: the inmates as well as the staff members articulate perceived conflicts of heroin maintenance within the institution after prior illegality and persecution, problems with coping with these contradictions can be observed, and there is jealousy based on perception of the dual standards.

First conclusions

Summarising our first impressions, we see that new forms of interactions within the penal system have risen due to the heroin maintenance (they are very different from the traditional interaction patterns between the two main groups of actors, staff and inmates; Kette 1991, Friedrichs 1979). More compliance and more contacts based on active care–taking seems to be one of the main results in the first period. We identified interdependencies between the participants and the penal institution, obligations and dependencies, involvement, engagement of the penal institution on behalf of the participants and intensified interactions within the organisation.

However, we can also show that this kind of development is not without contradictions (Borkenstein 1988). The illegality of heroin use outside prison walls causes contradictions during the heroine maintenance treatment inside the prison walls. Such contradictions are realised by both groups, inmates and prison staff. It will be necessary to find ways to cope with them if the effects of the project should be useful for the penal system.

Regarding our results we can see that the feasibility of heroin maintenance treatment within the penal system means also changes in the traditional role of the penal system in the rehabilitation. This change can be pointed out with the following remark: In order to implement the heroin maintenance treatment in the daily routine in a useful way, the penal system has to be able to move its topics from the primary goal of punishment towards the inclusion of care taking into their programme.

III Final Discussion

Clear guidelines from international organisations seem to carry little weight in the context of the security dominated world of penal systems. Pragmatic initiatives, as they have been introduced in some prisons in Switzerland, may enable the implementation of harm reduction measures even in a situation of political reservations against them. Without support by health authorities (e.g. in Switzerland by the Federal Office of Public Health) the overall level of health care in prison remains inadequate.

The comparable objectives of the two pilot projects presented above were first to prove that prevention measures already introduced in the community are also feasible in the prison environment, second to implement effective and necessary individual harm reduction measures in prison against uncontrolled consumption of illegal drugs as well as against risk behaviour concerning drug intake and sexual contacts, and finally to assist the institutions in coping with the drug problem inside prison walls. Syringe distribution has independently been demonstrated to be feasible and effective in a prison for male and female inmates – with one limitation: both prisons are of quite small size. None of the pre–suspected complications, such as misuse of syringes, injuries caused by undisposed syringes or elevation of drug consumption did occur. The preliminary results from the heroin prescription project in Oberschöngrün indicate that the implementation of this most disputed preventive measure seems to be feasible in prison, too. The introduction of so far–going harm reduction measures may therefore not any longer be refused by arguing on the level of pre–suspicions. In future, decisions should be based on clear political intentions only.

Implementation of such delicate prevention measures may in addition enforce prison institutions to cope with drug related problems and thereby improve their ability in solving the problems autonomously. This finally may lead to an efficient reduction of harm in prison, which is in the deep interest of all prisoners and of the institutions as well.

References

Baechtold A, Bürki B, 1995: Pilotprojekt Drogen– und HIV–Prävention in den Anstalten in Hindelbank – Schlussbericht des Projektrealisators. Bern, Amt für Freiheitsentzug und Betreuung.

BAG (Bundesamt für Gesundheitswesen) und Eidgenössische Kommission für Aidsfragen (Hrsg.), 1993: HIV–Prävention in der Schweiz. Ziele, Strategien, Massnahmen. Bern, Bundesamt für Gesundheitswesen.

Borkenstein Ch, 1988: Drogenabhängige im Strafvollzug. In: Egg R: Drogentherapie und Strafe. KrimZ, Kriminologie und Praxis, Wiesbaden, Bd. 3:235-244.

Brewer TF, Derrickson J, 1992: AIDS in prison: A review of epidemiology and preventive policy. AIDS, Vol 6(7), 623–628.

Council of Europe, 1993: Recommendation no. R(93)6 of the Ministers of Member States. Strasbourg, Council of Europe.

Dahle KP, Steller M, 1990: Coping im Strafvollzug: Eine Untersuchung zu Haftfolgen bei Jugendlichen. Zschr.f. experimentelle u. angewandte Psychol., Band XXXVII, Heft 1:31-51.

Dolan K, Wodak A, Penny R, 1995: AIDS behind bars: preventing HIV spread among incarcerated drug injectors. AIDS, 9, 825–832.

Dubois–Arber F, Barbey P, 1994: Evaluation der AIDS–Präventionsstrategie in der Schweiz: Vierter zusammenfassender Bericht, 1991–1992, im Auftrag des Bundesamtes für Gesundheitswesen. Lausanne, Institut univérsitaire de médecine sociale et préventive.

Friedrichs J, Dehm G, Giegler H, Schäfer K, Wurm W, 1979: Resozialisierungsziele und Organisationsstruktur. Teilnehmende Beobachtung in einer Strafanstalt. Kriminologisches Journal 3:204.

Gaube J, Feucht HH, Laufs R, Polywka S, Fingscheidt E, Müller HE, 1993: Hepatitis A,B und C als desmoterische Infektionen. Gesundheitswesen, Vol. 55 (5), 246–249.

Harding TW, 1987: AIDS in prison. Lancet, November 28, 1260–1263.

Keppler K, 1994: Sex'n Drugs'n Hepatitis. Anmerkungen zur Brisanz der Kombination Hepatitis, Drogenabhängigkeit und Inhaftierung. In: Heino Stöver (Hrsg.): Infektionsprophylaxe im Strafvollzug. Eine Übersicht über Theorie und Praxis. AIDS Forum D.A.H., Band XIV, Berlin, Deutsche AIDS–Hilfe e.V.:65–72.

Kette G, 1991: Haft. Eine sozialpsychologische Analyse. Hogrefe Göttingen.

Lamnek S, 1993: Qualitative Sozialforschung. Methoden und Techniken Bd 2. Beltz, Psychologie Verlags Union, Weinheim.

Mayring Ph, 1990: Einführung in die qualitative Sozialforschung. Psychologie Verlags Union München.

Nelles J, Bernasconi S, Bürki B, Hirsbrunner HP, Maurer C, Waldvogel D, 1994: Drogen– und AIDS–Prävention im Gefängnis: Pilotprojekt mit freier Spritzenabgabe in den Anstalten Hindelbank bei Bern/Schweiz. In: Heino Stöver (Hrsg.): Infektionsprophylaxe im Strafvollzug. Eine Übersicht über Theorie und Praxis. AIDS Forum D.A.H., Band XIV, Berlin, Deutsche AIDS–Hilfe e.V., 101–109 (*English translation available*).

Nelles J, Harding TW, 1995: Preventing HIV transmission in prison: a tale of medical disobedience and Swiss pragmatism. Lancet, Vol. 346, No. 8989, 1507–1508.

Nelles J, Waldvogel D, Maurer C, Aebischer C, Fuhrer A, Hirsbrunner HP, 1995: Drogen– und HIV–Prävention in den Anstalten von Hindelbank. Evaluationsbericht. Bern, Bundesamt für Gesundheitswesen (*Abridged report in English and French available*).

Rihs–Middle M, 1996: Ärtzliche Verschreibung von Betäubungsmitteln. Wissenschaftliche Grundlagen und praktische Erfahrungen. Bern/Göttingen/Toronto/Seattle, Verlag Hans Huber.

Schaefer Ch, Fäh P, Weibel U, Probst F, 1995: Feinkonzept für die Strafanstalt Kanton Solothurn. KOST: Kontrollierte Opiatabgabe im Strafvollzug. Strafanstalt Solothurn, Projektunterlage, unveröffentlicht.

Thomas PA and Moerings M (Eds.), 1994: AIDS in prison. Dartmouth, Aldershot, Brockfield USA, Singapore, Sidney.

Uchtenhagen A, Gutzwiller F, Dobler Mikola A, Blättler R, 1995: Versuche für eine ärztliche Verschreibung von Betäubungsmitteln: Zwischenbericht der Forschungsbeauftragten. Institut für Suchtforschung, Institut für Sozial- und Präventivmedizin der Universität Zürich, Zürich.

U.S. General Accounting Office, 1990: Case Study Evaluations. Transfer Paper 10.1.9, Gaithersburg M.D.

WHO (World Health Organization), 1993: Global Programme on AIDS. WHO guidelines on HIV infection and AIDS in prison, Geneva, World Health Organization.

List of authors ○ Autorenverzeichnis

Andrea BAECHTOLD, Prof. Dr. rer. pol, Vorsteher des Amtes für Freiheitsentzug und Betreuung des Kantons Bern, Schermenweg 5, Postfach, 3001 Bern, Schweiz

Pierre G. BAUER, PhD, Expert, AIDS Unit, Swiss Federal Office of Public Health, P.O. Box, 3003 Berne, Switzerland

Anja DOBLER-MIKOLA, lic. phil., Head of section, Insitute of Addiction Research in association with the University of Zürich, Konradstrasse 32, 8005 Zürich, Switzerland

Kate DOLAN, Research Officer, National Drug and Alcohol Research Centre, University of New South Wales, P.O. Box 1, Kensington NSW 2033, Australia

Josef ESTERMANN, Dr. phil. et iur., Lehrbeauftragter, Institut für Soziologie der Universität Bern, Lerchenweg 36, 3012 Bern, Schweiz, und: Orlux AG, Postfach 2817, CH–6002 Luzern

Andreas FUHRER, dipl. phil. nat, scientific collaborator, Psychiatric Services of the University of Berne, Bolligenstrasse 111, 3072 Ostermundigen/Bern, Switzerland

Monika FROMMEL, Prof. Dr., Institute of Criminology, Christian–Albrechts–University of Kiel, Olshausenstrasse, 24098 Kiel, Germany

Felix GUTZWILLER, Prof. Dr. med., Direktor des Instituts für Sozial– und Präventivmedizin der Universität Zürich, Sumatrastrasse 30, 8006 Zürich, Schweiz

Timothy W. HARDING, Prof. Dr. med., Director of the University Institute of Legal Medicine, University of Geneva, Avenue de Champbel 9, 1211 Geneva, Switzerland

Beat KAUFMANN, Dr. phil., wissenschaftlicher Mitarbeiter, Institut für Suchtforschung in Verbindung mit der Universität Zürich, Konradstrasse 32, 8005 Zürich, Schweiz

Chrisophe KOLLER, lic. sc. écon. et soc., fonctionnaire scientifique, Office fédeéral de la statistique, Secition santé, Schwarztorstrasse 53, 3003 Berne, Suisse

Joachim NELLES, Dr. med., Head Physician, Psychiatric Services of the University of Berne, Bolligenstrasse 111, 3072 Ostermundigen/Bern, Switzerland

Stephan QUENSEL, Prof. Dr. iur., Bremer Institut für Drogenforschung (BISDRO), Universität Bremen, Fachbereich 8, Postfach 33 04 40, 28334 Bremen, Deutschland

Ambros UCHTENHAGEN, Prof. Dr. med. et phil., Insitute of Addiction Research in association with the University of Zürich, Konradstrasse 32, 8005 Zürich, Switzerland

Francois WASSERFALLEN, M.A., Head of the AIDS Unit, Swiss Federal Office of Public Health, P.O. Box, 3003 Berne, Switzerland

Dina ZEEGERS PAGET, Doctor at Law, Scientific collaborator of the AIDS Unit, Swiss Federal Office of Public Health, P.O. Box, 3003 Berne, Switzerland